For the Love of Dogs
Suzanne Woods Fisher

Vintage Inspirations
An imprint of Vintage Romance Publishing
Ladson, South Carolina
www.vrpublishing.com

PUBLISHED BY VINTAGE INSPIRATIONS, an imprint of Vintage Romance Publishing www.vrpublishing.com

Dedicated to my sister, Wendy, and my two brothers, Dave and Tom. My siblings have been remarkably steadfast weathering our father's long and difficult battle with Alzheimer's disease.

Acknowledgements:

The cover photo of the yellow Labrador retriever has been reproduced with permission by Guide Dogs for the Blind in San Rafael, California, a non-profit organization dedicated to providing enhanced mobility to qualified individuals. For more information, visit the website at: www.guidedogs.com or call 800-295-4050. The royalties from sales of this book are being donated to Guide Dogs for the Blind.

A thank you to Dr. David K. Winter, Chancellor to Westmont College, the inspiration behind the fictitious character of wise Dr. Sommers.

A heartfelt appreciation goes to Vickie Kennedy, a Board Member for Guide Dogs for the Blind, who provided firsthand information about what it was like to lose one's sight to retinitis pigmentosa, a degenerative disease.

And, as always, a thank you to the Lord God for showing me the keys.

What Others Are Saying about *For the Love of Dogs*:

"Once again, I feel compelled to rave about author Suzanne W. Fisher's knack for developing a wonderful cast. Each character, down to the most 'insignificant' is full of life and color. In the end, Sam, Jack, Kathleen, and even irritatingly troubled Lucy, are more than just names on a page. They're my friends!" *Title Trakk*

"Apart from a compelling story, every novel needs an imperceptive tutorial, and author Ms. Fisher is always good for it. Raising guide dog puppies herself, she has intimate knowledge of the ins and outs of owning one of these gentle guides. Her expertise shines through, giving the reader a tiny taste of being blind and leaving only gratitude to the Lord for the gift of sight.

To sum it up, this novel will motive you to achieve your dreams despite the unpleasant odds." *Christian Fiction On-Line*

"You're responsible for keeping me up late at night! I couldn't put it down." Joanne Ritter, Marketing Director, Guide Dogs for the Blind

"This could be titled in *Awe of Dogs*. It is amazing what these guide dogs can do and the freedom they provide their blind companions. You don't pity blind people but reading this, instead stand in awe of what they can do." Linda Danis, bestselling author of *365 Things Every New Mom Should Know*

"This is a story of challenge, and great courage, depression, and hope. This is about us. It is a fascinating story, compelling us to read on. Even more, it communicates the special challenge of blindness, which is simply one expression of a rather common human experience, serious loss. And so we deeply enjoy knowing these good but struggling people and

also learn some profound truths about God, our lives, and priorities, shocking personal loss, and the dimensions of love."
David K. Winter, Chancellor, Westmont College

Late August...

Two churlish young men came up to Samantha and sat down, one on each side of her. They smelled strongly of stale cigarettes and...a slightly sweet smell that she couldn't quite place...almost like alfalfa hay...*all mixed up with the aroma of overly ripe arm pits.* She crinkled her nose and shuddered with disgust. Something about their oafish manner made the hair on her neck rise, even in the midst of a big party, especially when she realized they had been waiting until they could speak to her alone.

"We got a message for you to deliver to your husband," one of the men said. "Tell him that he's been warned. No more late payments."

"Whoa! Wait *just* a minute," Samantha objected indignantly. "I have no idea what you're talking about, and even more importantly, *that* man is *not* my—"

"Just remember to deliver the message," interrupted the other man. "Our boss is runnin' out of patience." Just as suddenly as they came, they disappeared.

Samantha remained glued to her chair, completely flummoxed. Those guys had obviously confused her with someone else. Jack's wife.

He's married? And he's involved in something illegal? Another couple of things to add to the list of what she didn't like about Jack. *On top of the fact that he stole Mr. Malcolm's property from us! I should have listened to my instincts that very first time I met him. I should have hopped off that bus and never looked back.*

That was just the start of how, six months later, Samantha found she had become a person she scarcely recognized, caught in a web of tangled circumstances, living a life she never would have chosen. And never knew she wanted.

Chapter One: **The Bus**

A few weeks earlier...

Something was missing from Samantha Christiansen's life, something she couldn't put into words. An awful emptiness. *I hoped that when I got Running Deer to this point, I'd feel...different,* she thought, walking to the bus stop. *Like I finally crossed the finish line. But...I don't. It just seemed as though there should be...more.*

Samantha had just delivered a forest of documents to apply for a sizable bank loan to expand Running Deer Ranch, her family-run premium olive oil company in Northern California. In a bold move, especially for one with such a risk-adverse nature, she had ordered a pricey state-of-the-art Italian Rapanelli mill before the loan with the bank had been guaranteed. She needed that mill in place, up and running, before harvest began in the fall.

She picked up her pace as she heard the squeaky brakes of the bus hurling around the street corner. *It was the right decision to get that loan, wasn't it?* she worried, biting her lip. She ran through the figures again in her head and reminded herself that this year's harvest looked especially promising after such a warm March.

She could hear her sister, Kathleen's, voice pipe into her thoughts: *What if Running Deer does more than just survive the year, but thrives? What if we get that loan paid off early? And what if the sky doesn't fall?*

Lately Samantha felt that her business was riding a heavy wave, impelled by recent publicity after being named "Artisan of the Year" by *Gourmand* magazine. Still, she knew she had to capture as much momentum for the company as she could, before the wave crested.

Samantha hurried to cross the street to meet the bus as it pulled up to the stop. She was half-way through the intersection when a car blasted its horn at her. She froze in fear, unsure if she should move forward or backward. Just in time, the car veered to avoid her. Samantha fell forward as the car whistled past her, breaking the fall by landing on her hands and knees.

"Get out of the road lady!" yelled the driver as he zoomed by.

The bus driver leapt out of the bus and ran over to her. "Sam, are you okay? Crazy driver. He nearly killed you!"

Samantha's heart was hammering. "I'm fine, Jimmy. Just shaken up a little. It's my own fault." She tried to scrape together a little bit of dignity as he helped her to her feet. "Serious thinking and crossing the street should never be tried at the same time."

Another man gently placed her hand on his elbow, guiding her to the bus.

Samantha spun around. "Wait! My cane!"

"Already got it," said the man in a deep, soft voice. He helped her up the stairs of the bus, down the aisle to a seat, and slid in beside her. A big man, he took up more than his share of the seat. "Ever thought about getting a guide dog?"

"What? Um, no," Samantha answered, still shaken and distracted, "but thank you for your help." The scrapes on her hands and knees started to sting.

"Near misses like that wouldn't happen."

"Well, near misses happen to everyone now and then," Samantha said. She had a sudden jolt of regret as soon as she heard that tone in her voice, the one her sister called the Madam Librarian tone. She didn't mean to sound so cross, but lately her words seemed to jump out of her mouth that way.

She reached in her purse for a tissue to wipe the gravel and blood off of her knees. She balled up the tissue in her hand and tried not to think about why she was turning into a crotchety old lady at the young age of twenty-nine.

"Ever been to the California Canine Academy for the Blind facility? It's not too far from here. You should take a tour someday."

Oh no! Not one of those guys who started sentences with "You should." Samantha was accustomed to comments about her blindness from well-intentioned strangers: people talking loudly as though she was hard of hearing, people trying to over-help her, misplaced and unwanted pity. But the "You should…" kind of guy, the type who seemed to be an Expert-on-her-World, the kind who was too self-assured, too cocky, well, that combination topped her try-to-avoid-at-all-costs list.

"If you don't mind, I have some reading to do," she said, pulling a book out of her briefcase. She fingered the Braille dots, not really concentrating but hoping he would take the hint and leave her alone.

"I don't mind at all," he responded pleasantly. "This is my stop, anyway. By the way, I'm Jack. Nice to meet you, uh, um…" He reached out his hand and brushed the back of hers, a known etiquette among the blind to signal a handshake.

Samantha looked up at him, startled that he would be knowledgeable about that nuance. As she shook his hand, she noticed that his was calloused and rough. *Not a guy who spends his days in an office,* she sized up quickly. But his touch was gentle, almost tender.

"She's Samantha, Jack! Friends call her Sam!" Jimmy volunteered over the screech of the opening bus doors.

"Maybe I'll see you again, Sam," Jack called out, bounding down the bus steps.

"He just started riding my line a few weeks ago," offered Jimmy. "Seems like a nice guy, don't ya think?"

Not really, she thought. But she gave Jimmy a benign smile.

"Sam, isn't this your stop, too?"

She could feel the heat of a blush on her cheeks as she threw her book into her purse, grabbed her briefcase and her cane, and scrambled down the stairs.

"Don't forget that the astronauts are going to land on the moon tonight, Sam!" Jimmy called out.

"How could *anyone* forget that?" she answered, grinning, waving to him as the bus doors closed.

"Sam! Sam! Over here!"

Samantha turned in the direction of her sister's voice. "Hi Kat! What are you doing here?" she asked, hopping into the passenger seat of her sister's station wagon.

"I was coming home from the supermarket and saw you get off the bus. I think I recognized that guy who jumped off the bus ahead of you, but I can't remember where I've seen him." Kathleen started up the car and turned onto the lane that led to Running Deer. "There he is. He's waving like he knows us! Should I offer him a ride?"

"No!" Samantha shook her head. "He's probably a Fuller Brush salesman, going door-to-door. Let's just get home." She felt for a chubby leg next to her. "Hi Lily!" She tickled her niece's leg and heard the toddler giggle as she tried to kick her hand away.

"Have a good day?" asked Kathleen.

"Well, I think I made a dent in the loan process. It's a lot of money we're trying to borrow. I just hope..." Samantha paused.

"Hope what?" asked Kathleen as she pulled into Running Deer's gravel driveway.

"Just that we're not biting off more than we can chew."

"*Why* must you always look for the Worst Case Scenario? You are *such* a chronic worrier."

Maybe. But you don't worry enough. Kathleen *never* worried. Worrying was Samantha's domain. Kathleen was born first, by a full ten minutes, but Samantha had always *felt* older. *Responsible. Boring, Kathleen would say. Kathleen, on the other hand, seemed to have the Fun gene pretty well locked-up.* Even as little girls, Samantha bit her nails while Kathleen made daisy chains. And now, Samantha wore a night guard to keep from grinding her teeth. *The only thing Kathleen puts near her mouth is a different shade of lipstick each day.*

Samantha exhaled, long resigned to their congenital claims. "Do you happen to know if Pete made any progress finding a contractor to prepare for the new mill?"

"I have no idea. I didn't get down to the office today. The baby was awake all night teething, and she wanted the rest of the world to keep her company. You know how tired I get when I'm pregnant. I had to nap when Lily naps."

Samantha rolled her eyes. She expected as much. Kathleen and her husband, Pete, didn't like the business side of the olive ranch; they felt it sullied them.

"I'll do it tomorrow. Hey, I sold more of Nonna's heirlooms to the antique dealer in town. In the last few months since she moved to Shady Acres, we have uncovered a treasure chest up in that dusty attic!"

"You're really getting into this, aren't you?" Samantha asked.

"*Love* it. I drop things off, and my money just rolls right in."

"Nonna's money," corrected Samantha.

"I *know* that," snapped Kathleen. She dropped Samantha off at her cottage before driving up to the farmhouse. "Come over for dinner tonight. Nonna's staying, too. She's up in the attic, weeding through more junk."

"Okay. I just need to take care of a few things first." Samantha walked to her cottage, paused as she held the key in the lock, and breathed in deeply. Star jasmine, wrapped around the porch rails, sweetly perfumed the air. Samantha loved her cottage. She called it 'Mise-En-Place.' Everything was in its place, just as she left it this morning and every morning. As she unlocked the front door, her Himalayan cat, Phoebe, darted past her and out the door.

Samantha changed into her jean cut-offs, dug out a carrot in the fridge, and went to the barn to feed her horse, Spitfire, who was hanging his head out his stall door.

"Hey, you big lug, how are you today?" Samantha asked with affection, stroking his mane. Spitfire shook his heavy head and shoved her with his nose. She laughed. "Are you mad at me? Stubbornness sure runs in this family." She put him in the corral to eat while she refilled his water bucket. "I wish I had more time to ride you, Spitfire. Soon. After the loan is finished," she consoled him as she led him back into his stall. "Let's just hope it works."

* * * *

When Kathleen saw Samantha cross the driveway from the barn, she propped open the kitchen door for her. "Phoebe is in here. She practically flew in the door. That stray cat was hanging around again today. He got into the cat food bucket in the barn today. Made a big mess."

"Oh no! I wish I knew who he belongs to. If Phoebe winds up pregnant, I will tar and feather that owner."

"You should have her fixed."

"Never! Not with her pedigree. I want to breed her one day." Samantha's face scrunched up as if in pain as she inhaled, crossing the threshold. "Something smells…rather…pungent."

"I know. I know," Kathleen said, closing the door behind Samantha. "I'm trying a new fondue recipe, but the cheese kind of stinks. Fondue is all the rage, you know."

"Isn't that what Jackie Kennedy served at White House dinners?"

Kathleen shot Samantha a look to see if she was trying to tweak her. Kathleen *adored* Jackie Kennedy. She was just about to make a snide comment in return when she noticed band-aids on her sister's knees. "What happened to you? Blood is seeping through."

"Just a little spill I took today. I was more embarrassed than hurt." Samantha slid her legs under the table. "A man on the bus told me that I should have a guide dog."

A slow, surprised smile played over Kathleen's face. "Really?" She picked up her spoon and started stirring the fondue. *Act cool,* she warned herself. She had wanted to suggest a guide dog to Samantha for a while now, but her sister resisted her efforts, calling them "over helping."

"Just today, I saw a blind person with a guide dog at the grocery store! He was really enthusiastic about it. He said he could never go back to a cane. Maybe…" she hesitated, glancing at Samantha to gauge her reaction, "you should consider it."

"No, no. I don't *need* a guide dog. I get around just fine. Besides, being a cane traveler isn't so bad. People usually scatter when they see me coming. Must have been how Moses felt, parting the Red Sea."

Kathleen smiled. She pulled out a kitchen chair and sat down next to her sister. "It seems like you're doing less than you used to. A lot less."

"I'm busier than I used to be."

Kathleen watched Samantha's jaw clench. Accustomed to her sister's resistance, she forged ahead, undeterred. "I don't mean that you aren't productive, I meant that you're not as adventurous as you used to be."

Samantha stood, got a glass out of the cupboard and then took a few strides to the freezer to reach for the ice tray. At the sink, she twisted the tray to release the ice cubes, plunked a few into her glass, and filled the glass with water.

"You're stalling," Kathleen said.

Samantha sighed, exasperated. "Kathleen, I can't see much anymore."

"Exactly! And you've gotten hurt more in the last few months than you ever have. Especially banging your head."

"I only bang my head in your kitchen because you always leave cupboards open."

"Well, that's my point. A cane can't help you with overhead dangers."

Samantha rolled her eyes toward the ceiling.

"Oh Sam, just be open to it! You could do so many more things with a guide dog. You wouldn't be as limited." She handed Samantha carrots, a chopping board, and a knife. "I need the carrots in half-circles for the salad. They *have* to be half-circles."

Samantha raised her eyebrows at Kathleen. "Any chance you watched *Julia Child* on television today?" She started cutting the carrots. In half-circles.

"As a matter of fact, I did," Kathleen answered airily. "Look, if we want to expand our business, we're going to have to go on trips and attend more events. Like the Award Ceremony on Saturday night." She picked up a toy Lily had thrown out of the playpen and handed it to her, smiling as the baby plopped down and started chewing on the toy. "You are really teething, aren't you?" she said, stroking her daughter's wispy hair.

Kathleen straightened and pivoted around. "Sam, I completely forgot to tell you! Guess what arrived today? An invitation to New York City by *Gourmand* magazine! For that Food Award! It's in early October. I can't go, not with the baby, and Pete needs to be here to supervise the harvest. You'll need to go to that, too."

Samantha stiffened her spine. "Maybe you and Pete should go; I'll look after the milling. Nonna and I can take care of Lily."

"Right," Kathleen said coolly. "Manage the mill while babysitting a one-year-old. Besides, Pete would never leave during harvest."

Samantha's eyes grew wide. "But I'm not really sure…I can…"

For a moment, Kathleen saw something pass through her sister's eyes—vulnerability? fear?—but it vanished before she could put a name to it. Her voice softened. "Sure you can, Sam. You've done it before."

"I haven't flown in a while. And I've only been to New York once."

Kathleen waved a hand, shooing away Samantha's worries as she would a mosquito. "It'll be fine! So about the guide dog…"

Samantha scowled at her. "Kathleen, I am *not* interested."

"We could at least visit the facility."

"You are like a dog with a bone," Samantha muttered under her breath.

"What was that?" Kathleen asked, eyeing her suspiciously.

"I said, I think your sauce is burning."

Kathleen jumped up, frowning as she peered into the sauce pan. She picked up a spoon and started stirring. "Boring Bob dropped by. He said to give him a call later tonight. He wants to come over and watch the moon landing." She tossed the burnt sauce down the garbage disposal, filling the saucepan with water to soak. "Watching your relationship with Boring Bob is like watching a leaf settle slowly to the bottom of the ocean. How long are you going to string him along?"

"I am not stringing anyone along," Samantha said coldly. "And stop calling him Boring Bob. You sound like you're in junior high."

Well, Bob is boring. "Bob is thirty-two and still lives at home."

"He's an electrical engineer. Living at home makes a lot of sense for him. His parents' house is huge, and they travel constantly. And, Kat, I am also nearly thirty and living at home." She gave her sister one of those wide eyed, butter-couldn't-melt looks. "Now that I think about it, so are you."

"It's different. We're running a business, and it's based at the family property." Samantha could be so frustrating. That girl never talked about a thing until she was good and ready to, and even then she put up fences you didn't dare cross. Cautiously, she added, "It seems…that Bob holds you back."

"Kathleen, talking to Bob is like having a set of *World Books* in the house. Up-to-date ones, too, unlike Nonna's. How could you possibly consider someone with his brain power to be holding me back?"

"Bob just seems to have a narrow view of the world." Kathleen pulled out a big wooden bowl for the salad. "And his idea of a big date is to come over and watch *Star Trek* with you."

Samantha rubbed her temples. "Today seems to have more than its fair share of lectures to improve my life," she said, under her breath.

"What was that? You're starting to mutter a lot." Kathleen frowned at her sister. "Anyway, I don't mean to point out the obvious, but you can't even see the television."

Samantha finished cutting the rest of the carrots. In sticks.

"I asked Boring Bob if he was coming to the Award Ceremony on Saturday night, but he said that he doesn't like shallow soirees, and he doesn't like to dance."

"So?"

"So…Running Deer is receiving an award, you're giving the acceptance speech, and Bob can't be inconvenienced to support you."

Samantha put her hands to her ears.

"It's going to be an incredible evening! This is so *big* for us!"

"I resent that you would ask him to an event without checking with me first. Honestly, is there *any* part of my life that you don't try to control?"

"Only the parts you need help in," Kathleen said pleasantly. "Like your entire personal life."

"Kathleen," Nonna warned in her don't-mess-with-me voice as she came into the kitchen, carrying a dusty box from the attic. "Let Sammy live her own life."

19

"Thank you, Nonna," Samantha said, visibly relieved by her grandmother's support.

Nonna unloaded an armful of heirlooms on the counter. She sniffed the air. "Something smells like—"

"I know, I know. I burnt the cheese sauce," Kathleen rued.

Phoebe followed in on Nonna's heels and settled in by Samantha's feet, waving her tail against Samantha's bare shins. "Kathleen, here are a few more things to try and sell. I'm assuming you girls don't want to keep these silver platters. They require *polishing*," she said provocatively.

In perfect unison, as if rehearsed, Kathleen and Samantha answered, "Sell them!"

"And look what else I found! Kathleen's box of S&H Green Stamps." She handed Kathleen a shoe box.

Kathleen peered into the box, gathering up the half-stamped booklets. "Think they're still good? I need new hot curlers. Mine just broke."

Samantha's eyebrows shot up. "Wait a minute. Those were my hot rollers."

Just then, Pete burst through the kitchen door, washed up at the kitchen sink, gave Kathleen a peck on the cheek, and went over to pick up Lily from the playpen. "Hey, ladies," he said cheerfully. "I was out in the orchards today, savoring my job as foreman of this ranch. I have never seen such a large harvest. Never in July. Never like this. I think Running Deer is about to gallop." He swung Lily around in the air until she squealed. "Phew! Something stinks in here. Like old gym socks."

"I know, I know! I burnt the fondue," Kathleen frowned. "Everyone seems to feel the need to point that out."

Pete plopped down in the kitchen chair, Lily on his lap, and said, "Sam, it would be great if we could nail down Malcolm's property and plant those new Spanish olive trees before the competition is all over them. Can't you try one more time to sweet talk Mr. Malcolm into selling?"

"I've tried and tried; I'll keep trying," Samantha answered. "He just won't discuss it with me. He's got some kind of burr under his saddle about the subject."

"What about the Mitchells' property?" Pete asked.

"They said they aren't ready to move."

Kathleen had her head in the fridge, looking for lettuce for the salad. When she closed the fridge door, she noticed a cat-in-the-cream smile on her grandmother's face. "What's up, Nonna?" she asked. "What are you grinning about?"

"Oh nothing," Nonna answered with a mysterious lilt to her voice and a twinkle in her eyes. "Just happy to have all of you together in one room."

"We're *always* together," Samantha said, puzzled.

Pete ignored the diversion and turned back to Samantha. "How did the bank talks go today?"

"Promising," she answered. "I have a nagging worry that I should be going to a larger bank in the city, but then I go back to thinking that it's best to stay with the bank that has supported Running Deer ever since Gramps started it up."

"What's to worry about?" Pete asked, snatching a carrot stick from her.

Samantha bit the corner of her lip. "It's such a small bank. Their loan policies are laced with all kinds of iron-clad covenants."

"Covenants?" Pete looked confused. "I'm not following."

"It means that they've put some loan requirements on us that we have to meet. A minimum amount of cash has to stay in the business account. They take the loan payment directly out of that account. Another requirement is we have to promise to not take out any other outstanding loans anywhere else," she explained.

Pete let Lily gnaw on the end of the carrot stick. "That shouldn't be hard."

"Well, it also means that no one taps into the account unless it is for the business. Not even in a *dire* emergency. No one," Samantha answered, pointing a finger toward Kathleen.

Kathleen rolled her eyes. "Oh for heaven's sake!" she said with disgust. "One dining room table and six little chairs that I bought out of the business account...and you're *still* stewing over it."

"You'll be stewing, too, if we get audited and thrown into jail because you needed a new dining room table and *eight* chairs," corrected Samantha.

"What would happen if we had an emergency?" Pete interrupted, a concerned look on his face.

"If we broke covenants, they would call in the loan," Samantha said. "It would have to be paid back in full...or...we could face bankruptcy. Either way, Running Deer would be more like... well...like Roadkill Deer."

Chapter Two: **The Award**

A few days later, Samantha was waiting for the bus, ready to head home after finalizing negotiations at the bank for the business loan.

"Hey there, Sam," Jimmy said as she dropped change into the bus' fare box. "Did you see it?"

"Well, no, but I heard it, Jimmy!" She covered her mouth with her fist, a makeshift microphone. "One small step for man...static static static...one giant leap for mankind."

Jimmy laughed. "Man o' man. Never thought I'd see the day when a man walked on the moon."

"That's just what my grandmother said. Now you're sounding like an old man," Samantha teased as she moved down the aisle.

"Second seat on the right is open, but watch the—" Before Jimmy could finish his sentence, Samantha tripped over a package that someone had tucked under a seat and half-way out in the aisle. The loan papers in her notebook flew up in the air as the contents of her purse spilled on the floor, rolling under bus seats.

A passenger jumped up to help and steered Samantha carefully to an empty seat before picking up the things she had dropped. "Here you go, Sam," said a soft, deep voice as he handed her the papers and purse.

No! Not the Dog Guy. She gave him a polite but curt thank you.

Jack interpreted her under-the-breath thanks as an invitation to sit down. "That's just the kind of thing that could be avoided with a guide dog," he offered cheerfully.

Samantha stiffened. *Not again. I think I am going to scream.* In a crisp tone, she said, "Yes, well, I'm sure you're right."

Jack didn't notice her crisp tone. "Say, do you know the difference between having a cane and having a guide dog?"

23

She wondered if the bus window was too small to jump out of. "Why no, I don't." *But I'll bet you're going to enlighten me.*

She was right. "The purpose of a white cane is to *look* for obstacles. The purpose of a guide dog is to *avoid* obstacles." Jack leaned back in the seat and crossed his arms. "Mind if I guess the cause of your blindness? Is it RP?"

Samantha's eyebrows shot up. "What makes you think that?"

"I can tell that you have a little bit of vision. The way you look directly at a person. Kind of like you're looking down two paper towel holders. Am I wrong?"

He was describing her vision with an eerie accuracy. She tilted her head toward him. "How do you know about retinitis pigmentosa? Do you have a family member with RP?"

"Nope," he answered, without elaborating.

"Well, Mr—"

"Jack," he interrupted. "Call me Jack."

"Jack, I appreciate your concern, but I really am *not* interested in having a guide dog."

"Any particular reason?"

Samantha racked her brain for a solid excuse. Finally, the truth seemed simpler. "I'm afraid of dogs."

"No kidding?!" he asked in disbelief. It seemed like the first time in his life he had ever heard of such a thing. The bus lurched to a stop. "Oh, here we are."

Briefly, Samantha wondered if she could just stay on the bus and let it take her anywhere but here until Jimmy, trying to be helpful, piped up, "Tuscan Ketchup, Sam!"

Jack waited for her at the bottom of the steps. "Why did the bus driver call out Tuscan Ketchup?"

"He's trying to be funny. He's referring to the olive oil ranch down this lane." She switched her briefcase to her right hand so her left hand could direct the cane. "Italians call olive oil 'Tuscan Ketchup'." As Jack walked along beside her, Samantha noticed he had a slight limp.

"I heard a lot about that olive oil farm from the guy whose house I bought. You live nearby?" he asked.

"Ranch, not a farm. And yes, my family runs the ranch." Then she stopped abruptly. "Wait a minute." She spun around to face him. "There are only three houses down this road. Mine. The Mitchells'…and I know they're not interested in moving. And Mr. Malcolm's."

"That's the one! I bought Mr. Malcolm's place. I got *really* lucky. We met at the supermarket last month. His sister in Florida had just broken her hip or arm or something like that, so he was in a hurry to move there and help her. Gave me a great deal, too, furnishings and all. Threw in an oriental rug if we could close the deal in thirty days. Worked for me. It's just what I was looking for, location and price and size." Jack stopped. "Well, here's where I turn-off. Good night, Sam. Glad to know we're neighbors."

As Samantha took in the upsetting discovery that Mr. Malcolm had sold his property to a stranger—without ever discussing it with Running Deer despite the many times she had begged him to sell to her—she felt her heart start to race.

Then, a new thought burst into Samantha's head, squeezing out Mr. Malcolm. "It's *your* cat! A cat just appeared on my doorstep a few weeks ago, and it's making my cat certifiably crazy! My precious, pedigreed, un-spade cat! And, and, and—" she stuttered as her breathing accelerated, "—that horrible cat of yours is getting into the cat food that I store in the barn!"

"Nope, not me," Jack said pleasantly. "I'm not really a cat guy."

As she heard Jack limp down his gravel driveway, she felt as though a three-hundred-pound gorilla just landed on top of her.

* * * *

Kathleen was upstairs, folding clean diapers, when she heard her sister storm into the farmhouse. "Kat! Where are you?!" Samantha screamed.

Kathleen flew down the stairs and into the kitchen. "Quiet! You'll wake the baby! What's wrong?"

Samantha stood planted, her hands on her hips. "Do you remember that guy on the bus who told me to get a guide dog after that near miss?"

"What near miss?" asked Kathleen, forehead wrinkled in concern. "You told me about a man on the bus, but you never said you had a near miss. Nearly missed *what*, Sam?" She glanced down at Samantha's knees, frowning. She *knew* something had happened to her the other day.

Samantha waved her hand to brush off that worry. "That's not important. What's important is that man...that *crazed bus guy*...has *bought* Mr. Malcolm's house. *Our* Mr. Malcolm's house! The one we planned to put the new Spanish olive trees on!"

"*What?* You've *got* to be kidding! How could Mr. Malcolm sell it without talking to us first? We've been neighbors for decades!" Kathleen plopped down in a chair. "Do you think the crazy bus guy offered him a fortune? More than he could refuse?"

"No! He said he got a *great* deal on it! Not only did we lose the property—this important, *strategic* property—but we have a very *strange* new neighbor."

Kathleen looked skeptically at Samantha. "Oh Sam, is he really that bad?"

"Yes! He asks personal questions and offers unwanted advice and keeps badgering me about this guide dog thing." Samantha shuddered and made a face. "He's weird, Kat. Weird like...Zodiac Killer-weird. And he appeared out of nowhere. Maybe we should call the cops and let them know we might have a serial killer in the neighborhood."

She turned to open the refrigerator to find the iced tea pitcher but stopped as she thought of something to add. She whirled around and pointed a finger at Kathleen. "A serial killer *with a cat*. I just know that stray cat belongs to him. He denied it, but I'll bet he was lying."

Chin propped up on her elbow, Kathleen watched Samantha pour a glass of iced tea. *I want to meet this crazy bus guy. There aren't too many people who get under Sam's skin like this guy has. Either he really is weird...or maybe, just maybe—*

"Listen, Kat, I need a favor," Samantha interrupted Kathleen's musings. "An appraiser is coming to Running Deer for a property assessment on Monday. The loan officer wanted to see the property, too, so I invited them both to stay for lunch." She slid into the chair and tilted her head, giving a wide-eyed look of sweet innocence. "I thought you wouldn't mind whipping something up for everyone. One of your specialties? To help smooth the loan process."

"*Whip* up a fancy lunch?" Kathleen asked, eyebrows lifted. *Here's my chance.* "Okay, Sam. I'll make you a bargain. Come Saturday, you go with me to take a tour of the California Canine Academy for the Blind, and on Monday, I'll make your lunch."

Samantha sat straight up in the chair. "Kathleen, you *know* how I feel about dogs."

"These dogs aren't aggressive, Sam. You can get over it."

Samantha covered her face with her hands.

"So Saturday, we'll go?"

"Do I really have a choice?" Samantha snapped, muffled behind her hands.

Kathleen felt triumphant. "Not if you want a fancy-schmancy meal to woo over your loan guys." She reached out and finished the last of Samantha's iced tea, silently plotting a way to meet this curious new neighbor.

* * * *

On Saturday morning, Jack rode his bike to work to check on a few things he hadn't had time for during the week. He had to swerve out of the way of an enormous Country Squire station wagon, complete with fake wood paneling, as it came barreling into a parking lot. After he hopped off of his bike and started to lock it at the rack, he noticed two women getting out of the station wagon. He watched them for a while, amused.

One kept up a steady chatter, arms waving like a symphony conductor, carrying on an animated one-sided conversation. Even unfolding a baby stroller didn't stem her flow of words, he noticed. The other woman, with a toddler hoisted on her hip, seemed to be generally ignoring the arm waving talker. By the time he reached them, both women were bent over the stroller, tucking in the kicking toddler.

Glancing over as he passed them, Jack did a double take. "Sam?"

27

The two women popped up at the same time, trying to locate the voice. Jack's eyes darted from one woman to the other, confused. He thought his eyes were playing tricks on him. They were mirror images. Same long brunette hair pulled back in a ponytail. Same large, luminous eyes that had dazzled him the first time he met her on the bus.

Why was that woman stuck in his thoughts? He couldn't get her out of his mind—but which one was she? Then one woman's face erupted into a big smile as the other stayed frozen, like a deer caught in headlights. Instantly, he identified Samantha.

The smiling one jumped in. "I'm Kathleen. Sam's twin."

"No kidding?" Jack asked. "Identical twins?"

"Well, if we were identical, Kathleen would have RP, wouldn't she?" Samantha said tartly, her tongue and her brain back in synchronization.

He gave a short laugh. "Excellent point! Kathleen, my name is Jack Shaw. I'm an instructor here."

"An instructor? A *dog* instructor?" Samantha's mind seemed caught on the word. "Why didn't you just tell me you were a dog trainer on the bus?"

"A *guide* dog instructor," Jack corrected, his masculine pride kicking in. "Didn't I? I must have. I bet I did. I'm sure I did." He scratched his head, trying to remember. "But I'm really bad with details."

"Jack Shaw. That name seems so familiar. Have we met?" asked Kathleen.

"Not that I remember, but apparently I'm your new neighbor. I bought Mr. Malcolm's house." Jack bent over to say hello to Lily. "Sam, is this your baby?"

Samantha sputtered for words until Kathleen chimed in. "This is my daughter, Lily." Lowering her voice, she added, "Sam's not married."

Samantha jabbed Kathleen with her elbow.

"Say, did you take my advice and come for a tour?" Jack seemed pleased. "How about if I show you around?"

"No, no," objected Samantha, a little loudly. "I mean, you must have work to do."

"Not really. Just came in to check on a few things. I'll be right back." This day had just taken a very interesting turn of events, he decided, grinning.

* * * *

As he disappeared into the building, Kathleen turned to Samantha. "*That's* the crazed bus guy? Sam, he's adorable! Huge, too."

"But why didn't he just tell me that he was a dog trainer?" Samantha asked. "Doesn't that seem odd to you?"

"No. You're just paranoid. He didn't want you to feel intimidated."

"Didn't *want* me to feel intimidated? He's *stalking* me. He's everywhere I go! Let's leave. Please, Kat. Now!"

"No way, Sam. I got you this far. We're going to check out having a guide dog. You agreed," Kathleen added bossily. "Hush. Here he comes."

"All set. Follow me," Jack boomed as he burst through the doors. He led them first to the kennels where a chorus of barking greeted them.

Samantha felt startled, vulnerable, not sure where the barking was coming from. "The dogs are all in secured kennels," Jack said to reassure her. "They're just saying hello."

"I think my hearing will be permanently impaired," said Samantha, covering her ears.

"Ha! Imagine if you worked here. First, I want to take you over to the puppies. This will cure your fear of dogs. Lily will love this part, too." He led them down a sunny aisle to the puppy yard. "Go on in the yard and sit on the grass. I'll be right back."

Samantha heard the clinking of the kennel gate and turned to Kathleen. "See what I mean? He gives orders like a Marine Sergeant."

"I think he's wonderful," Kathleen said decidedly.

Why does that not surprise me? Samantha thought.

Jack came back out with a soft, yelping little pup. "Sam, hold out your hands." Gently, he placed the puppy in her hands.

As she smelled the puppy breath, touching the soft little leather soles of his paws, holding the puppy close to her face, something melted inside of her. It reminded her of the first time she held Lily.

"The ears are like velvet," Samantha whispered.

"Feel the paws?" Jack said, smiling. "New shoes." He went back in and brought out another pup for Lily to pet. Soon the pups wiggled to get down and play with each other. "Next, I want to take Sam over to see a larger dog."

"Actually, puppies are enough for me," she quickly injected.

"Nonsense! You need to understand the whole picture." He crouched down to scoop up the puppies in his large hands and carry them back to the kennels.

He took Kathleen and Samantha and Lily over to another part of the kennel area to find a dog-in-training. "Sam, this yellow lab is named Azure. She's nearly two years old and has a very gentle nature. Put out your hand."

Tentatively, Samantha held out her hand. Azure sniffed, then licked her hand. Samantha couldn't hold back a grin. "Feels just like Spitfire's tongue."

"Spitfire is Sam's horse," Kathleen piped up helpfully.

"Do you mean to tell me that you ride a *horse* named Spitfire, but you're afraid of a *dog*?" Jack asked.

"I had a...a negative encounter with a dog once," Samantha answered defensively. "I've never felt comfortable around dogs since."

"Now's the chance to get to know another kind of dog," Jack said. "These dogs are bred and raised for intelligence, calmness, and a strong work ethic. Sam, try patting Azure's back, stroking her from head to tail."

Cautiously, Samantha stroked her as Azure's tail thumped back and forth. "She likes you," Jack said.

She couldn't say why, but Samantha felt pleased.

"Azure, down. Stay." The dog promptly went into the down-stay position with Jack's commands. "Okay, next thing I want you to do, Sam, is a game called 'Juno.' Juno is just a name for a pretend dog. Grab hold of this harness, and I'm going to lead you just like Juno is in the harness. Ready?"

Samantha held on to the firm leather harness in her left hand. Jack started moving, pulling her along with him as she held on to the harness. "Wait! You're going too fast!"

"That's how quickly the dogs move."

"Like a runaway locomotive?"

Jack gave a short laugh. "No, they move briskly because they know where they're going. A dog becomes your eyes, Sam. You don't have to be preoccupied with every step, the way you are now. Right?"

Slowly, she nodded.

"Juno is doing the work for you, so you can trust the dog and just keep up. It's that simple."

Somehow, I doubt that last remark.

With great sincerity, Jack asked, "Samantha, is there anything more I can do to help make this easier for you?"

Maybe tomorrow she'd be back to being suspicious of him, but at the moment she felt he was being genuine. "No, but…thank you," she answered.

"Aw, Sam," Kathleen started, sounding disappointed.

"It's okay," Jack interrupted. "You made a lot of headway for one day." He picked up Azure's leash, gave her the okay to get up, and said, "I'll take Azure back to the kennels, and we can finish up the tour." He stopped suddenly and turned to Samantha. "Oh, about that cat. Mr. Malcolm happened to call the other day to ask about him. His name is Rascal. Turns out that he was part of the package for buying the house. Mr. Malcolm said he told me about him, but, uh…it must have slipped my mind."

Samantha gave Kathleen what she hoped was a "Didn't I tell you so?" look.

"If it's any consolation, he said Rascal has been fixed," Jack offered.

"Thank you, Jack. It's a great consolation," said Kathleen.

"I don't suppose either of you would be interested in having another cat?" Jack asked tentatively.

In perfect unison, the sisters answered, "No!"

Later, on the drive back to Running Deer Ranch, Samantha was quiet.

"Interesting, don't you think?" Kathleen prompted.

"Yes, very interesting," Samantha echoed, but her mind had drifted off to planning for the Award Ceremony. "I'd like to get to the venue early so that I can practice walking up and down from the podium."

"Fine. We'll take my car and leave early. Pete can come later. Actually, that works better for me because then Nonna can get home sooner. She's babysitting Lily tonight. And I know Pete will want to stay later."

Around five o'clock that evening, their grandmother arrived. "Oh my, girls, look at your glossy tresses!" she said.

"Nonna, no one says 'glossy tresses' anymore," Samantha said teasingly. "You've *got* to stay hip."

"Really? Well, that's a shame. It's such a good phrase. What *should* I say?" she asked.

"Probably that we might be mistaken for Raquel Welch," said Kathleen.

"Minus the cleavage," Samantha added.

"Who's Raquel Welch?" Nonna asked.

"Ask any guy!" Kathleen tossed over her shoulder as she and Samantha went to the car.

As soon as they arrived at the venue, Samantha went straight to the platform and started counting steps with her white cane.

"Three small stair steps, turn right, then about seven steps to the podium," said a male voice that was becoming all too familiar.

Samantha whipped around. "Jack? What are *you* doing here?"

"Your sister invited me this morning."

Kathleen came bustling up right behind him. "We had an extra ticket, Sam," she rushed to say, "and I thought it would be a small way to thank Jack for the private tour this morning. And to welcome him to the neighborhood. Seemed a shame to waste the ticket, you know, since your friend was unable to attend. Guess I forgot to mention it to you." Under her breath she whispered to Samantha, "Stop gaping like a hooked fish."

Samantha clamped her lips together and cast what she hoped was a searing look at her.

"You both look especially lovely tonight," Jack said pleasantly

"Well, thank you, Jack," answered Kathleen. "Your tuxedo looks brand new. I hope you didn't have to rent it."

"No. I keep one ready at a moment's notice just in case of emergency high society events like tonight," he answered amiably.

That remark gave Samantha a small measure of relief. At least he might have some sense of the dignity of tonight's event. He struck her as the kind of guy who tucked his napkin under his chin like a big lobster bib.

"Oh, I see Pete!" said Kathleen, conveniently excusing herself. "He just arrived. See you both at dinner! Sam, our place cards are at table four, farthest to the right of the platform."

Jack turned and watched her go. "I like your sister. She's—"

"Intrusive? Meddlesome? Devious?"

"I was going to say she's fun." Jack turned back to Samantha. "Where were we? Oh yes, scoping out the steps to the podium. Not planning to use the white cane to accept the award?"

He had read her mind. Effortlessly, he acted as a human guide, placing her right hand on his left elbow as he guided her up the steps. "Okay, three up. Stop, turn right. Let's count the steps. Four, five, six, seven, eight. Feel the podium? Let's turn and go back and try it again."

After dinner, the lengthy Award Ceremony, many photo opportunities of the winners in each category, and countless congratulatory hugs, Samantha whispered to Kathleen, "Have you seen that Jack guy?"

"Yes, he's straight across from us, talking to people. He seems to know everybody here, or they know him. I just *know* I've seen him before."

"Kathleen, it wasn't fair to invite him to this. Not to him, not to me. You have to stop this habit of throwing me under the train. I think you enjoy it."

Pete was standing next to them and explained reasonably, "Look at it this way, Sam. If we're friendly to him, maybe he'll sell the property to us."

"Hush," whispered Kathleen. "Here he comes."

"There you are," Jack said as he approached Samantha. "Thought I'd lost you to your adoring crowd. May I have this dance?" He gently took hold of one of her hands but waited for a response.

Surprised by his gallantry, Samantha slowly nodded. Gracefully, Jack led her on to the dance floor as the band started to play a new number.

Should she say something?. "Jack, Kathleen might have misled you," she started in a carefully crafted 'let's-clarify-things' speech.

"Actually, Sam, *you're* the one who is misleading me. Right now. Can't you just relax and let me lead?"

"Oh. Sorry." Embarrassed, she stumbled for a few steps before catching on.

"There! Much easier than having us both lead," he said. "You did a great job accepting the award. Excellent speech. Very professional."

With unmasked interest, she asked, "Really? You're not just saying that?"

"I have never once thought about olive trees being so old."

"Olives have been around a long time," she said. "They don't have rings in the wood, but there are living olive trees today that date back six thousand years."

"I liked the part when you mentioned that it was the olive branch that the dove brought back to Noah after the great flood. Come to think of it, there are actually a lot of references in the Bible to olives."

Samantha tried to cover a smirk. What would a dog trainer know about the *Bible*? "Yes, well, they're the oldest known cultivated trees in history."

"No kidding? The black kind that's in the can?"

Samantha gave him a bemused look.

"What? What did I say wrong?"

"Well," she explained with professorial patience, "they're only black in the can because they have been exposed to air after lye extraction."

"Oh."

"Don't feel badly. Many people are olive ignorant," she said magnanimously. Then she lowered her voice. "Jack, when I went up to the podium, did I appear blind?"

"No, you didn't. Why should it matter?"

"I want people to focus on our company. I don't want anyone's pity." She raised an eyebrow at him. "Not *anyone's*."

"What?" he asked, catching her innuendo. "I don't pity you, Sam. I felt a little sorry for you when you were nearly run over by the car. Maybe a little when you tripped and fell in the bus. But why would you think that I pity you?"

"I guess I don't know *what* to think about you, I met you a few weeks ago on a bus, and you seem irrationally insistent to have me get a guide dog, and now you're suddenly my sister's new best friend."

Jack laughed.

She had to admit she liked his laugh. It was the kind of laugh that made her smile. A contagious laugh. "Is it even possible to insult you?"

"Nope. I've got a pretty thick hide," he said. "But I don't think I would ever pity you." He twirled her around until she couldn't help but start to smile. "So...why is the olive farm called 'Running Deer'?"

"Ranch. Not a farm. My grandfather named it because we have so many deer on the property, and they seem to always be on the run."

Jack burst out laughing again as if Samantha had made a joke. She scrunched up her face, puzzled. She didn't make jokes. "Why is that so funny?"

"I figured there was a really cool story behind it like your grandfather was an Indian chief."

"With a name like Christiansen?"

That only got Jack laughing even more. "More like a Viking, huh?"

After the song ended, Kathleen interrupted them. "I'm going to go now and relieve Nonna. Sam, stay and have some fun; Pete's planning to bring you home. Thanks for coming, Jack. You're quite a smooth dancer. You even make Sam look like a good dancer." She turned and left before Samantha could object.

As the band started up its next song, Samantha broached an important subject. She smiled, too sweetly. "Jack, is there any chance you would consider selling us Mr. Malcolm's property? For a profit, of course."

"It's now *my* property, no longer Mr. Malcolm's. And no, no chance at all," he said, just as sweetly.

As soon as the music ended, he asked if she would mind sitting down. Bending down to rub his knee, he asked her, "Can I get you something to drink?"

"Just sparkling water, please."

Jack left to go get their beverages. Suddenly, two churlish young men came up to Samantha and sat down, one on each side of her. They smelled strongly of stale cigarettes and...a slightly sweet smell...she couldn't quite place it...almost like alfalfa hay...*mixed with the aroma of overly ripe arm pits.* She crinkled her nose and shuddered with disgust. Something about their oafish manner made the hair on her neck rise, even in the midst of a big party, especially when she realized they had been waiting until she was alone.

"Hey lady, we got a message for you to deliver to your husband. Tell him that he's been warned. No more late payments."

"Wait *just* a minute," Samantha objected indignantly. "That man is *not* my—"

"Just remember to deliver that message," interrupted the other man. "Our boss is runnin' out of patience." And just as suddenly as they came, they left.

Samantha remained glued to her chair, completely flummoxed. Those guys had obviously confused her with someone else. Jack's wife.

Another couple of things to add to the list of what I don't like about Jack. He bought Mr. Malcolm's property. He's married. And he's involved in something illegal.

She shivered, though the night was hot.

Chapter Three: **The Academy**

Samantha dreaded these appointments. She'd rather be just about anywhere else. On a hot August day, Samantha sat in her eye doctor's office for a routine appointment. Routine, for her, meant she would be informed about the percentage of vision loss she had experienced in the last six months. As if she didn't know! She could barely see anything anymore—just fuzzy shapes and shadows—and there was *nothing* she could do about it.

Dr. Freeman, a tall, thin wisp of a man with wire-rimmed glasses, scribbled down notes after examining her eyes. "So, Sam, have you been following this Woodstock festival?" he asked.

"A little bit," Samantha answered. "It's on some dairy farm in upstate New York, right?"

"Yes. Hundreds of thousands of flower children." He sighed and closed her chart. "No doubt my son is there."

Samantha had gone to Dr. Freeman for eye exams ever since she was a teenager. His son had participated in the "Summer of Love" in San Francisco two years ago and never returned home after that. "Have you heard from him lately?"

He leaned back in his squeaky chair, releasing a weary sigh. "Once in a great while, he calls us—collect—to ask us to send money."

"Oh." Samantha wasn't quite sure what to say. "That dairy farm will never be the same. Imagine the smells—a mass of humanity among a mass of cows...in August!" She wrinkled her nose.

Dr. Freeman snorted. He opened her chart again and started to ask her questions about how she was coping with her diminishing vision. "Sounds to me like anxiety," he suggested, after she admitted she was having trouble sleeping. "Not unusual when you're adjusting to vision loss."

Samantha squeezed her hands together and asked the one question she had never wanted to ask Dr. Freeman. It was time to know the answer. "How much longer can I expect to have some vision left?"

He swiveled around in his chair to face her. "Hard to say, Sam. Your visual field lost another five percent in just six months. That's about double what I would have expected. Could be stress related. Anything new?"

"Not really," she shrugged. "The business is expanding, but it's not stressful. Not bad stress, anyway."

"Accommodating reduced vision can be stressful." His chair squeaked as he rolled back and forth. "It hasn't been proven, but there's strong indication that trauma or stress accelerates vision loss. It's your weak link."

She drew a deep breath and squeezed her eyes shut for a moment. "There's a part of me that wonders if it might be a relief to finally be completely blind. Having a little bit of light and shadow in one eye, and the other eye feels like there's a screen in front of it, and colors are gone in both…well, maybe it will be easier when it's finally gone."

"Other patients have said the same thing."

Chin to her chest, Samantha quietly added, "My sister wants me to get a guide dog."

"What do you think?"

She gathered her words carefully. "I was almost hit by a car a few weeks ago. I was crossing the street to catch the bus, and I didn't see the car coming. That's the first time I've had such a close call. I haven't really slept well since."

Dr. Freeman scratched his chin. "I'm going to give you a prescription for something to help you sleep. Just to take the edge off." He scribbled on a prescription pad and tore off the sheet to hand to Samantha.

She held the thin paper in her hand and frowned. "I really don't want to start taking medication. I can handle this."

"Okay. Just keep it, though. We all need a little help sometimes. Give some serious thought to the guide dog idea, Sam. I've had lots of patients who have had wonderful experiences with guides." He patted her on the back as he headed to the door. "See you again in six months."

She lifted her chin. "I hope you'll hear from your son soon. That he's coming home."

"Thanks. I hope you're right."

Later that week, Samantha was folding laundry when her phone rang. Juggling a stack of towels in one arm, she reached for the receiver to answer it.

"Sam? It's Jack. Jack Shaw. Your new neighbor. Remember me?"

How could I forget? "Vaguely. How did you get my phone number?"

"It's right here on the paperwork you sent in."

She tucked the towels in the linen closet. "What paperwork?"

"The paperwork you sent in to apply for a guide dog."

"What?"

"We've had a cancellation in the next class."

Her heart kicked into overdrive as she tried to stay calm. "Jack, I—"

"Class starts tomorrow at 3 p.m.," he interrupted. "You're very fortunate, Sam. This process usually takes months. There are people ahead of you, but since you're local and we're within twenty-four hours of class starting, it's too late to give notice to people who live far away. I was given the green light to fill the slot with you."

"Jack! *Please* listen to me. I never sent in the paperwork!"

"Sure you did. Your signature is right here."

"No! No I didn't! My sister forged it! Look at the 'S.' She always makes a curl on top of the S. I never do that."

"She *forged* your signature?"

"Yes! She does it all the time."

She heard Jack take a deep breath. "Wow. Wow. Wow. Is that a twin thing?"

With teeth gritted, Samantha answered, "No, it's a *Kat* thing." She briefly pondered how many years in prison she would have to serve if she murdered her sister but then decided that no jury would convict her. *They would understand, even sympathize.*

"Well, well. That changes things."

From somewhere deep inside, not aware of making the decision, Samantha blurted out, "Wait! Jack, wait! Um...give me an hour to think about it?"

"Absolutely!" He sounded pleased, which annoyed her. "Just get back to me by five o'clock one way or the other."

Slowly, she put the phone back on the receiver. *Why didn't I just say no?* She was astounded at herself. *Where in the world did that flicker of uncertainty come from?* She was a woman who lived by lists, who didn't like surprises. And now, she had just surprised herself. Plus, she still had an enormous decision to make. A slow burn started rising within her. Getting mad felt easier than making a decision, so she turned out her cottage lights and headed to the farmhouse.

* * * *

Nervously, Kathleen kept one eye on the cottage, expecting Samantha to come storming over at any moment.

"Here she comes," Nonna told her in a warning voice, looking out the window as Samantha slammed her cottage door. "You shouldn't have done it."

"But she never would have done it herself!" Kathleen reasoned. She could tell Samantha was furious; her mouth had a tight, pinched look, and her hands were clenched in fists at her side as she marched toward the kitchen. Kathleen opened the door, bracing for the onslaught. "So...I take it that Jack got hold of you?" Kathleen said meekly, when Samantha reached her. Kathleen cleared her throat. "He called here first, looking for you."

"How could you?! How dare you!"

Kathleen bit her lip. Samantha seemed angrier than she had expected her to be. Her mind whirred with excuses, but then she decided to try a different approach than deception. "Sam, I plead guilty to everything, but you still have to go tomorrow."

"I haven't even decided yet if I *want* a guide dog." Samantha plopped down in a kitchen chair.

Kathleen exchanged a look of surprise with Nonna. She hadn't expected Samantha's tirade to wind down so quickly. And she had assumed that Samantha wouldn't even *consider* attending the program. This was a good sign! Emboldened, she was ready to pull out all of her persuasion tactics. "Sam, try it! Just *try* it. Jack said that the spot would go empty; it's too late to bring someone else in."

Nonna sat down in a chair facing Samantha, covering Samantha's hand with her own. Softly but firmly, she said, "Sammy, Kathleen might have overstepped a little—"

"You think so?" Samantha asked sarcastically.

Kathleen rolled her eyes.

"—but she did so with the best of intentions. Honey, you need more help than a white cane can give you."

That Samantha couldn't deny. She stood up and walked over to lean against the kitchen counter. "Even if I did think about getting a guide dog...the timing right now is terrible! The *ranch!* The *loan!* And the new mill needs to be installed in the processing facility by harvest time."

"Pete and I will take care of it," Kathleen offered.

Samantha groaned and covered her face with her hands. "In one month, you could run this company into the ground."

"Oh Sam, you're not leaving the country," Kathleen said. "It's only twenty-eight days. Samantha, trust us. You *need* to do this."

Samantha remained silent.

"And you haven't taken a vacation in years."

Samantha's chin snapped up. "This *hardly* sounds like a vacation, Kat! It sounds like a tremendous amount of work. I know nothing about dogs. I'm afraid of dogs! And the end result is to completely change my life! That is *not* a vacation." Samantha turned to face the window, arms crossed, biting her lip in deep thought.

Kathleen opened her mouth to say something when Nonna silenced her with a warning glance.

Finally, almost whispering, Samantha turned her head slightly and asked, "Nonna, do you think I really need it?"

Nonna stood up and walked over to Samantha, gently gripping her upper arms. "I do, sweetheart." The words came soft and unhurried. "Sammy, you're so young. You have so much living still to do. But your world has begun to shrink. You hardly leave the ranch anymore unless you have to. As if it's the only place that you're safe. That's not *you,* Samantha."

Samantha hung her head for a long moment and then gave a deep sigh of resignation. "Okay. Okay. I'll try it." She squinted her eyes at Kathleen. "It's time you keep your sticky little fingers off of the controls."

"Oh, Sammy, you know you can't stay mad at me for long." Kathleen jumped up and rubbed her hands together, thrilled at this outcome. She never dreamed her sister would agree to go without a fight! "I've already packed for you. I found your hidden key to your cottage."

"Nonna, remind me to hide my key in a better Kat-proof place," Samantha muttered.

"There goes that muttering again!" Kathleen scowled at her. "Anyway, we're going to have a special dinner. Nonna promised to bake her world famous mint chocolate brownies, didn't you, Nonna?"

"Already bought the ingredients," Nonna said. "I just need you both to leave the kitchen so I can bake in peace."

"Then we'll go," Kathleen said, standing up. "By the way, Sam, I've even invited Boring Bob."

Samantha folded her arms on the table and slammed her head against them, over and over, defeated.

Five minutes before five o'clock, Samantha made the call to Jack. The giant and automatic smile in his voice only irked her. At least, she realized, comforted by the thought, he would be back in the kennels with the dogs. She could avoid him. He was a dog trainer not a people trainer.

* * * *

The Christiansen family ate dinner al fresco, on the patio, enjoying a perfect, bug-free, humidity-free California summer evening, bathed in purple twilight. At least it *was* a perfect evening until the reason for the special dinner came up in conversation.

"You mean, you filled out the paperwork and sent it in without Samantha's knowledge?" Bob asked accusingly. "That's just *wrong,* Kathleen."

Kathleen ignored Bob and passed the salad to Nonna. She could tell he was glaring at her, but she didn't care. Bob always thought he knew what was best for Samantha.

"Bob, let me give you some advice," said Pete, laughing amiably. "Don't interfere with twins."

"Good advice from a guy who has long been comfortable in his role of being the filling in the sandwich," Kathleen said, leaning over to pick up the food Lily had thrown on the ground.

"This is not a laughing matter," persisted Bob. "This is inexcusable. Kathleen, you had no *right* to make that kind of a decision for Samantha."

Now Bob had crossed the line; Kathleen was getting steamed. Bob never did understand the connection between twins, she thought, glaring at him. It was one of the main reasons she didn't want Samantha to marry him. "Well, Bob, this isn't *your* decision," defended Kathleen, rising up in her seat. "This is Sam's decision."

Bob stood up to face her. "You should talk! You *filled* out the application without her knowledge. You *forged* her signature. You *packed* her bags. What kind of interference is that?"

"Enough!" said Nonna, holding her hands up in the air as a warning. "Samantha is right here and can speak for herself on the matter." The charm of her voice neutralized the static electricity in the air.

Slowly, like two boxers circling each other in the ring, Kathleen and Bob backed down, resuming the meal.

"Thank you, Nonna," Samantha said, smoothing her napkin over her lap. She turned toward Bob. "I'm going to go ahead and try it. I hate to admit it, but Kat's probably right. I never would have done it myself. Maybe it's just as well that it has happened so suddenly. I would talk myself out of it."

"Maybe there's a reason. Maybe having a dog isn't right for you," objected Bob.

"Maybe so," Samantha said, "but I'm going to find out for myself. I need to try. I've lost a lot of vision this year. I don't want to be dependent on anyone not anymore than I have to be."

"You *don't* need a guide dog, Sam!" insisted Bob.

Kathleen slammed down her fists on the table. "Let Samantha be the judge of that!"

"Well, you seem to have already made the decision for her!" Bob argued back.

An awkward silence fell over the table, thick and uncomfortable.

As if on cue, the phone rang in the kitchen. Pete jumped up, looking relieved to have an excuse to leave. "I'll get it. Be right back," he said, heading into the house.

Samantha turned to Kathleen and Bob. "Please, let's not spoil the dinner. This meal is delicious, and it's my last one with all of you for a month." She smiled, a little uncertainly, quelling the tension. "Now, where are your mint brownies, Nonna?"

Nonna blinked several times, as though this was something she should know and didn't. "I'm sorry, dear. You never said anything about mint brownies," she said.

"Yes I did. Don't you remember? We were in the kitchen today," said Kathleen. "Sam, you heard me, didn't you?"

Tilting her head toward Nonna, looking concerned, Samantha gave a slow nod.

"No, Kathleen," Nonna answered, waving the thought away with her hand. "You must be mistaken."

Kathleen sighed and went into the kitchen to scrounge up some ice cream from the freezer. Pete hung up the phone with a bang, looking distracted and agitated.

"What's wrong?" she asked him.

"Nothing," he said curtly. "Just a problem about a missed delivery." He glanced at his watch. "I'd better get up to the office and check on it." He grabbed the truck keys on his way out.

This evening wasn't going the way Kathleen had hoped, she groused out loud, unaware that the kitchen window was open and everyone could hear her.

* * * *

The next afternoon, Kathleen, Lily, and Pete helped Samantha unpack in her dormitory room at the California Canine Academy for the Blind.

"First meeting is in the Day Room at 4 p.m.," said Lisa, an instructor who led them to Samantha's room.

After shoving Samantha's empty suitcase on the top shelf of the closet, Pete said, "Kat, we should go and let Sam get settled."

"Call if you've forgotten anything, and I'll run it over." Kathleen reached over to hug Samantha.

Over Kathleen's shoulder, Samantha listed last minute instructions to Pete. "You should be getting a call within a week or two when the mill is through Customs and ready for delivery. I have the check already drafted. It's in my locked desk drawer. You're the only one who knows where the key is hidden." She pulled away from Kathleen, casting a suspicious look at her. "The building site is almost completely prepared. It should be seamless."

"Let us worry about Running Deer, and you worry about learning how to work with a guide dog," Pete said in a big brotherly tone. "Kat, let's go before we end up causing her to change her mind." He gave Samantha a quick hug and pulled Kathleen from the room.

"Make lots of friends!" she heard Kathleen call to her from down the hall.

As soon as they left, an ominous quiet filled the room. *I have to make friends?* Samantha thought, starting to panic. Growing up with a twin sister, she didn't need to work that muscle used to make friends. She wasn't even sure she had that muscle.

Samantha had a firm desire to be elsewhere. *What am I doing here? What have I gotten myself into?* She balled up her fist and rubbed the place between her ribs, feeling that dreaded knot in her stomach start rising up in her. *Maybe I could slip out without anyone noticing.* She put her hand up on the closet shelf to reach her suitcase just as someone walked into her room, interrupting her plan of escape.

"Bienvenue! You must be Zamanza. I am Etienne. Your roommate!" said an elderly woman.

Relinquishing her escape plan with some reluctance, Samantha said, "Hello, Etienne. What an unusual name. I've never heard it before."

"I am ze fifth generation Etienne. My muzzer, my grandmuzzer, my great grandmuzzer, my great-great grandmuzzer! I am Etienne Number Five!" She sat down on the bed. "Iz it not exciting? Here I am, seventy-two yearz-old, ready to get my first guide dog! Ozzer service dog organizations have age limits but not zis one. Fantastique, no?"

"Fantastic?" Samantha said weakly. She put down her white cane and sat on her own bed. "Or terrifying? I'm not really sure this is right for me."

"Zamanza, we must be willing to get rid of ze life we have planned zo az to have ze life that iz waiting for uz."

Well, Samantha consoled herself, *at the very least I will have a roommate with a to-die-for French accent.* "I'm impressed, Etienne. Is that original?"

"Goodnezz, no. I collect quotes. I zink of zem as little lightz along our path."

A little bell went off in the clock next to Etienne's bed. "Four o'clock," Samantha noted, steeling herself. "I guess it's time to get this show on the road." She took a deep breath and reached for her cane.

In the Day Room, the students sat in a large circle as Lisa started introductions.

"My name is Kenny. I race sailboats," explained one young, energetic-sounding man. "I live up in Puget Sound and sail around the Orcas Islands."

"Could you explain a little about your experience as a blind sailor, Kenny?" encouraged Lisa.

"We have a crew of two blind sailors and two sighted sailors. The key to a crew's success is communication. I have to rely on all of my senses on the water. I even listen to how close other boats are to me by listening to their movement through the water and the luff of their sails."

"Ever had a collision?" asked another student.

"Oh, a few close calls. It's not one hundred percent accurate, but you'd be amazed at how much you can see by listening." Kenny explained that he had been born prematurely and suffered a ruptured optic nerve after receiving too much oxygen in his incubator.

"How about you, Anne?" prompted Lisa to the woman seated next to Kenny.

"I have macular degeneration," explained Anne. "I knew I would be facing blindness at mid-life; my father had macular degeneration, too. He used a guide dog. I saw how much freedom he was able to have."

"Ray?" asked Lisa. "What about you?"

"I'm a mechanic," Ray answered in a husky Texan accent, "but in my spare time, I hunt."

"You hunt?" Samantha blurted out. "With a gun?" She hoped his hunting companions weren't blind, also.

"I grew up huntin'," Ray answered patiently. "I had always learned to rely on my own instincts. I decided there just wasn't no reason to quit the sport after losing my vision. I lost my sight completely when I was twenty-five because of RP." He crossed one leg and slapped his knee. "But y'all can relax. I do everything but actually pull the trigger."

"Ray, have you ever heard of modified hunting rifles?" asked Lisa. "We've had other blind hunters use them. The rifle allows a blind person to shoot while a sighted person aims and steadies the gun."

"Yeah, I know. I've tried 'em. But I don't think the rifle is accurate enough to kill a target on the first shot. In my mind, that's a hunter's duty. Besides, shootin' is only a small part of hunting. I can usually hear my prey long before my partner can. He's distracted by other sights, but I'm listenin'. And heck, I can drag the game out of the field with the best of 'em."

Samantha thought nothing could top the blind sailor or blind hunter story, until she heard Ed's story. "I'm a parachutist," he explained. "I've jumped over five hundred times since I lost my vision to a degenerative eye disorder."

"So tell us how it works," Lisa asked.

"Most times, I'll jump with a partner so we know when to pull the cord. But when I do solo jumps, I rely on a two-way radio to tell me when to pull the parachute and where to land."

The most intriguing person for Samantha, however, was a gentleman in his sixties, Dr. David Sommers, a college president for a small Christian college in Southern California. He didn't have a dramatic story; he had recently lost his sight to nonarthritic ischemic optic neuropathy and blamed his vision loss on stress. He explained that he and his wife were getting ready to leave on a vacation when he noticed some gray spots in his eyesight. Over the next few days, the dots grew into large blind patches; within weeks, he had lost ninety percent of his sight. He could see shapes in bright light, but he was essentially blind for life.

But then he made a comment that filled Samantha with awe: "I believe that blindness has made me a better person."

How could any one come to that conclusion? Instantly, she knew that she wanted to get to know him better. She *needed* to get to know him better. *Maybe that's why I'm here. To meet Dr. Sommers.*

Despite her misgivings about being at CCAB, Samantha couldn't help but be fascinated by the interesting and varied assortment of students. Etienne, at seventy-two, was the oldest, blind from glaucoma; Jon, at nineteen, was the youngest, losing his vision from RP like Samantha. Jon had already made plans to hike the entire Oregon Trail with his soon-to-be-partnered guide dog.

The one common thread she noticed was each person desired a full and independent life. And everyone was eager about getting a guide dog, looking forward to the enhanced freedom the dog would provide for them.

Everyone. Except for me.

* * * *

Glancing at his wristwatch, Jack hurried to get to the Day Room to meet the new group of students. He frowned when he realized how late he was. Lisa was always on his case for being late. He wanted to make a good first impression on the students, especially Samantha. He could tell she didn't think much of him, especially after she found out he bought her neighbor's property. The cat didn't help, either.

He quietly opened the door, hoping to sneak in, unnoticed, when he heard Lisa ask, "And Samantha? What's your story?"

Jack glanced around the room to find Samantha. He had to hold back a grin when he saw her. She was biting her lip, arms crossed tightly against her chest, looking like she would rather have a root canal, minus anesthesia, than be here. He wasn't surprised. After finding out her sister had filled out the paperwork, he had been shocked when she agreed to come. He was glad he didn't have sisters.

"Well, um, my family runs an olive ranch," Samantha said softly.

"Jack!" said Lisa, spotting him. "Late as usual! We just finished introductions, so I'll pass the meeting off to you."

He noticed that Samantha's head jerked up like a fish on the line when Lisa mentioned his name. *Was that a good thing? Probably not.*

* * * *

Samantha's throat pinched tight at the mention of Jack's name. *What is he doing here? He said he worked in the kennels! Back with the dogs!* Her feeling of dread intensified. She thought about making a break for the door like a sailor in a capsized boat who spied a lighthouse. She wondered if anyone would notice. *Of course not!* she decided, comforted by the thought. *They're blind, too.*

"Hello everyone, I'm Jack Shaw, an instructor here," Jack started, interrupting Samantha's muse. "Welcome to California Canine Academy for the Blind. To put it in terms that everyone can easily understand, consider this month to be football training camp. You're in conditioning for the upcoming season."

A couple of the athletes murmured enthusiastically as Samantha leaned over to Etienne and whispered, "*What* is he talking about?"

"Je ne sais pas. I do not know," Etienne answered. "Football in France iz zoccer."

"By the end of this month," continued Jack, unaware of the stir he had created, "I can guarantee you'll leave here with more self-confidence and independence and better skills to be competitive in a sighted world. The next best thing to having your sight back will be having this guide dog at your side. You will be able to go wherever you want to go. You'll be an unstoppable team. It may be hard to believe right now, but by the end of this month, your guide dog will become an extension of you."

Jack went on to explain the purpose of the next few days before the official "Dog Day" of student/dog pairing scheduled for Wednesday. "We're going to be developing your skills, getting you prepared for your dog by working with the commands you're going to be using, doing some Juno skills, and evaluating which dog from our strings is best suited for you." He walked around the circle as he spoke. "Now... it may seem as if each day, we keep moving the goalpost on you..."

Again, Samantha gently nudged Etienne with her elbow. Etienne nudged her back.

"...but there's a good reason for that," continued Jack. "At the end of each and every day, through different exercises, you are going to keep developing confidence in yourself and in your dog so that when you leave here, you're ready for any situation. We have assigned groups of one instructor per four people. I'm going to read out the names, and the instructors will come up to you to start your tour."

As Jack called out the groups, one by one, the room emptied. Soon, only four students remained. "Dr. Sommers, Samantha, Etienne, and Jon. You've been assigned to me," he said.

Samantha's stomach started churning. Jack made her very uncomfortable. She couldn't forget that strange situation with those ruffians at the Award Ceremony. But mostly, she still hadn't forgiven him for buying Mr. Malcolm's property.

For the next two days, the students woke up at six thirty, ate breakfast, sat through a lecture, practiced commands, rehearsed Juno, and ate lunch. Then, they sat through another lecture, practiced skills, ate dinner, heard another lecture, were asked innumerable questions about their lifestyle by the instructors, and fell into bed, exhausted and overwhelmed by the steep learning curve.

"How am I ever going to remember all of this?" Samantha moaned to Etienne as they were getting into their beds one night.

One of the instructors explained that this month wasn't about training the dogs, but training the students. "These dogs have already been trained. You're the ones who have to be trained to learn how to read your dogs. That's what we're going to prepare you to do." The lectures covered every imaginable dog-related topic from grooming to health care to what to do if their guide dog was ever attacked by an aggressive dog.

During one exercise, the students were told to line up with their leashes attached to a chain link fence to practice the proper way to give corrections. "Snap. Pop. Release. Okay, keep trying until it becomes automatic," said Jack, walking along the line of students.

At lunch, Samantha sat down next to Lisa. "Do you think you could help me figure out how to hold a harness properly?" she asked, stretching out her aching left hand. "It feels so cumbersome."

"It won't be long until it's comfortable to you," Lisa said between bites of her sandwich. "Jack could probably work with you after lecture tonight."

"Well, um, I was thinking that, well, maybe I should change instructors."

Lisa put the rest of her sandwich into her paper bag. "Why?"

"You see, Jack is actually my neighbor and—"

"No kidding? Cool! He can help when you get back home." She hopped up to get another cookie.

That wasn't exactly what I was hoping for.

Later in the day, as they were working around obstacles and practicing commands yet again, Jack came up alongside Samantha. "So word on the street tells me that you want a different instructor."

Thanks a lot, Lisa, Samantha silently fumed. "Uh, what exactly did she tell you?"

"Something like...I'm so handsome that you're having trouble concentrating."

Samantha's eyes widened. "Blind jokes? You make *blind* jokes with your students?"

Jack laughed. "Look, Sam. There's a reason you're in my group. The four people assigned to me have had no experience with dogs. They always give me the rookies. I like the challenge." He grinned and socked her gently on her arm. "So buck up, Private. Only twenty-six days to go."

Chapter Four: **Azure**

The first Wednesday of each new class was called "Dog Day." The instructors had carefully matched the class-ready dogs to the needs of each student. The assigned dogs were getting bathed and groomed while the students waited anxiously in their rooms for the instructor to come and bring their dog to them.

Jack found Samantha in the hallway, dialing the dormitory phone.

"Ready, Sam?" Jack asked. He noticed she always froze, like a squirrel caught in traffic, when she heard his voice.

"So soon?" she asked. She put down the receiver, took a deep breath, and stood up. Jack placed her hand on his elbow and guided her up the long hallway to the Day Room.

Half-way down, Samantha suddenly stopped and faced Jack. "What if this dog doesn't like me?" she whispered.

The earnestness on her face caught him off guard. It was one of the things he found puzzling and intriguing about Samantha. At times, she seemed cucumber cool, competent and confident, like when she was giving the speech at that ceremony. That speech blew him away. Everyone else, too. She delivered it flawlessly like she gave speeches every day.

But there were other moments, like this one, when she seemed shy and insecure, vulnerable almost. An odd feeling came over him when she looked at him like this. He thought he was seeing the real Sam. There was an echo of sadness in her eyes. She just seemed so…real. But it also made him want to protect her, and he knew that's where he needed to be careful. A sweet smile spread across his face. "Sam, more importantly, what if this dog does?" he whispered back.

Jack described the dog assigned to Samantha. "I've got a yellow lab picked out for you with big brown eyes and a coffee cream colored coat, dark for a lab. She has a very gentle disposition, can handle a lot of distractions, and has a good temperament for travel. I think she's just right for you, Sam. She's an 'every down player' type of dog."

"What does *that* mean?" Samantha tilted her head at Jack. "Wait…a girl? I have a girl dog? What's her name?"

"I'll tell you in a minute as soon as I bring her in." He led her to a chair. "Well, Sam, are you ready for your new partner?"

"I think so. I hope so."

"Better know it, Sam," he intoned solemnly.

* * * *

An eternity later, Jack returned. "Here she is." The dog went straight up to Samantha, thumping her tail, licking her face.

Samantha framed her hands on the dog's head, holding her back from licking her, when something familiar struck a chord. "Jack, is this…? Could this be Azure?"

Jack laughed. "Sure is. She suits you the best. Plus, she already likes you so for a person with acute dog phobia, it seems like an added bonus." He put her hand on the harness.

Tentatively, Samantha picked up the handle on Azure's harness, aware of the gravity of the moment. The first of many times. She stood to return to her room and confidently gave Azure the hand signal to go forward.

"Uh, opposite direction, Sam," Jack said. "Straight behind you, third door on your left."

Embarrassed, Samantha spun around, surprised at how attuned Azure was to her movements. Once in the dorm room, Samantha lifted off Azure's harness. Azure began sniffing and didn't stop until she had sniffed every square inch of the room then curled up into a ball. Samantha sat down beside her on the floor, stroking her head, listening to Azure's peaceful, steady breathing. As it deepened into gentle snores, Samantha thought the sound was almost achingly beautiful. Her dog. Her partner. Her companion.

The next week sped by. Each day was carefully planned to help the students develop confidence in all kinds of situations. At first, they stayed close to campus.

"Your dog is trained to navigate obstacles, so he takes a wide path around objects in your path. Trust your dog and start reading his movements," explained one of the instructors.

"Remember, that's the main thing you're trying to learn in the next few weeks. *Learn to read your dog's movements*."

Sunday, even at CCAB, was a day set apart. Volunteers for CCAB offered to drive students to church, to the wine country, or to other places of interest. Samantha had planned to spend the day catching up on Running Deer work, but Etienne had other ideas. She signed them both up for an afternoon outing to Point Reyes National Seashore.

"Et will be zuch fun, Zamanza! Pleeze come wiz me. I want to zee every zing in California zat zer iz to zee before I return to my daughter'z house in Nevada. I have never zeen ze Pazific Ozean! We have been working zo hard; we need ze break. Just a few hourz. Come. Pleeze come. I do not want to go wizout you. Iz good for uz. Oui?"

As Samantha tried to think up an iron-clad excuse to remain at the dormitory, Etienne deftly slipped the harness on Azure, scooped Samantha's jacket off of the bedpost, and gently pulled her along. Samantha grimaced. Her entire afternoon had just been high-jacked by this tiny little French roommate. Smiling weakly, she climbed into some kind-hearted volunteer's mini-van and tried not to fret about Running Deer.

* * * *

Leaving sunny Santa Galena, they entered a microclimate of bitter cold fog as they drove to Point Reyes, a triangle of coastline, forest and grasslands. The first stop was the Lighthouse's Visitor Center.

"Welcome, welcome," said the portly ranger, his voice deep and resonating. "This park has more avian diversity than any other U.S. national park, and the birds are protected here, too, so they're easier to spot." He stopped abruptly, and his eyes went wide. He cleared his throat, suddenly embarrassed, as it occurred to him that he was describing bird watching to a group of blind people. "Ahem, I mean, um, to hear."

Noticing the ranger's awkwardness, Jack jumped in to help. "Blind people would rather not have you adjust conversation for them. Just use the same words, the same inferences." It always amused him to see how uncomfortable people could be around blind people. *Like blind people don't know they're blind!*

Obviously relieved, the ranger finished his welcome speech, encouraging them all to return in January to watch the migration of the whales. As soon as the words left his mouth, he slammed the palm of his head to his forehead.

"Don't worry about it," Jack said reassuringly. "Maybe we'll be back for those whales."

Afterwards, the students walked down the cliffs to get to the beach. At the base of the cliffs were heaps of surf-worn rocks and little sandy alcoves. Beyond that lay the dusky blue of the Pacific Ocean.

Jack followed behind, making sure everyone traversed safely to the beach. He loved the ocean. Today was his day off, but when he heard about this trip to Point Reyes, he offered to attend as an accompanying instructor. He never missed a chance to get to the sea. Standing on the sand, gazing at the ocean always made him feel closer to God. Someone told him once that the love of God is like the ocean; you can see its beginnings but not its end.

"Smell that salt air," said Jack, inhaling deeply, as he came up and stood next to Samantha and Azure. "Listen to those waves crashing! Wish I'd brought my surfboard."

Samantha smiled absently, lost in a memory.

He studied her for a long moment. "Glad you came?" he asked, wondering what she was thinking about. Her eyes were distant and a little mysterious. Half dreaming, half sentient.

"It reminds me of the ocean where I spent my childhood," she said softly.

"Which one?" Jack asked.

"The Bismarck Sea."

Jack's eyes went wide with surprise. Normally, he would ask 'Where the heck is the Bismarck Sea?', but he didn't say anything. He was pretty sure she might clam up if he showed too much interest in her. She still seemed pretty jumpy around him.

She lifted her head toward the sky. "Listening to those sea birds…I'd forgotten about the sound of birds, of how loud they can be. Incredible sounds that nearly drowned out everything else. Parrots with feathers that look like a rainbow of neon lights, eagles, birds of paradise ..." Her words drizzled into thoughtful silence.

"Birds of paradise? Huh. I thought that was a flower."

"The flower was named *for* the bird. Birds of paradise have been hunted for centuries for their plumage. For ladies' hats."

"No kidding?" Jack said good-naturedly. "Sounds like you grew up in a jungle."

Samantha smiled at him as if he was a very dense child. "Not a *jungle*," she said, as if it were obvious. "A *rainforest*." She and Azure headed down to the water, leaving Jack behind.

He watched her go, rubbing his chin. The more time he spent around Samantha, the more he found himself fascinated by her. He kept discovering new aspects to her personality, layer by layer. But then his smile dimmed. After watching her hesitation as she interacted with Azure over the week, he just wasn't quite sure she was ready for a guide dog.

* * * *

A few days later, the students started to go out into the town to practice real-life situations with their guide dogs. Outings were carefully planned to cover every kind of traveling experience that a student and guide dog might encounter: escalators to buses to trains. They even went on a few night walks. "Despite being blind," lectured their thorough instructors, "despite the quiet of an evening, anytime you walk at night, you're going to hear different sounds and face different situations than you will during the day."

The next week, as they walked down yet another street in Santa Galena, Azure stopped suddenly and wouldn't budge. "Let's go, Azure." Samantha made the hand motion to go forward. "Let's go." She said it again with more determination. Azure remained statuesque. "Forward!" Azure wouldn't budge. Samantha bent down to take hold of the leash to lead her forward.

A large hand reached on top of hers.

"Sam," Jack said quietly but firmly. "Lean down carefully, and put your hand forward onto the ground."

As she did what he asked, she discovered that there was an open manhole right in front of her.

"Azure was trying to *keep* you from moving forward," Jack said. "It's called 'intelligent disobedience'. She just saved you from a serious accident. But you completely missed reading her movement."

Mortified, Samantha re-clipped the leash and stroked Azure's head.

"Tonight, Sam, we need to talk," Jack said solemnly.

Samantha was quiet during dinner, unsure of what to expect from Jack. His voice had sounded ominous to her. As soon as the evening lecture on grooming was over, she felt his hand on her elbow.

"Let's go have that conversation," he said.

Samantha, Azure, and Jack went out to a small bench under the redwood trees. The world had shrunken to just the two of them. Samantha kept her attention on Azure, waiting for Jack to begin. She could tell that he was watching her, but she kept her head down. With more bravado than she felt, she said, "Okay, Jack. Let me have it."

Uncharacteristically, Jack remained silent.

"I know you're disappointed with me about this afternoon. I made a mistake."

He leaned forward on his elbows. "It's not just about today, Sam."

"What do you mean?"

"I've worked with you for over a week now. I think you're struggling with a fundamental issue."

"What 'issue?'" she asked defensively.

"Trust. We can't say that enough. You *have* to trust your dog."

Samantha was quiet for a while. "This is all new for me, Jack."

He leaned back and crossed his arms against his chest. "Is it?"

Samantha raised her head indignantly. "You hardly know me!"

"Well, why is *that*, Sam? It's back to the same problem. Trust."

"*What?!* First, within minutes of meeting me, you tell me I need a guide dog. I finally agree to get one. And now you're telling me I'm not *capable* of trusting a guide dog."

"That's not what I said," Jack said calmly.

"Then what *are* you saying?"

"I didn't say you weren't *capable* of trusting Azure. I think you need to make a *choice* to trust her. This dog has been trained to be your eyes for you. When that harness is on, she is on-duty. You have to trust her, just as she trusts you to care for her. You're a team. And there is no 'I' in team. Sam, either you decide to trust her, or—"

"Or what?" Samantha said faintly, not sure if she wanted to hear him finish that sentence.

"Or..." he paused, struggling to find the right words, "maybe having a guide dog isn't right for you. It isn't right for everybody. Using a cane might give you all of the help you need...or want." He leaned back. "I know your sister kind of boxed you into this."

Samantha turned to him, wide-eyed, not quite hearing. Deep within her, after just a few days with Azure, she knew that she could never go back to a white cane again. "I'll work harder."

"But that's my point, Sam. You shouldn't be working harder. Not everything in life can be solved by working harder. Let Azure do her job. That's what she's trained to do. You don't completely control her." He stood up, deep in thought for a moment. "Look, it's like this. Have you ever played any football?"

She groaned. "Is this another blind joke?"

"No. Bear with me. I used to play a little. There were times when I had to make a pass, and I couldn't see the open receiver. I was being blocked too tightly. So I had to throw the football where I last saw the receiver and trust he was there." He sat back down again. "Now do you understand?"

Samantha wrinkled up her face.

Jack sighed. "Sam, you have to be willing to trust Azure, trust that she will be open to receive the ball when you throw it. Do you get it now?"

Slowly, Samantha shook her head.

"I thought I was making it so clear," said Jack, sounding crestfallen. He exhaled in despair. "Well, Sam, the bottom line is that if you really *can't* place your trust in Azure, then it's definitely not going to work."

She turned her head away from Jack. *Now* she grasped the challenge.

"Some people are worthy of your trust, too," he said gently.

Right. Like I'm going to trust a guy with two thugs on his tail. Not to mention a wife at home while he's tomcatting. She didn't actually know whether that was true or not, but the notion was hard to ignore. She stood up to leave.

"Is that it, Sam? Am I the problem?" he asked, sincerely wanting to know. "Would another instructor make a difference?"

Samantha sighed and sat back down.   "No, Jack. It's not you. I mean, you're incredibly opinionated and infernally full of advice, but you're a good instructor."

"What is it then? What makes you think you can't count on Azure?"

When she finally turned to him, her face was full of expression. "The problem is…" she paused. *What was the problem?* she heard a little voice ask. *Haven't I pondered this very question on several sleepless nights?* "The problem is…that up until a little over a year ago, I was doing pretty well with a cane. Then my vision made a rapid descent. I've been able to adjust to the technical adaptations that I have needed to make…but there's one part of being blind that I am struggling with."

Nervously, she fingered the leash in her hands. "I used to consider myself to be a pretty good judge of character—I could size someone up by watching their eyes and observing their expressions. That's all gone, now. And I haven't figured out a new way to assess people or situations." She struggled to express herself correctly. "I'm always off-kilter. I find myself…holding back. Or as you call it, not trusting anyone."

She turned to him, her face full of honest expression. "But I don't *want* to be this way. I think that's why I was willing to let Kathleen coerce me into coming. I want to figure out how to

59

make this transition and still be the person I've always been. Or become an even better person."

Jack sat quietly, deep in thought for a long moment, before he slapped his hands on his knees. "Okay," he said at last, conviction in his voice. "Let's keep trying."

"Jack?" asked Jon as he approached them. "Could I get some help with something with Arbor?"

Samantha used the interruption to go back to the dormitory. And to think.

* * * *

The conversation Jack had with Samantha weighed on him. He didn't want to discourage her, but he could tell that she wasn't connecting to her dog in the way she should be. She simply didn't believe the dog knew what it was doing. Even the poor dog looked confused, like it wanted to say, "Are you *kidding* me? Do you not get that *I'm* the one who can see?"

Sam surprised him, though, by what she said, about not wanting to let blindness beat her. About wanting to be a better person, in spite of it. Even the way she looked as she said it tugged at his heart.

Dang! There was something about that girl that had gotten under his skin. She looked so open, so vulnerable, longing to find a way to fill the emptiness. He had to hold back from wanting to scoop her into his arms and tell her everything would be all right. The truth was, he didn't know if it would be all right. He admired her determination, but he didn't really know if she could ever hand over control to Azure.

He felt as though he had poked a raw wound in her. *But maybe that's good. Maybe that's how the wound will finally heal.* One thing football had taught him is that pain can teach you important lessons. You can try and ignore it for a while, but sooner or letter, pain acts like a megaphone. It gets your full attention.

* * * *

The next evening, Samantha took Azure out to relieve before going to bed. On her way back to her room, she passed the open door of the Day Room and paused, listening to someone play the piano.

"Sam?" asked Dr. Sommers.

She leaned against the piano. "How did you know it was me?"

"I smelled your perfume."

Samantha smiled at his perceptiveness. "I do that, too. I mean, I identify someone by smell. You always smell like *Old Spice*. My grandfather used the same aftershave. Etienne smells like *Chanel #5*. And Jack always smells of soap."

"I've noticed that about Jack. He must use an industrial strength laundry detergent."

"You play beautifully," she said. "Mind if I ask you something?"

"Anything," he said kindly.

She came closer to where he was seated. "Do you find it difficult to trust Zadok?"

"To trust him?"

"Well, you've managed without a guide dog. Isn't it hard to shift your confidence to a dog?"

"Ah. I see where you're going. I think of it as a different kind of trust. Sort of like a different way of seeing."

"I understand about *seeing* differently. About using my senses. But how do I *trust* differently?"

"Trust in what you don't see. It's like faith. You don't see the wind, but you know it's there. You feel the effects of it. We don't see God, but we feel His effect. We don't see what our dog sees, but we benefit from the effects." Then he added, "Sam, do you mind if I ask you something personal?"

"Of course not." But she wondered what kind of personal question he meant.

"Do you believe in God?"

Oh. That kind of personal. She got Azure settled next to Zadok and sat on the chair facing Dr. Sommers, stalling. "Well, sort of. I guess there's Something up there." *I'm just not positive He's down here,* she thought but didn't say.

"Were you raised with any faith?"

"Yes," Samantha answered. Should she say more? Dr. Sommers waited patiently, expecting her to expand her answer beyond one word. After squirming a little, Samantha said, "My parents are missionaries in Papua New Guinea. My sister and I were born there. I was around ten when I started having problems with my vision, so they sent us to live with our grandparents in the states so that I would attend a school for the blind." She paused. "In some ways, it was the best thing for us. Especially for me. My grandmother never saw me as a handicapped person in the way that my parents did. But..." she hesitated to finish the sentence.

"But what?"

"Well, being sent off right as I needed them the most, well, it felt like..." her voice trailed off.

"Like the Great Commission was more important than taking care of their children?" finished Dr. Sommers.

Exactly. "It seemed...like God must be pretty disinterested."

"Might be that you just didn't look for Him."

"I don't follow you."

"Could be that He's been there all along, all of the time, but you weren't paying attention. You weren't noticing."

Samantha was quiet for a moment.

"Well, for example, to finish growing up with your grandmother's attitude toward your blindness instead of your folks'. That could have been providential even if it didn't feel like it at the time."

Zadok stood up and yawned, stretched and lay down again.

"Sam, what a person believes about God has a profound affect on his or her behavior. If you don't *believe* God is trustworthy, that might be the reason why you have trouble with trust."

This conversation just crossed that thin line into getting too personal, Samantha decided as her palms started to sweat. Her right hand reached over and touched her watch to read the time. "I should go. I need to catch up on work tonight." She stood up to leave.

"You know, Sam, when we get that part right, about God, then everything else finds its rightful place." Dr. Sommers calmly resumed playing the piano then stopped abruptly. "Zadok! I just remembered where I had heard of your name." He placed his hands intuitively on the right notes of the piano, reminded of a hymn by George Frederick Handel entitled "Zadok the Priest."

Chapter Five: **The Bicycle**

By mid-September, a little past the half-way point, Samantha was feeling overloaded. She had expected more spare time. After lecture one evening, Samantha hurried to her room, anxious to catch up on Running Deer business.

As her mind jumped to the ranch, she felt apprehension rumble to life in her stomach. Normally obsessively efficient, she was woefully behind in returning phone messages and extremely concerned about things she'd left pending. Like the loan. Like the media kits that needed to be proofed and returned to the printer. Like the expensive new mill. Like launching the mail order business.

Just as she had a hand on the door to go find a phone and call the office, she heard a knock at her door. "What?" she groaned, distracted and annoyed by the interruption.

"Hi, Sam!" Jack poked his head in the door opening. Azure thumped her tail at the sight of him. "Come with me. There's something I'd like you to try. Leave Azure on tie-down just this once. Do you mind?" he asked as an afterthought.

Samantha wanted to tell him *'Yes, I do mind. I'm off-duty and want to be left alone,'* but there was something in his voice that sounded like a delighted young boy. Reluctantly, she reached for her white cane.

"Just leave it. You won't need it," he said. He took her hand, put it on his elbow, and guided her to the back of the dormitory. "Okay." He placed her hand on the seat of a bicycle. "Hop on."

"What?"

"It's a tandem."

"A what?"

"A tandem! A bicycle built for two. You hop on the back...unless you want to pilot."

"Ah, more blind humor. Very amusing," she said. She climbed on the bicycle and waited for Jack to hop on.

"Okay? We're off!" Jack called to her. As he started pumping, Samantha barely needed to pedal. After a while, she didn't bother. "Hey, are you working back there?" he yelled to her.

"Sure I am!" she hollered back. *Well, sometimes I am.* The wind whipping her hair against her face, flying through the streets, she started to forget about Running Deer and relax, completely safe behind Jack as they zoomed through the neighborhoods. After a long ride, they stopped to get an ice cream cone and sat to eat it on a bench.

"Having fun?" he asked.

"Yes!" she answered, surprising even herself with her enthusiasm. "I've never ridden a tandem before. I haven't even ridden a bicycle since I was a kid. I didn't...I didn't feel blind! It's how I feel when I ride Spitfire up at the ranch. Or it felt just like when you and I were..." Abruptly, she clamped her lips shut.

"When we were what?" he asked. "What, Sam?"

"Dancing," she said almost inaudibly. She felt her cheeks flame up.

Jack sat up straight. "Yes! That's exactly the point I wanted to make! It should be the same way with Azure. Same as dancing or riding a tandem bike. If you're doing it right, you forget you're blind. But you have to let her do the leading. Just like when we were dancing and you kept trying to lead. When you finally let me lead, it became easy. Fluid. We worked as a team. Let Azure be the guide she needs to be, Sam. Hence the name," he added wryly, giving her a nudge with his elbow, "*guide* dog."

He let her take that in for a moment. Then he added, "Sam, if I could put this into football terms—"

Samantha groaned.

He ignored her. "—you're over-thinking. Very common in football. Study the playbook, memorize the systems, and then simply react to situations. Just react."

Samantha clasped both hands to her cheeks in exasperation. "Please! No more football metaphors. Etienne and I have to find a translator after each of your lectures. They're *completely* incomprehensible to us."

"But Sam, football *is* a metaphor for life." He sounded hurt.

She couldn't help but smile at his seriousness. "I understand what you're trying to say. You've been drilling the teamwork concept into us since we first got here. I just have to get it in my head."

"One of the hardest heads I've ever had the pleasure to know," Jack said, knocking gently on her head. "Come on, we'd better get back. The sun is starting to set."

* * * *

As Jack steered the bike into the parking lot of the CCAB campus, he saw the president, Mr. Collins, heading to his car.

Jack slowed the bike to a stop. "Hi, Mr. Collins. You're working late. On the weekend, too."

"Seems that so are you," said Mr. Collins.

Jack turned to Samantha. "This is Samantha Christiansen. She's a student here this month."

"Christiansen? Samantha Christiansen of Running Deer Ranch? The olive oil company? The one that's winning all of those awards?"

"Why, yes. That's me," Samantha answered, pleased. "I mean, that's my company."

"I'd like to talk to you, Samantha. I'm out of the office for a few days, but then I'll give Jack a call to set up a meeting. See you both then." He hopped in his Peugeot and drove off, tooting his horn lightly to say goodbye.

"What do you suppose that was all about?" wondered Samantha.

Jack watched him zoom away. "Business. He's all business."

As she hopped off the bike, she asked, "Jack, should you be concerned that your boss saw you out bicycling with one of the students?"

He glanced at her, surprised. "Nope. Should I be?"

"Well, you're not taking everyone out on a bike ride."

"But no one else needs a tandem bike ride to understand how to work with a guide dog."

Samantha rolled her eyes.

He grinned. "Besides, Etienne is ninety-nine. And if I rode tandem with Dr. Sommers or Jon, everyone would question our manliness."

"Etienne is only seventy-two and could ride circles around the rest of us." She grew solemn. "Seriously, Jack, I don't want you to get into any kind of trouble."

Jack laughed. "Seriously, Sam. What makes you think that this is trouble?"

Suddenly, she blurted out, "Well, then, doesn't your wife expect you home on a Saturday night?"

"My *wife?*" Jack was stunned. How did Samantha know about Ellen? He never discussed her. Not with anyone. "I don't think so. She passed away a few years ago."

Samantha's jaw dropped open, but no sound came out.

Without waiting for a response, Jack parked the bike and guided Samantha back to the dorm. "Here's your door. Sleep well."

The light hearted mood of their outing had skidded to a halt.

* * * *

As Samantha lay in bed that night, unable to fall asleep, she mulled over Jack's remark that his wife had died. *Why did those two guys think I was his wife? Or...did they assume I was his wife just because we were dancing?*

At breakfast the next morning, Dr. Sommers asked Samantha if she'd go to church with him and a few others. "A volunteer offered to drive; she's coming to pick us up in the parking lot in one hour." Sensing her hesitation, he added, "What have you got to lose?"

"Okay. I'll try it," she said, smiling. She got ready to go, slipped the harness on Azure, and went outside to meet Dr. Sommers.

"There you are!" Dr. Sommers said as she met him by the car. "I think that's all," he said to the volunteer driver. Students and dogs climbed into the van, and the driver started up the engine. Then they heard a voice yell breathlessly from outside of the van, "Wait! Wait for me!"

Jack. Samantha groaned.

* * * *

Jack jumped up into the van and sat in the backseat next to Samantha and Azure, jostling them. Azure sat up quickly to

67

greet her instructor as Samantha shifted over on the bench to make room for Jack.

"Sorry I'm late, folks," Jack said.

"Sheesh, Jack," Jon yelled lightheartedly from the front seat of the van. "You're always late."

"Nah. The rest of the world is just a little early," Jack hollered back, a grin in his voice.

"Don't tell me that you're a church go-er?" Samantha whispered to Jack, raising a skeptical eyebrow.

"Sure. Never miss it."

He almost laughed out loud at the surprised look on her face. "Why, Sam, I'm hurt," he said in mock despair. "Do I seem like such a heathen?"

Her face scrunched up. "Well, sort of."

With that, he burst out laughing.

The van took them to the nearby Santa Galena Community Church. Jack saw Samantha hold back as everyone marched right up to the front row. He could read discomfort on her face. "What's wrong?" he whispered, close enough to smell her shampoo.

"I'd rather just sit in the back."

"Why?"

Nervously, she fingered the leash, her eyes lowered. "I, uh, I've forgotten what you do in church. When I need to stand up or sit down or kneel." She lifted her face to him. "And then there's Azure. I mean, how will she react to the organ? What if she yawns loudly during the sermon?"

That earnest, searching look on her face caught him off guard. *Dang!* This girl was getting to him, despite his intention to keep this relationship entirely professional. He could even feel heat run up the back of his neck, like he was a teenager asking a girl to prom.

He leaned over to quietly tell Samantha, "Azure's puppy reports said that her raisers took her to church every week. So she's not a problem. And this isn't a church where people kneel anyway." He touched her elbow. "Come on; let's join the others."

Samantha sat down next to him in the front pew. Azure laid down and settled in for a long nap, obviously comfortable in this environment. As the organist sat down and began to play, Jack whispered loudly to her, "Great Scott! He looks like he's doing the tomahawk chop on the organ. I think Azure could do a better job."

Samantha covered her mouth with her hand, trying to suppress a giggle.

Jack glanced to his left, aware that she was appraising him. He leaned toward her and whispered, "I'm tall, dark, and devilishly handsome."

He couldn't hold back a grin as Samantha jerked her head forward to face the minister, her cheeks flaming.

* * * *

"There's a few paragraphs written from Frederick Buechner's book, *Whistling in the Dark,* that I wanted to read as I begin today's sermon series," said the minister as he launched into his sermon. He coughed to clear his throat.

"At the end of the book of John," he continued, "the disciples go out fishing on the Sea of Tiberias. It is night. They have no luck. Their nets are empty. Then they spot somebody standing on the beach. At first they don't see who it is in the darkness. It is Jesus. The darkness of John is broken by the flicker of a charcoal fire on the sand. Jesus has made it. He cooks some fish on it for his old friends' breakfast. On the horizon there are the first pale traces of the sun getting ready to rise."

The minister turned the pages of his sermon notes. "This little cook-out on the beach is almost too ordinary to take seriously. Yet if Scripture is to be believed, enormous stakes were involved. By sheltering a spark with a pair of cupped hands and blowing on it, the Light of the World gets enough of a fire going to make breakfast. It's not apt to your interest in cosmology or even in theology that draws you to it so much as it's the empty feeling in your stomach. You don't have to understand anything very complicated. All you're asked is to take a step or two forward through the darkness and start digging in."

The minister's words felt like arrows aimed at Samantha. *That empty feeling in my stomach.* She knew that feeling *so* well. *An emptiness that couldn't be filled.* Unbidden, her eyes swam; fat tears spilled down her face. *What is the matter with me lately?*

Deeply embarrassed, Samantha leaned over to scratch behind Azure's ears. As soon as the prayer began, she slipped out to find the ladies' room. She tried to hurry and mop her face before anyone would notice her absence. When she left the bathroom, she nearly bumped into Jack, waiting for her in the narthex.

"I told them to go ahead without us," he said. "We can walk back."

She felt trapped. "Has the van already left? I should really get back and use the afternoon to get caught up on my work—"

"Let's get some lunch," he interrupted.

Silently, they walked over to a nearby deli. "What would you like?" Jack asked.

"Turkey on wheat, please. Just a half," she said. "And water."

He repeated her order to the man behind the counter then ordered a large roast beef sandwich on a sourdough roll for himself with chips and soda.

As soon as they went back out in the sunlight, Samantha reached quickly for her sunglasses, eyes wincing from the bright light.

"Does sunshine ever give you headaches?" Jack asked.

"Sometimes," she admitted.

"Are you taking vitamins? New research is showing that vitamins can slow down the progression of RP."

Samantha nodded, trying not to roll her eyes.

"Especially Vitamins A & E," he continued.

"But stressful instructors speed up the progression of RP," she shot back.

He laughed. "Really? I hadn't read that in the latest literature."

They walked over to a park and sat down on the lawn. Azure sprawled out contentedly in the shady grass.

"So, what made you get emotional in church? You must have had a reason," Jack asked, disturbing the peaceful moment.

Samantha was taken aback. She didn't consider Jack to be a man overburdened with perception. Quiet for a long moment, running her fingers along Azure's leather leash, she gave a cautious answer. "I guess being in church just churned up a few things."

"Such as…" prompted Jack.

She wasn't sure how much she wanted to share with Jack. Azure rolled over and yawned loudly.

"Such as…" Jack repeated.

"After you and I had talked the other night, Dr. Sommers and I had a chat about how hard it is to lose your sight and rely on others. And to trust a dog with your life." She gently stroked Azure's back. "He thinks blind people who have lost their vision have to re-learn how we trust. Using our heart, instead of our eyes. He said that's how God sees us. He even had a verse in the Bible about it, something about man sees one thing, but God sees something else."

"The Lord does not look at the things man looks at. Man looks at the outward appearance, but the Lord looks at the heart," filled in Jack.

"Yes, that's the verse. That's it exactly!" She hadn't expected Jack to be biblically literate. *Not that I am.*

"Go on, Sam," Jack encouraged. "So Dr. Sommers told you that verse…"

"Well, then, this morning's sermon…about that empty feeling in your stomach. Like you're missing something. I…feel that way. It just seemed to hit the same nerve."

"Sermons have a strange way of doing that," Jack said, sounding sincere.

"I seem to keep getting the same message, lately. There's something the cosmos is trying to tell me, but I just can't seem to get it."

Jack gave a short laugh. "The cosmos?"

"Kat calls it the cosmos."

"What about you?"

"I haven't given the topic much thought to tell you the truth." She tilted her head. "What about you? Is religion important to you?"

71

"Not religion. But God is. The most important part of my life."

That was the last thing she expected him to say. Intrigued, she asked, "Why is God so important to you?"

"A few years back, my wife was killed in a car accident."

Samantha listened carefully.

"I couldn't have made it without God's help…" Jack's voice trailed off. "That's all. I couldn't have made it. My relationship with God means everything to me now."

Azure stood up to stretch and walked over to lick Samantha's face. "Okay, Azure, okay! That's enough."

Jack took the dog's leash and pulled it gently over to him. Azure curled up next to him, resting her head on his knee. "By the way, Sam, how did you know I had been married?" he asked, stroking the dog's velvety ears.

She bit her lip. "At that Award Ceremony a few months ago, two young guys came up to me and said something about you being married."

"*What?*"

"Probably just a case of mistaken identity."

He waited for her to elaborate.

"They had a message for you."

"What kind of message?"

"It was sort of strange. I just didn't want to get in the middle of it."

"What *did* they say?" he asked.

"After we had danced, I sat down while you went to go get something to drink. Two guys sat down next to me. They told me…they said to tell my husband that they'd given him fair warning and that the extension was running out. I assumed that they thought I was your wife."

"What?! Why didn't you tell me this?"

She shrugged.

"So you've been thinking all along that I was up to something *crooked?* And guys were threatening to rough me up?"

She nodded.

"And that I was *married?* Out *cheating* on my wife?"

"Yes," she said meekly. "Sorry."

"Hmmm. Strange. No wonder you haven't trusted me."

"Precisely!" Samantha nodded in agreement.

"You could've just asked me, you know," he said, laughing.

Perplexed, Samantha couldn't figure Jack out. She was amazed he wasn't offended.

Somewhere in town, a church bell chimed two rings. He gasped. "Two o'clock! I've got to meet Lucy in an hour. She gets mad if I'm late. We've got to get back."

Suddenly, Azure stood up, hair hackling down her back. In one graceful motion, Jack caught her leash and corrected her quickly. "She was fixed on a squirrel with an evil thought in her head," he explained. "We'll have to watch that in her. Prey instinct. Hard to overcome." He helped Samantha to her feet, all business now.

As they walked through the gates of the Academy, Samantha heard Bob call her name. "Sam! I've been waiting for you! Where have you been?" He ran toward her and grabbed her for a hug before Azure started jumping up on him.

"What's *wrong* with that dog?" Bob asked, pulling back from Samantha.

"I don't know! She's never jumped up on me," said Samantha.

"You really shouldn't approach a blind person like that," Jack said in his instructor's voice.

"Azure, sit," commanded Samantha. Obediently, the dog sat. "Okay, Bob. Let's try this again." She turned to introduce Jack to Bob, but Jack was gone.

* * * *

Later that evening, Kathleen sat cross legged on the sofa with the telephone in her lap and a can of Tab in one hand. "How's everything going, Sam? Are you enjoying your dog? What's her name again?"

"It's Azure. The color of a blue sea. Oh, Kat, I love her. I never dreamed I would say that! She's an awesome dog. You can't *believe* how many places we've been to: every downtown street in Santa Galena, Point Reyes, everywhere!"

"Point Reyes?" *Hmmm,* Kathleen thought. *Pete hasn't taken me to Point Reyes in years. We need to have more fun together,* she decided right then. She took a sip of her Tab.

Samantha continued on, bubbling with enthusiasm. "You would be *amazed* at all that we've done! We've gone on ferries, buses, trains. They want us to feel prepared for any situation once we leave here. We even went to the San Francisco airport so that we'll be comfortable walking the dogs to the gates."

Kathleen smiled, relieved to hear her sister sound so...happy. "So, Sam, glad you're there?" *In other words, glad I made you go?*

"I think so. It's a little overwhelming, but I'm learning a lot, about a lot of different things." Samantha paused. "Kat, do you ever think about God?"

Kathleen frowned. "About God? What exactly are they teaching you there?"

Samantha laughed. "It's not like that. There's a college president here who is a Christian, and we've had some interesting talks together. I just haven't thought much about religion since we left Papua New Guinea. I sort of...left it on the island with Mom and Dad. So what do you think?"

Kathleen thought she heard the baby cry from her crib. She stood up and walked to the door to listen. Distracted, she answered, "Well, you know how I feel about the cosmos, somehow trying to help us all muddle through."

"A random cosmos?"

Satisfied that the baby was still asleep, Kathleen sat back down. "I don't know. I never really gave it much thought. Anyway, let's talk about more important things." In a flat, bored tone, she asked, "Has Bob come by?"

"Uh, yes." Samantha sounded reluctant to elaborate.

For once, Kathleen didn't either. Her voice perked up. "So have you seen much of Jack?" She grinned when Samantha didn't answer right away. She *knew* there was a spark between those two! She just knew it. Samantha would never admit it, though.

"Oh, just a little. Once or twice. Listen, I'm not getting much extra time to stay caught up on Running Deer business.

Is everything going okay? Have you ordered the bottles yet? You and Pete haven't forgotten to feed Spitfire, have you?"

Aha! She's trying to change the subject! "Everything's fine. I'm still deciding on the bottles. I've narrowed it down to two. Spitfire's fine. Pete rode him last evening. Listen, Sam, guess what I found out about your Jack Shaw?" She grinned, knowing that Samantha would bristle at how she phrased that.

"What are you talking about?" she asked coldly.

"Better still, I'm going to read this article out loud to you. You'll be blown away. I *knew* that I had recognized him! He's famous, in a way!" Kathleen picked up a clipping she had cut out of a magazine and read it over the phone to Samantha until stopping abruptly. "Uh oh, Lily's crying. I'd better go. Bye. Love you!" She slammed down the phone and hurried up the stairs to her daughter.

* * * *

The next morning, Samantha felt a little uncertain about how Jack might act towards her after yesterday. After church. After thinking he was a cheating scoundrel. After accusing him of being a mobster. After Bob.

But Jack was the same as ever.

"Today, we're heading down to San Francisco to walk the streets," Jack announced to the group. One by one, the instructors walked each team to the van.

Alarm began to grate in Samantha's stomach as she thought about facing a busy city, filled with traffic and cranky, impatient businesspeople who took themselves very seriously, on a Monday of *all* mornings.

Too soon, they arrived in the city. Samantha decided to volunteer to go first and get this exercise over with. As she walked along Powell Street near the St. Francis Hotel, a homeless person followed behind, calling out to her, whistling to the dog, not making any sense. She struggled to concentrate on Azure and not let the man unnerve her.

"Sam, Azure won't get distracted. She won't let you down," reassured Jack.

Samantha hoped he was right. She and Azure continued down the street to the cable car turnaround then back to the van.

Afterwards, on the ride home, students and dogs were mentally and physically drained from concentrating so intently; soon, all of the dogs and many of the students fell asleep. Seated next to Samantha, Jack's voice dropped to a deep bass as he leaned in close to her ear. "Riding on the van kind of reminds me of how we first met."

"When you burst into my life to tell me to get a guide dog?"

"That's not exactly how I remember it." He scratched his head. "I remember risking my neck to save you from getting hit by a car."

"*What?!*" Samantha's eyes went wide. "I believe that's called *revisionism.* As in, revising history." They were quiet for a few minutes before she asked, "Jack, why don't you ever drive the van?"

Jack flinched, as if stung by a bee. "I just don't," he answered curtly, slamming the door on that subject.

What's so bad about that question? Why would he bristle at that? I accuse him of being a cheat and a scoundrel, and he laughs. I ask him why he doesn't drive a van, and he suddenly gets huffy. She tried to smooth over the awkwardness, "You never mentioned that you played professional football."

"Didn't I? Are you positive? I'm sure I've mentioned it."

"I especially loved the quote from one fawning reporter: 'Shaw infused every situation with a sense of urgency'," Samantha stated. "Well, *that* is an excellent summary of your personality."

"Any good quarterback creates a sense of urgency," Jack responded, sounding pleased that his student had researched him.

A thought suddenly dawned on Samantha. She gasped. "Was Mr. Malcolm aware that you played football?"

"Why, yes." He shifted on his seat to look directly at Samantha. "He recognized me in the grocery store. When I told him I was looking for a house, he offered it to me right there next to the bananas."

Samantha was floored. "So *that's* how you did it! Mr. Malcolm is crazy about professional football. Especially *your* team." She winced. "What did you do to get such a good price? Give him your Superbowl ring?"

"Don't be ridiculous! Of course not!" Jack said indignantly. Then he added, "Besides, I retired in '66, three years ago. The first Superbowl was in '67."

Samantha shifted in her seat to turn away from him, in stony silence, inwardly fuming.

Wednesday of that week was Samantha and Kathleen's thirtieth birthday. Kathleen called the dormitory telephone at six in the morning, waking up Samantha and Etienne and all of the other students, too. "I knew I had to call early, or you'd be gone. Happy birthday! We're going to come tonight around eight o'clock to see you. I know we're only supposed to be allowed to visit on Sundays, but I already cleared it with the Academy. It's only fair, too. How many times does a person turn thirty? Tell everyone we'll bring cake."

Samantha stifled a yawn. "Happy Birthday to you, too! You're bringing Lily, aren't you? I miss her so much." She *really* did. "Kat, can you believe we're thirty?"

"Nope. It's entirely unconscionable. So I'm going to pretend it isn't happening."

Samantha grinned, long familiar with Kathleen's coping strategy of denying anything she didn't want to face.

At breakfast, the instructors sang *Happy Birthday* to her and gave her a plate of scrambled eggs with a lit candle in the center. "Kinda fitting. A new decade. A new beginning," Jack noted.

More than anyone might realize. Samantha's thoughts drifted off to the conversation she had with Bob the other night.

Bob had a specific reason for stopping by on Sunday. After Samantha showed the campus to him, he asked if there was a private place to talk. Samantha led him out back to the patio behind the dormitory. They sat down, facing each other. She couldn't think of anything to say to him, which surprised her.

"Look, Sam," Bob started out. "You've given it a good shot. No one could say you haven't tried."

"What are you talking about?"

"You don't need to stay. I'll take you home tonight. I can deal with your sister."

Samantha wrapped Azure's leash around and around her hand, stalling. After gathering her thoughts, she asked, "Why don't you want me to have a guide dog?"

Bob gave a sarcastic snort. "You're the one who didn't want one, remember? This was your sister's big idea."

"I remember. But why don't *you* want me to have a guide?"

He hesitated. "You don't *need* one. I can be your guide."

"But I won't have to be as dependent on Kat and Pete, Nonna, you, or anyone else. I can travel and do more for the business."

His voice held a trace of disgust. "You're going to end up looking like one of those dog ladies."

"*What?*"

"You know, the type who has a dog in her lap when she drives or in her purse when she shops. The kind that talks to her dog like it's a person. You know the type. A dog lady."

"Are you *serious?* This isn't like having a pet! This is about independence."

He grabbed her hands and intertwined his fingers with hers. "But I don't *mind* that you're dependent on me. In fact, I like it."

She suddenly felt like she was suffocating, as if she had been swimming underwater, holding her breath, and needed to get to the surface before she drowned. It wasn't a new feeling, she realized. She yanked her hands firmly out of his. "But I don't *want* to be dependent. Not on *anyone*. Ever."

Bob stiffened. "What are you saying…?"

A strange image flashed through her mind like a slow moving dream. She saw herself swimming toward a life preserver that someone had thrown out to her. What bothered her was that Jack was the one who had thrown it to her. She didn't even know what Jack looked like; she just knew it was him. She shook her head to clear the image. "Bob, it's just not going to work out between us."

"But, Sam…"

"I'm sorry if I misled you."

Bob's voice sounded like a guitar string, wound too tightly. "Wait a minute. You're overreacting."

"No, I'm not."

He swallowed. "You can't be serious."

"I am."

Bob stood up. "Then I guess this is good-bye, Sam." His voice shook, very upset or very mad. She couldn't quite tell which.

"Bob, I'm sorry," Samantha called out as she heard his footsteps hurry away. But she wasn't all that sorry, not really. As much as she hated to admit it, her sister was absolutely right. She wasn't in love with Bob.

* * * *

After dinner that evening, Kathleen, Pete, Lily, and Nonna arrived, bringing the promised birthday cake. The other students had heard Samantha talk about Kathleen's cooking ability, so they hovered in the dining room for a piece of cake. After seeing how involved Samantha was with holding Lily, Kathleen quietly left the cafeteria and poked around the dormitory, hunting for Jack. She found him on the patio, working with a student. "Jack!" she called out.

He jackknifed to his feet when he heard her voice. For a split second, she could tell he thought she was Samantha. It was a trick Kathleen loved to play on unsuspecting victims ever since she was a kid. Samantha never played it; she was far too moral to have anything to do with a deception, no matter how innocent it could be. Today, Kathleen caught a certain look in Jack's eyes before he realized his mistake. She saw, too, the smile that lit his face. Here and then gone. Kathleen felt triumphant. "Come for cake!" She waved to him. "You, too!" she added, pointing to the student. "There's plenty."

"I thought I smelled cake." Jack answered, heading right over to the cafeteria.

Kathleen pulled out a chair for Jack next to Samantha. "Jack, do you remember Pete?" Kathleen asked.

Jack reached across the table and shook hands with Pete then sat down in a different seat next to Nonna, far from Samantha.

Kathleen put her hand on Nonna's shoulder. "Nonna, this is Jack, the instructor I was telling you about. Sam met him on the bus. Remember?"

"No, I'm sorry I don't," Nonna said, glancing sideways at Jack.

Kathleen frowned. "He's the one who bought Mr. Malcolm's property. I told you all about him."

Nonna rolled her eyes. "You tell me all sorts of things and expect me to remember them, Kathleen," she said, as she passed Jack a large slice of birthday cake. "Enjoy, Jack. This cake is a family tradition."

Kathleen tilted her head, watching Nonna. A feeling of portent rocked through her. Then the moment passed, and she dismissed it as nonsense.

* * * *

Jack and Nonna talked for quite a while. Samantha tried to overhear their conversation, but Lily was in her lap, trying to stuff cake into Samantha's mouth. Kat finally rescued Samantha and scooped up Lily, whispering, "Wow, that Dr. Sommers looks like a retired astronaut."

Samantha decided not to point out to Kathleen that astronauts were such a new career that no one had retired yet. Instead, she wiped her mouth with a napkin and said, "Pete, tell me about the new mill."

"It's a beauty! I know it's expensive, but it's just what Running Deer needs."

"If this year's harvest keeps looking good, I think it'll pay for itself. I'd really like to pay down that debt as soon as we can." Samantha furrowed her brow, reminded of Running Deer.

"I'm sure the new mill is as good as paid for," he said. "For now, let the other problems wait."

Samantha tilted her head, alarmed. "*What* other problems?"

Just then, Kathleen called Pete over to help clean up the paper plates. Pete hopped up to help. A little too quickly, Samantha noted.

Later, Nonna whispered to Samantha, "I like that Jack. He says you're his favorite student."

Samantha put her hands to her face, exasperated. "Nonna, I highly doubt he said that."

"Maybe...it was that you're his most stubborn student."

Samantha laughed. "Now *that*, I believe."

Jack and Samantha walked her family back to the car to say goodbye. On the way back to the dormitory, hands shoved in his pockets, Jack said, "Your grandmother is pretty special."

Samantha nodded.

"She said that you put a new lock on your cottage and won't let anyone in unless they're invited. No one else has a key."

"She told you that?" Samantha frowned. "Well, you would, too, if you were visually impaired and had a twin sister who borrows things and doesn't return them, like my hot rollers on the day I was supposed to meet with *Gourmand* magazine for an important interview."

"I don't know if I would. I don't have that much hair left." He patted his head. "So...you're writing a novel."

Samantha froze in her tracks. "Did Kat tell you that?"

"No. Nonna did."

"She didn't!"

"She did! She says you are a gifted writer."

Samantha was astounded! It was *so* unlike Nonna to divulge personal information. Kathleen would tell anything to anybody. But *Nonna*?

"So what's it about?" Jack asked.

Samantha narrowed her eyes. "About a bossy guide dog instructor who keeps telling his blind student how to manage her life. Oh, and she has a very interfering twin sister and grandmother."

"Really?" he asked, undisturbed. "Sounds like a runaway best seller. How does it end?"

Samantha stopped, pretending to be deep in thought. "I haven't decided yet. I might have the blind woman kill everyone off and disappear on a beautiful tropical island to live out her days in peace and quiet."

"Hmmm...I think she would be haunted by guilt from her well-meaning relatives and her beloved instructor."

"I said he was a *bossy* instructor."

"I think you said beloved instructor," Jack said good-naturedly.

Samantha frowned. *I didn't, did I?*

"Refreshing logic, though. If someone irritates you, you 'off' them. Keeps life simple."

Glancing sideways at her, he saw a smile creep over her face. Walking along in companionable silence, Jack said, "I saw that uptight little guy leave the other night. He didn't look happy."

"Bob? No, I suppose not," Samantha said.

"Everything okay?" he asked with genuine concern.

Samantha nodded.

"Will he be coming back?"

Slowly, she shook her head.

"Good," he said. "Azure didn't like him."

Chapter Six: Graduation Day

It was hot. One evening, Samantha and Dr. Sommers plopped down on chairs in the Day Room instead of going back to their stuffy rooms.

Now seemed like a perfect opportunity. No one else was around, and Samantha could ask him a private question, well, privately. Leaning forward in her chair, she asked, "Do you remember when you said that becoming blind made you a better person? What exactly did you mean by that?"

Dr. Sommers bent over and moved Zadok away from Azure. Lying on their stomachs, the two dogs had been inching closer and closer toward each other and now were nose-to-nose. As he straightened up, he asked in a compassionate tone, "Having a hard time with it, Sam?"

How was he able to do that? See right through me? Suddenly, Samantha's words bubbled up and couldn't be contained. "I miss the simple things, like picking up the newspaper, sitting down, and reading it in the morning with a cup of coffee. I miss colors and sunsets and expressions on people's faces. And most of all, I miss knowing what the new faces look like that come into my life. Important faces, like my niece's. She's only one, but I'll never know what she looks like." She sighed. "But above all, I miss my independence."

Dr. Sommers listened patiently. "Sam, have you ever been to a foreign country?" He slapped his palm to his forehead. "What am I saying? You grew up in Papua New Guinea!"

"The United States felt like a foreign country."

"Think back to how you felt when you first moved here. Probably overwhelmed, frustrated, missing home and friends. That's how I felt when I became blind. Like I was dropped into a foreign country, didn't know the language, *and* didn't want to be there in the first place. After a while, I realized that if I stopped fighting it and tried to embrace it, anything was possible. Anything at all."

Could it really be that simple? To just stop fighting it?

83

The door opened, and Jack burst into the Day Room, waking up the dogs. They leapt to their feet to greet him, whole bodies wagging with excitement. "Sorry to interrupt, but Sam's been summoned to the principal's office. Mr. Collins wants to see us."

Annoyed with Jack's interruption, Samantha said, "I'm sorry, Dr. Sommers. Maybe we could finish this conversation later."

Meeting Jack and Samantha at his office door, Mr. Collins gave her a handshake that could make a man out of a boy, she decided, trying not to wince. "Samantha Christiansen! I've had Running Deer olive oil. Excellent stuff. My wife loves it. Says I need it for my heart. Jack, how are you? How's that bad knee? Good? Good! Sit right down, and let's get started."

Samantha hoped he would stop to take a breath, but he just kept on talking.

Mr. Collins pulled out a chair for Samantha. "So let's get to the point. A television program wants to do a profile on a local student; you know, follow the student for a day, attend a graduation. When I saw you the other night, Samantha, I thought you'd be ideal."

Oh no! So that's what this is about. Panic started to cramp her stomach. *Think fast, Sam.* "There are others who would be far more interesting. Dr. Sommers, for example. He's a college president who recently lost his eye sight. He's catching on much more quickly than I am to handling dogs."

"But he's not local," Mr. Collins said.

Samantha swallowed past the rising lump in her throat. "Then there's Etienne. She's ninety-nine."

"Only seventy-two, Sam," Jack interrupted. "You should know that. She's your roommate."

Samantha hissed at Jack, "Don't you ever take *anything* seriously?"

Jack feigned shock. "Absolutely! A good steak. That is a *very* serious moment for me."

"Man...that does sound good," said Mr. Collins. "A T-bone? With mashed potatoes on the side?"

"Yep. Nothing better," Jack agreed.

Samantha scrunched up her face. *Where was this conversation floating? The wise thing would be to take control and end this.* "Excuse me for interrupting your idyll, gentlemen, but could we get back to the business at hand?"

"Yes. Yes, of course." Mr. Collins cleared his throat. "Now where were we?"

"Mr. Collins, there are so many interesting students here. You could profile any one of them. There's Kenny. He's a blind sailor. A sailor! And then there's Ray, the hunter, and Ed, the parachutist. *They're* the ones to interview. Athletes who push the limits. *That's* the angle you want." She was pleased with herself for being so persuasive, on the spot, without forethought.

"Hmmm," pondered Mr. Collins, sounding intrigued.

"Those men are much more fascinating than my story," she reiterated. "Plus I wouldn't come off well in an interview."

"Why not?"

"Well, for one, Jack says I have a problem with trust." *There! That should take care of it. Relationship problems made men nervous.* She smiled, silently congratulating herself.

"Huh," Mr. Collins said thoughtfully, rubbing his chin. "Now *that* could make an interesting angle. Remind me to mention that to the interviewer."

Jack started chuckling as Samantha's eyes widened with horror.

Mr. Collins seemed to finally notice Samantha's discomfort. "Look, Samantha," he coaxed, "this would be wonderful exposure for your company."

Oh no. Not that! He found my weak spot. My Achilles heel! She could never say no to anything that would benefit Running Deer. She exhaled, resigned to her fate. "Oh, all right. I'll do it."

"Excellent! Jack, I'll get in touch with you after I hear back from the television station." He stood up, ready to dismiss them, then stopped and sat back down again. "Samantha, you might just be on to something. What if we did a newspaper article, profiling these athletes?"

"Great idea, Mr. Collins!" Jack turned to Samantha. "So what do you think?"

"What do I think about what?" she asked, confused.

"About writing up those articles?" Jack turned back to Mr. Collins. "How did you know that Sam was an experienced writer?" He slapped his hands on his knees. "That's why you're the president, I guess."

Too stunned to react, Samantha felt her chest lock tight. The headline of her obituary danced across her mind: *Samantha Christiansen, aged 30, died of a massive heart attack brought on by severe shock...*

Mr. Collins clapped his hands. "Well, Jack ol' boy, that's how you get ahead in this world." He went over and opened the door to his office, adroitly signaling the end of the meeting. "Samantha, I'll get back to you as soon as I speak to the newspaper, and Jack, I'll call you when the date for the television interview gets set up."

As soon as Samantha and Jack were outside of the building, she whipped around to face him, eyes blazing. "How could you do that to me?"

"Because I've noticed you can accomplish anything you set your mind to."

"But I didn't set my mind to this! *You* set my mind to this!" She covered her face with her hands. "An experienced writer? Are you *crazy*? I have *started* a novel. *Started!* That's *all!*"

"That's more experience than I have."

She crossed her arms against her chest. "Oh, I have definitely decided on the right ending for this novel. I am *so* 'offing' the instructor."

"Wow," Jack said calmly. "Vikings have surprisingly hot tempers."

Later that night, as Samantha lay wide awake in bed, listening to Oriole's and Azure's whiffling snores, she fought back rising waves of anxiety. Yet she couldn't deny that, deep down, despite feeling completely overwhelmed and inadequate for the job, there was a part of her that was *thrilled* to be writing this article.

Three evenings later, she let Dr. Sommers read the first draft of her article she had typed on the Braille typewriter that was in the library. "This is good, Sam," he said as he finished it.

"You're not just saying that? It's only the first draft."

"I mean it. It's excellent."

"Be honest. Ruthlessly honest. I don't want to be like those *Amateur Hour* wannabes who think they can sing and dance because their friends and family are too nice to tell them they can't."

Dr. Sommers laughed. "Relax, Sam. I love the part about how the dogs are well suited to their athletic partners. Like describing the parachutist's guide dog as having high-octane exuberance." He handed the papers back to her. "You did a fine job."

As Samantha went back to her room to get ready for bed, she found a note in Braille Etienne had left on her bed. Samantha ran her fingers along the raised dots: "Tout es question d'equilibre."

She smiled. "Thank you for the note, Etienne. But I don't understand French."

"It iz ze mantra of ze French. It meanz: Everyzing iz a matter of balanz." Etienne came over to Samantha's bed and sat down on it. Earnestly, she said, "Zamanza, sometimez I worry zat you are not in balanz. You work and work. Too serious, no?"

"My sister has shared that same thought with me once or twice, Etienne." *Or a couple of hundred times.*

"Ze French, we like ze balanz. A little work, a little play. Iz good. Iz better."

Samantha put the note up on her bureau top so it wouldn't get misplaced. "I'll save this and put it on my office bulletin board to remind myself to have more fun."

"Bon! Très bon! And zink of me and my Oriole." Etienne sat on her bed. "Zamanza, have you noticed how my Oriole crossez her pawz? Jez like a little lady. Iz it not charming? Oui?"

Samantha crouched down to pat Oriole, which inspired Azure to come over to her. Soon, both dogs were trying to lick her face. "Oriole is a perfect match for you, Etienne."

"Can you believe zat we are graduating next week? Iz it not exciting? No?"

Samantha laughed. "Oui! Absolument, Etienne Number Five!"

As Etienne prepared to go to bed, Samantha smiled fondly, soothed by her roommate's absent minded humming. She was enchanted with Etienne and not just because of her gorgeous accent. It was her attitude. Even at her age, she remained open to new experiences. In return, life seemed to treat her well. *Why can't I be more like that?*

On Sunday, Samantha decided to take Etienne's advice and relax, at least for an hour. She joined the others and went to church. Afterwards, the volunteer driver dropped some students at a street fair, but Samantha stayed in the car, planning to get back to the campus and work. She was pleased with herself that she could check "relaxation" off her day's to-do list.

Jack held the car door open for her. "*What* is so important that you can't enjoy a beautiful Sunday afternoon? Come down to the street fair with the others. Come on. You've been working hard. So has Azure. She needs a break."

Reluctantly, Samantha stepped out of the car.

As the students wandered through the street fair, they picked up a few things for lunch. Jack kept getting sidetracked into friendly chats with the produce sellers and soon the group tired of waiting for him. Samantha decided to tell him that they were leaving without him. What she was really thinking about was finding a pay phone to call Pete and check on the harvest.

"*What?* Everyone's leaving me?! Sam, stay and we'll eat on that little bench over there."

Before she had a chance to object, he ran to tell the others to go on without them. Samantha quietly complained to Azure, who listened attentively.

* * * *

When Jack returned, he steered them to the bench. He had bought some cheese, bread, two soda pops; Samantha had purchased two perfectly ripened peaches and a box of strawberries. Nearby were a guitarist and two singers, crooning a warbled rendition of *Puff the Magic Dragon*.

88

"This is amazing!" Samantha said, "A feast! All from a street fair."

"And don't forget the serenade," Jack added. "Though I'm thinking of offering them money to stop singing." He flicked off her soda pop top off and handed it to her.

She took a sip and asked, "What is this?"

"Uh," he leaned over and read the can. "Fresca. It's new."

Keeping her head low, she asked shyly, "So that interview went pretty well the other day, don't you think?"

He glanced at her, trying not to notice how the sunlight made her hair look coppery. "It went great. You're doing much better with Azure. You're starting to read her movements. I think you just may graduate after all. You've earned your snaps."

"My *what?* My *snaps?* Oh, never mind." Samantha took another sip of her soda pop.

Jack realized that Samantha had turned a significant corner ever since that bicycle ride. Watching her this morning, he noticed she seemed more confident with Azure. Maybe they were finally gelling into a team.

A smile played at the corner's of Samantha's mouth. "I didn't realize you were such a hot shot wide angle receiver guy."

"The term is wide receiver and, anyway, I played quarterback. Second string." He took a bite of his peach. "You know nothing about football, do you?"

"Not a thing."

"Did I hear you say Azure means the world to you in that interview? I seem to remember that not so long ago you were sure you didn't want a guide dog."

Samantha rolled her eyes, her smile fading away. "Oh, you sound like my sister."

He took another bite of his peach. "So Collins said your newspaper article was outstanding."

"Oh? Well, that's good."

"He thinks it might even be reprinted in the other syndicates."

"Oh?" Samantha appeared dispassionate.

He wondered, though, if she was trying to hide how pleased she felt. One thing he had figured out was she wasn't as self-assured as she seemed. She was really very soft, very kindhearted. More than a few times, he had caught her helping the other students practice their exercises. He could tell that Samantha was a person others could depend on. He shook his head, realizing that his train of thought had just derailed. "You didn't want me to look it over?"

"Dr. Sommers edited it for me. I didn't need a third opinion."

"A third opinion? Or *my* opinion?"

She kept her eyes lowered, not answering.

"Still mad at me for volunteering you to write it?"

"I'm getting over it."

"I never realized Vikings take so long to thaw out."

"They do. A carryover from Arctic survival," she said, lifting her head, smiling smugly.

After lunch, they spent some time wandering through the street fair. They were both amazed to realize it was nearly time for dinner when they arrived back at the campus.

* * * *

The next morning, the students and dogs gathered in the Day Room to head out for the day. "Team," Jack started in, clasping his hands together, imitating Coach Vince Lombardi before a big game, "today is a '4th quarter moment' for everyone. We're going to take you out into the streets of Santa Galena and expect you to find your way back to campus. We'll give you verbal directions, but you're on your own."

The students started murmuring amongst themselves.

"You can always ask help from any stranger you might pass," continued Jack. "Please don't feel like we're letting you hang out to dry. If anyone is seriously lost or worried, just send out a 'hail Mary'. Okay, let's load up the van."

"Zamantha? Have you any idea what he just zaid?" whispered Etienne.

"No!" Samantha whispered back. "Not all of it, anyway. I think he means that we're going to have to figure out how to get back to the campus alone." Noticing Etienne's nervousness, she said reassuringly, "We can do this, Etienne."

"Zat iz an encouraging thought," said Etienne. "But I do hope zat ze 'Hail Mary' means zat zomeone iz watching."

"I have an idea," she said, digging through her wallet. "Listen carefully to the instructions and count how many blocks you'll have to walk. Each time you walk down a block, take a quarter from one pocket and put it in another pocket. That will help us remember how many streets we need to go and how many we've gone before we need to make a turn."

Etienne picked up the quarters out of Samantha's open palm. "Zamanza! You are brilliant!"

Samantha and Azure were the last team to head out. As Samantha gave Azure the command to go forward, she felt fairly confident. At the first intersection, she asked a man waiting at the corner for street names. With that information, she identified her location. *Only five blocks to campus.* Planning her route, she realized that only one street was a main thoroughfare with heavy traffic. The last street.

Three blocks later, she reached into her pocket to see how many quarters were left. *Two to go. So far, so good.*

One block later she reached the final street, the main thoroughfare that worried her. Even more discouraging, she discovered construction workers using jackhammers, digging up a walkway to a building on the street corner. The noise muffled out the sound of the traffic. She waited and waited, biting her lip, letting the lights change a couple of times. She hoped a pedestrian might chance along. She couldn't hear a thing over the sound of the jackhammers, only the swish of cars as they zoomed past.

Should I flag the instructor for help? No. I can't. She knew this was a big moment for her and Azure. *There won't be an instructor trailing behind me for the rest of my life*

Finally, Samantha took a deep breath and said to Azure, "Well, girl, it's up to you." She bent down to stroke her. She could feel Azure's entire body stiffen, preparing for action. Azure looked left, then right, then left, then right again, then started forward as Samantha followed her lead, trusting that they would get safely to the other side.

When Samantha stepped onto the CCAB campus, she leaned down to hug Azure. Jack ran up to congratulate her.

"Jack! Did you see? Did you see what Azure did?" Samantha asked triumphantly.

"I saw it all!" he answered, a giant smile in his voice. "I was behind you the entire time."

"Are Etienne and Oriole back yet?" she asked eagerly. "And Dr. Sommers and Zadok? And Jon and Arbor?"

"Yep! They must all be in the cafeteria having lunch. Looks like everyone made it."

As Samantha turned to go join the others in the cafeteria, she stopped and said to Jack, "You were right, Jack. I read Azure's body and trusted her. We communicated!"

"She didn't let you down, did she?"

"No." Adding with a grin, "I don't think I would be here if she did."

He laughed, draped an arm around her shoulders, and squeezed. "Sam, you did great. You're ready to graduate." He dropped his arm but not before she happened to notice that her shoulder fit perfectly under his.

That evening, Samantha and Dr. Sommers made a point to have one last farewell chat in the Day Room. She couldn't believe that the month was over. *What a month.*

"Samantha, do you remember that talk we had about adjusting to blindness?" asked Dr. Sommers.

"Of course I do. I've thought of it often."

"It got me thinking back to when I was first losing my sight. I felt such a loss because I couldn't have a physical perception of a person like I used to just by looking at them or watching their eyes. Do you know what I mean?"

"I know *exactly* what you mean," answered Samantha, interest growing. She crossed her legs on the couch and leaned forward a little.

"Since then, I've decided that there might even be a benefit or two tucked in. I think that as we can accept and adjust to our vision loss, we might actually become *better* judges of characters."

"How so?"

"Being blind, I have no pre-judgment of an individual. No idea of what he looks like, what color he is, what size, or how he dresses or carries himself. I have to make a decision on a person based on how he or she relates to me. And as a result, I think I am *more* fair. *More* objective."

Samantha turned that thought over and over in her mind. "Well," she finally said, "I've been going blind for twenty years, and you've been blind for two, yet you've figured it all out."

"That might have something to do with this gray head of mine. There *are* a few consolations for age besides creaky joints," he said, laughing.

"But just one thing, Dr. Sommers, I want the truth," she said firmly. "Jack told you to talk to me about this, didn't he?"

Dr. Sommers didn't respond, shifting in his chair uncomfortably. Finally, he meekly confessed, "Yes."

* * * *

The next afternoon after the reception for the Graduation Ceremony, Jack knocked on Samantha's door. "Etienne already left?"

Samantha was folding her clothes and putting them in the suitcase. "You just missed her. She and Oriole had a train to catch."

Jack folded his arms and leaned against the door jam. "Azure's puppy raiser seemed nice."

"She is! We're going to keep in touch."

"When are you heading home?"

"Kat said she'd be back by four o'clock. She had an errand to run while I finished packing."

"That was really nice of Kathleen to bring Running Deer olive oil to all of the students."

Samantha gave him a sly grin. "Ulterior motive. Expands our customer base."

He put his hands in his pockets. "Sam, I'll need to come by to do a follow-up call on you and Azure."

Samantha said nothing and kept packing up.

"Unless, of course, you might have a question or two before then. You could always call."

"Right. I've got the switchboard's number memorized." She zipped up her suitcase.

"I mean, you could even call my house. Or…I could call you. Just to see how you and Azure are doing. Just to make sure you're remembering to feed her."

"I won't forget to feed her," Samantha laughed. "She won't *let* me forget to feed her."

"Well, you might forget how to put the harness on."

"Nope. I've done it so often now I could do it in my sleep."

"You might forget to give her heartworm medicine on the first of the month."

"Wait a minute, Jack. That's tomorrow. October 1st is tomorrow."

"See?" He raised his hands up in the air. "I *knew* it. You've already forgotten. It's settled then. I'll call you tomorrow to remind you."

Finished with her packing, she turned and gave him her full attention. "So, Jack," Samantha said, her voice dripping with honey, "would you at least give some serious thought to selling Mr. Malcolm's property to us?"

"You mean *my* property," he corrected. "Absolutely! And then after I've thought about it, to whom should I say 'no'? You or your sister?"

Samantha frowned.

Just then there was a knock at her door. "Sam? Still here?"

"Hi, Dr. Sommers. Jack's here, too."

Jack moved away from the door as Dr. Sommer and Zadok walked in.

Dr. Sommers handed Samantha a package. "There's something I want you to have. It's a *Bible* on audio tape."

Samantha reached out to Dr. Sommers a hug. "Thank you. I'll treasure it."

"Just promise me you'll listen to it. Soon you won't be able to get enough of it." Dr. Sommers paused for a moment. "I thought about getting you a Braille *Bible*, but you would've needed a donkey and a cart to get it home."

Kathleen had come into the room and had overheard the conversation. "What do you mean?"

"A Braille *Bible* is huge," Samantha explained. "It takes up an entire shelf in the dormitory library."

Samantha described to her sister, almost verbatim, the lecture Jack had given to the students about how the Braille alphabet system of fingertip dots was created. A Frenchman born in 1809, Louis had been blinded in an accident in his father's harness workshop. At the age of three, he had grabbed an awl in the tool shed and hurt his eye, resulting in an infection that caused total blindness. As a young teenager, Louis stumbled on an alphabet code of twelve dots used by the French Army for night messages. Inspired, he found that code to be too cumbersome and trimmed it down to six dots, but the dots still required a large amount of space for fingertips to decipher the letters.

As Jack watched Samantha's animated face as she told Kathleen the story, he was again amazed at how she had changed in this last month. He remembered giving that lecture, convinced she wasn't even listening.

Jack reached over and shook Dr. Sommers's hand. "Call anytime with questions, Dr. Sommers. I'll be in touch soon for the follow-up." He leaned down and stroked Zadok's large black anvil head. "You behave yourself, boy. Make us proud."

As Dr. Sommers turned to leave, he said, "Just promise you'll send me an invitation."

"To what?" Samantha and Jack asked in unison.

Dr. Sommers chuckled to himself. "Ha! And they call me blind?" he muttered under his breath as he strode up the hallway.

Kathleen gave Jack a catlike smile, which made him uneasy. "Where's Pete?" he asked, wanting to change the focus.

"Working. Just a foretaste of milling time; we'll never see him." Kathleen reached over and picked up Samantha's suitcase. She gave him a beguiling look. "So, Jack, don't be a stranger. Just walk up the street and join us for dinner sometime. I'm a great cook."

Jack caught Samantha's glare at her sister and decided he should make an exit. "Thank you, Kathleen. I might just take you up on that. See you soon, Sam." He took Samantha's hand and squeezed it gently as he passed her to go to the door.

"I saw that," Kathleen whispered to Samantha as he left the room.

Overhearing her, Jack slapped his palm to his forehead. *What is wrong with me? Where is my professional detachment? She's my student! And that sister of hers has eagle eyes.*

But then a smile spread slowly across his face. As of tomorrow, Samantha would no longer be a student. Tomorrow, she would be his neighbor.

Chapter Seven: Home

Azure stood posted like a sentry guard beside Samantha's bed early Sunday morning, breathing noisily, waiting patiently. Samantha sensed the immediate concern behind those two large brown eyes staring at her, wondering what time to expect breakfast to be served around these new digs.

"Guess this is the way it's going to be now," Samantha said, petting Azure's soft head. "You and me." Phoebe, her cat, was perched on top of the refrigerator, offended that a dog had moved in. Samantha felt the hands on her watch. "Azure, what would you think about trying that little church down the road today? I haven't been there in years. If we leave pretty soon, I think we could make it. Are you in?"

Azure thumped her tail, which Samantha took as a 'yes.'

As they walked to the little church, Samantha didn't really know what was propelling her, she just felt she *had* to be there. She knew something was missing in her life. She still wasn't sure what *it* was, but she was ready to stop ignoring the feeling and try to find out. If she had learned anything this last month, it was that she needed to face her fears head-on. She had always thought of her fears as giants, dragging big clubs behind them. Oddly enough, they weren't quite as potent as they seemed.

A well meaning usher tapped her on the shoulder. "Don't you want to sit up front so that you can hear better?"

She wanted to ask the usher why he assumed a blind person was hard of hearing. Instead, she politely answered. "Thank you, no. The back row is fine." She slid into the back pew so she could leave when the sermon grew boring.

"Today's text is from the gospel of Matthew when Jesus walked on the water," began the minister.

Relieved that she recognized the story, Samantha leaned back in the pew.

"Imagine the thoughts running through Peter's mind as Christ invited him out on the water. 'I want to, Lord, but I just can't.' And Jesus beckoning to him, 'But you can, Peter! Just try!' So out Peter walked, talking first one step then another. He kept his eyes on Jesus' face, and he was walking on water! Then suddenly Peter's mind overtook him. It's impossible to walk on water, he thought. I know about that. I'm a fisherman. I've been around the sea my entire life! I'll sink! I'll drown. He felt the wind. He knew the effects of wind."

The minister's voice dropped an octave, deftly switching his role from actor to narrator. "Remember, he was a fisherman. He believed in the wind, something he couldn't even see, but he could feel it. And you know what happened?"

Now the minister started winding up again; his voice picked up speed and intensity and excitement. "Peter started to sink. His faith failed him. His circumstances overwhelmed him. But did the Lord let him sink? No! Jesus reached his hand out and grabbed Peter. Even with Peter's small effort of faith, of trust, the Lord rewarded Peter. He rewarded him with what he could do right then. He didn't ask for a leap of faith. Just a step." He lowered his voice to a whisper. "Just a step."

This is getting creepy. Her palms started to sweat. She slipped out before the benediction.

At lunchtime, Jack called to ask if he could drop by while out on a bicycle ride just to be absolutely sure Azure was surviving a day alone with her.

"Why don't you come by at dinnertime? Kathleen is planning a big welcome home supper tonight because Pete couldn't be with us last night. She really is a good cook." *Plus,* she reasoned, *if he sees the ranch, maybe he'll reconsider selling us Mr. Malcolm's property.*

"How could I refuse? Just tell me when."

"Five o'clock."

"Is six okay? I'm busy until then."

Bet he's busy with that Lucy woman. But all that she said was, "Six o'clock is fine."

* * * *

Around half past six, Jack bicycled up to Samantha's cottage. He rested his bike against the wall and joined Samantha and Azure on the front porch.

"So *this* is where you live?" he asked, glancing around him. The farmhouse, a two-story Craftsman style building, was

For the Love of Dogs

situated across the driveway. Jack's gaze circled around, ending with Samantha's cottage. "But that looks like a two-stall cow barn."

"It's a cottage. I call it 'Mise-En-Place.' That's French for—"

"Everything in its place," interrupted Jack. "A restaurant term. I know it well. A brother of mine runs a restaurant. He has an insane but brilliant chef who screams out 'mise-en-place' right before the dinner crowd is due in."

"Come inside," she offered.

As they walked inside, Jack stopped and looked around curiously. "It's like a dollhouse. And so clean. Painfully clean." He sounded amazed.

"That's how I like it." A cat wove around Samantha's legs.

Jack stepped back from the cat. He thought the cat was glaring at him. "But it's so pink. A pink dollhouse."

"There's not *that* much pink. Besides, the light colors make the room lighter. It's easier for me to see things." Samantha scooped down to pick up her cat. "Didn't you grow up with any sisters?"

"Nope. Three brothers." He walked slowly all around the room, taking it all in. "Even your sofas are little. And there are flowers all over them." He was floored. He never would have anticipated Sam in a frilly little house. With a cat. He scratched his head. This woman kept surprising him.

"They're called loveseats, and they are *very* chic," she said, looking a little offended. "They're covered in cabbage roses. Didn't you ever have upholstered furniture?"

"No. My mother gave up. We had furniture that she could hose down."

Samantha winced. "Sounds like a kennel."

The cat jumped out of her arms and waved her tail, eyes fixed on Jack. He thought that cat looked a little diabolical. "I'm not sure I can stand up straight in here."

"Well, I'm not a six-foot-nine football linerunner."

"Six-foot-two. Quarterback. Second string," he corrected her absently as he peered into the little kitchen. "And the term is linebacker." He started rubbing his arms. "I think I'm starting to break out in hives."

"Colors don't cause you to break out in hives."

"I think my throat is tightening up."

A little smile broke out in Samantha's face. "Let's go outside before you start to hyperventilate."

"Your cat keeps staring at me. With an evil look in her eyes."

Samantha rolled her eyes. "You are *such* a big baby."

As they walked over to the farmhouse, Jack said, "I noticed a tape recorder on your desk. And were those Bible cassettes next to it? The ones from Dr. Sommers? Looked like the package was opened."

Her eyebrows shot up. "You didn't miss much despite nearly passing out from an overdose of femininity."

"It was the cat. I think she's got it in for me." He would not want to be in a closed room with *that* cat.

Samantha laughed. "I went to church today; when I got home, I tried to find out what the minister was talking about."

"Good sermon?" he asked, pleased that she had taken that initiative without anyone's coaxing.

She told him about the part when Christ encouraged Peter to walk on the water. She bent down to stroke Azure and said shyly, "I sort of understand how Peter felt. Wanting to believe but doubting at the same time."

Jack bent down to pat Azure so that he was on the same level as Samantha. He knew that what she had just told him was significant. "There are a lot of people in the *Bible*, too, who had doubts."

Samantha popped back up. "Doubters?" she asked him with suspicion. "In the *Bible*?"

"God can handle doubts, Sam." He let that sink in for a while, gently patting Azure's head before standing up to go to the farmhouse.

As they approached the kitchen, Kathleen opened the door to greet them with Lily on her hip. "Hi, Jack! Come in. You remember Lily and Nonna."

"Hello, Mrs. Christiansen. We met a few weeks ago," Jack put his hand out to shake Nonna's hand.

"We did?" Nonna asked, cocking her head. Her forehead wrinkled in concern.

"You remember, Nonna. At CCAB. On my birthday," Samantha prompted.

Jack walked over to look at a drawing hung on the kitchen wall. "I noticed one like it in Sam's cottage. You almost want to reach in and grab one of the green apples. Who's the artist?" he asked, unable to find a signature.

An awkward silence filled the room. Finally, Nonna said, "Samantha. She's quite artistic. Pastels are her favorite medium."

"Were," Samantha said, matter-of-factly. "Pastels *were* her favorite."

"And here I am with twenty-twenty vision, and I can't even draw a stick figure. The Universe kind of blew it when it passed out gifts," said Kathleen, as she whisked the salad dressing with her one free hand.

Jack studied Samantha in amazement. *Was there anything she couldn't do?*

"Kathleen, just because a gift has a short season, that doesn't make it any less of a gift," said Nonna. "There are a number of Sammy's drawings framed in other parts of the house, Jack, if you're interested in seeing them."

"Thank you, I'd like that," Jack said, following behind Nonna for a tour. *I'd like that very much.*

* * * *

After they left the kitchen, Samantha whispered to Kathleen, "Doesn't it seem odd that Nonna didn't remember Jack? She met him just a few weeks ago when we celebrated our birthday at CCAB. They had a *very* long conversation at CCAB. *Way* too long."

Kathleen handed her the salad dressing. "She's been a little forgetful since her move."

"Have you noticed other things?"

Kathleen turned off the oven temperature. "She keeps losing things. Like misplacing her car keys. Leaving the tea kettle on. That kind of thing."

"That's not like her," Samantha said, starting to fret.

"Sam, you worry too much. A move is a big deal for someone her age." Kathleen pulled the lasagna out of the oven. "We may have to start without Pete. He's running late. Some equipment keeps breaking down. Toss the salad, and I'll carry the lasagna to the table."

They were half-way through the meal when Pete joined them. He washed up, sat down, and reached out a hand to shake Jack's hand. "Welcome, Jack. Sorry I'm late."

"Kathleen, this lasagna is delicious," said Nonna. Then she turned to Jack. "So Jack, tell us about your work."

That's more like Nonna, thought Samantha, relieved. The consummate hostess.

Jack explained his work, how a string of dogs is trained for class over a four-to-six month period then a group of students are brought in for a month of training. "We work in cycles. We train the dogs from when they're recalled from their puppy raisers then prepare them to be class-ready. When the students arrive, the instructors practically live at the dorm for a month while the students are there then take some vacation time or do follow-up and start again with a new group of dogs. I'm not taking vacation now; I'm saving it up for Christmas."

"Do you enjoy your work?" asked Nonna.

"I do."

"Is it difficult to work with blind people?" asked Kathleen.

"Well, it takes patience and understanding," Jack said, then paused before adding, "but I like a challenge."

Suddenly, Kathleen and Pete burst out laughing. It took less than a split second for Samantha to realize that something just transpired she missed. Even Nonna, usually Samantha's advocate, couldn't keep from laughing. "I'm sorry, Sammy," Nonna explained, "but Jack pointed at you as he said it."

Samantha flashed an indignant glance at Jack, which only got everyone laughing harder. She felt the heat in her neck rise to her cheeks.

Just then, the phone rang in the kitchen and Pete excused himself to answer it.

"Oh, Sam," remembered Kathleen. "The travel agent sent your ticket. Your trip to New York is all set up for the end of this week. Pan Am, your favorite airline!"

"No kidding? You're going to New York?" asked Jack, pleased.

Samantha tried to sound nonchalant, but her throat felt dry. "I guess I am."

"I didn't know that olive oil has its own conventions," Jack said, reaching for a second helping of lasagna.

Both Samantha and Kathleen had to stifle a grin as Kathleen explained, "It's not a convention. Every year, *Gourmand* magazine gives out twelve 'American Food Awards,' and, this year, we've received one of them. They toast everyone's achievement during a gala dinner at a very posh restaurant in New York. Pretty heady stuff."

As Kathleen talked, Samantha grew increasingly preoccupied with the trip. She wondered if the lasagna in her stomach was turning mysteriously into concrete.

Samantha was awfully quiet. Noticing, Jack leaned over and whispered reassuringly, "Sam, you can do this New York trip. It'll be fine. You'll have Azure with you."

For a man who did not seem very sensitive, Samantha was once again surprised by Jack's perceptiveness.

After dinner, Jack and Samantha walked outside, lingering to talk by his bicycle. "Pete was on the phone for a long time."

Samantha shrugged her shoulders. "What's so odd about that?"

"He seemed upset with whomever was on the phone. Then he slammed the receiver down. Didn't you notice?"

Samantha shook her head. She was too busy worrying about what to pack for New York and what to do if Azure needed to be relieved while they were 30,000 feet in the air.

"I just got thinking about those thugs at that Award Ceremony and wondered if maybe the thugs had confused you with Kathleen."

"*What!?*"

"From a distance, you look identical. You were both there, she left early, you didn't use your cane. I just wondered if it was you that they had mistaken. Not me."

"You're accusing Pete of being involved in something? Just because he had a phone call?"

"Just a thought." He pulled his bicycle around. "But Sam?"

"What?"

"Have you checked the books for Running Deer lately?" He climbed on his bike. "I'd better go. Thanks for dinner." He rode off, whistling down the long gravel driveway.

No, I haven't checked the books lately because I have hardly had a minute to myself for over a month.

Kathleen came outside and stood next to Samantha. "I was watching from the window. Did you two have an argument?"

Samantha looked at Kathleen with disbelief. "Oh my gosh! You are turning into Gladys Kravitz from *Bewitched!*"

Kathleen ignored her. "You know what I like about Jack? When we started talking about the New York trip, he encouraged you. It reminded me of the way Nonna would give you a pep talk before a horse show."

Samantha ignored her.

"Boring Bob would've fed your insecurities and talked you out of going."

Samantha turned to leave.

"What's happened to Boring Bob, anyway? I thought he would have swooped in by now."

"Kat, mind your own business," barked Samantha.

"Well, aren't we a little peevish," said Kathleen.

Samantha woke up early Monday morning eager to get caught up on Running Deer. After taking care of Azure, feeding Spitfire, and turning him out in the corral, she prepared for a few hours of catch-up work before heading to her office. She knew a Goliath-sized pile of work waited for her. She should have gone into the office yesterday, but her mind was full, still processing all that she had learned during the month at CCAB. And, to her surprise, she felt relaxed.

At least she *had* felt relaxed up to the point when Jack suggested that she check Running Deer's books. From that point on, she felt a needling concern.

As soon as she finished breakfast, she changed from her sweats into khaki trousers with a blue shirt and walked with Azure over the hill to the office. At the door, she braced herself to face Lena, her part-time office assistant. Lena was fiercely loyal to Samantha, carrying orders out diligently and literally. But Lena was not a woman overburdened with initiative. She could not or would not make a single decision without clear direction from Samantha. Very, very clear direction.

"Oh, Miss Sam!" Lena ran over to hug Samantha. Despite Samantha's repeated request, despite being considerably older than her, Lena refused to call her anything but 'Miss Sam.' "Welcome back! And look at this *beautiful* pooch." Lena bent over to give kisses to Azure on her mouth which Samantha thought was disgusting.

On her desk, Samantha found four huge mounds of paper, neatly piled.

"Now, Miss Sam, I put everything in order for each week you were gone." Lena was very good at making piles.

Samantha had expected something like this. "Okay, Lena. Get yourself some coffee and pull up a chair. The goal is to locate my desktop before the end of the day."

Samantha and Lena started on the first pile, trying to skim through as many papers as possible. Azure rested her head on Samantha's feet, content. The phone rang often, interrupting, but Samantha didn't mind; it felt good to be back at work and finally get on top of things again.

The advertising agency called with new ads prepared, waiting for approval to place the ads in media trade journals. The bottle vendor called to confirm the bottle order; they should arrive within the month.

Good! Samantha thought. *Kathleen actually followed through on something.*

The insurance company called with a quote for a higher premium for the new mill.

The printer called: The labels hadn't been proofed yet, and the printer needed them immediately if they were going to be ready in time for bottling.

Why hadn't Kathleen proofed those?

At lunchtime, Samantha took a quick break to stretch, ate a crunchy green apple, then got back to work. The afternoon sped by. Samantha felt such a deep satisfaction, such pleasure in her work...until Lena read the last few phone messages:

"Please contact Alice Lawton at the bank immediately about a situation with Running Deer."

"What situation?"

"Oh, I don't know, Miss Sam," Lena answered. "I just write down the messages. I don't read them." She paused. "Oh! Wait! I remember that day. There were a number of calls from the bank. The lady wanted to talk to you and wouldn't leave any message. Finally, she did, though. It was a very hot afternoon, and the air conditioning unit wasn't working so Pete told us to go home early and—"

"Lena, what did the messages say?" Samantha interrupted, frustrated.

She rummaged through the pile of pink message slips. "A check for Running Deer had bounced."

"What?! A check *bounced*?" She grabbed her wrist and felt the dial. It was after three and the bank was closed.

"Then, the next morning that bank lady called again...it was already hot that morning, and the air conditioning unit, remember, wasn't working so we had some fans going and they kept blowing the messages off my desk—"

"Lena...*what* did the bank lady say?"

"She said money had been deposited to cover the loan payment."

Completely confused, Samantha decided she needed to go find Pete to ask if he knew anything about the bounced check when her phone rang.

"Sam? It's Jack."

"Oh," she said in a flat tone, still smarting a little after last night's conversation. She covered the phone and whispered, "Excuse me a moment, Lena."

Lena got up and closed Samantha's door as she left.

"I only have a minute," Jack continued. "I'm on a break. Look, I'm sorry if I said anything out of line last night. About Pete."

"Actually, something odd..." she started, her mind still stuck on the bank, but stopped herself. She scratched her head. "Never mind. Anyway, thanks for apologizing. Bye." She started to hang up the receiver but stopped when she heard Jack call out.

"Wait! How's Azure today?"

"Hot. It must be close to one hundred degrees. Good for the olives."

"Good for olives, but bad for dogs in fur coats. Be sure to give her plenty of water."

"I will. Bye."

"Wait! Maybe I should drop by tonight and check to see if she's okay."

"Jack, you have no confidence in me. And you're the one who taught me everything I know about dogs!"

"Well, just to be safe. She's a valuable commodity, you know."

"Trust me. I do know." A smile tugged at the corner of her lips. "Okay. See you tonight."

That evening, Samantha was watering plants on her porch when she heard Jack bicycle up to the cottage. He rested his bike against the cottage and leaned down to pat Azure affectionately before stepping up on the porch.

"Satisfied?" Samantha asked him. "She's fine."

"I never doubted you."

Samantha gave a short laugh.

"Want to take a walk?" he asked Samantha, lifting the large watering bucket out of her hands.

Awkwardness covered Samantha like a blanket. She knew Jack was interested in her, but she wasn't sure how she felt about those intentions. She wasn't really sure *how* she felt about Jack. Although she hated to admit it, she had begun to enjoy his company. But on the other hand, she felt equally as aggravated by him. *And then...there is Lucy. What do I really know about him, other than he's good with dogs?*

Unaware of Samantha's interior dialogue analyzing his shortcomings, Jack led her up a trail with Azure in harness. They walked along, up and over the hills, in silence. Finally, Jack broke the quiet. "Have you noticed how short the days are growing?"

"Sadly, yes," she answered. "It's hard to let summer go when you're a rancher. Autumn is our busiest time. Harvest is exhausting. We're ready to keel over by Christmas morning."

She felt his eyes on her. Maddeningly, her face started to flush so she picked up her pace and walked faster.

He quickened his stride to match hers. "What did you do today?"

"Tried to get caught up. There's so much to coordinate before harvest begins. And I waded through four enormous stacks of papers."

Jack whistled in appreciation. "Sounds awful. I hate paperwork."

Without thinking first, Samantha blurted out, "But something funny happened while I was away. A check from the business account bounced. It must have been written by Pete or Nonna." She clapped her hand against her mouth. *I'm getting to be just like Kat, saying anything that's on my mind. No filter.* She shuddered.

Jack stopped. "What about your sister?"

"Oh no! She's not allowed to get anywhere near Running Deer's finances. She's not even on the signature card for the bank account."

"What about Pete? Have you spoken with him?"

"No. I didn't have a chance to talk to him today. When the harvest starts, he virtually lives in the orchards. Equipment is always breaking down, and workers need direction. I tried calling Nonna but she didn't return my calls..." She realized Jack wasn't listening so she stopped talking.

Jack remained silent, as though he didn't want to say aloud what he was thinking.

A hammer tripped in Samantha's mind. She stopped abruptly, hands hooked on her hips. "Why don't you like Pete?"

Jack hesitated. "He's very likeable. But I think he might have some things going on that he isn't being straight about."

"I'm sure there's a reasonable explanation."

He crossed his arms over his chest. "Tell me again exactly what those men said to you at the Award Ceremony."

Samantha told him.

Jack exhaled. "Sam, you've got some homework to do. Things aren't adding up."

Samantha frowned, regretting that she had ever brought up the bounced check. *Jack can't possibly understand how a family business works...how complicated it can be with family...but that won't stop him from telling me what to do.* A wedge of geese passed overhead, honking down at them. She decided to take their advice and change direction. "So what do you know about olives?"

He gave a short laugh. "They come in a jar with slimy little red things stuck in them."

"There's more to olives than that!" she answered. "Did you know that olives have been found in Egyptian tombs that are over two thousands years old?"

"No kidding?"

"Did you know that at the ancient Olympic Games, winners were given olive wreaths as trophies?"

"Come to think of it, I can just picture a wreath on the head of some guy in a toga." He stopped at the top of the ridge to look at the valley. "It's a beautiful piece of property," he remarked admiringly.

"My grandfather bought these orchards over fifty years ago." She sat down on a large rock. "The land was part of the original mission that's near here, founded by the Spanish priests in the 1700s. The missionaries had planted those Spanish Mission olive trees hundreds of years ago."

"Seems odd. Why would a Viking end up with olive trees?"

"My grandmother knew all about them. Her parents were from Spain."

"Ah! That explains your hair and eyes. And skin."

A stain of flush brushed Samantha's cheeks. She tried to ignore his remark and return to the subject of olives. "My grandmother knew that olive trees were like grapevines; they could produce the best and most concentrated fruit under benign neglect. So, together, my grandparents cared for the Spanish olive trees."

She gestured out to the hills, knowing exactly where she was. The olive leaves rustled silkily around them. "Jack, look at the design of the rows of olive trees. They're almost like a quilt pattern with stripes of silvery green. See how they follow the contours of the hills?"

"So your grandfather made olive oil?"

"No. He just farmed the olives and sold them to a large producer for canning. He scratched out a living but just barely. He died when Kat and I were in college. He left the ranch to us because my parents didn't want it."

"Then how did you get into making olive oil?"

"You *extract* olive oil; you don't *make* it," she corrected. "Kat and I had a plan in college to talk Nonna into letting us try and extract olive oil. Kat did her senior college project on the health benefits of olive oil; I did mine on creating a brand. There has been so much research proving how beneficial olive oil is—because it's so high in monounsaturated fat—that we knew we had a pretty good shot at success. Monounsaturated fat is the good kind," explained Samantha, sensing Jack's confusion. "It lowers LDL cholesterol. Think 'L' for lousy—LDL clogs up arteries."

"Go on," he said, interested.

"So, after college, Kat and I talked Nonna into giving it a try. Took a lot of hand-wringing, but she finally agreed. We have been ahead of the curve; olive oil is just becoming popular in California. It still isn't used as much as it could be, but we're hopeful it will catch on. For the first few years, we had the milling done off-site, but as we bought up neighboring properties, we had room to add a processing facility close to the orchards. I bought a secondhand mill, which worked pretty well, but this year we were able to purchase a new mill. An Old World new mill, I should say," she said. Briefly, she wondered if she was talking too much. She loved talking about Running Deer. Jack didn't seem to mind, though.

"What does that mean?"

"Well, artisanal producers favor the Old World method of a stone wheel to smash the fruit and extract the oil. Gravity does its work, causing the oil to drip into a collector."

"So where do Nonna and Pete fit in?"

"Nonna has a better head for business than Gramps ever did. She's indefatigable." Samantha's enthusiasm faded. "At least she was until six or eight months ago. She decided it was time to retire and move to the retirement facility. She thought that if she stayed at the ranch, we'd be pulling her back in on every decision." *She was probably right.*

Samantha was pensive for a moment, thinking of her grandmother. "Anyway, Pete is the ranch manager. He handles the farming side of the business and tends to the trees. He even propagates olive trees from cuttings."

She sat down on a rock. "Pete started eight years ago with Gramps' original nine thousand trees; we've added three Tuscan varieties as we've bought up new acreage. Tuscan style olive oil has a unique, peppery flavor because it's harvested early before the frost hits. The Spanish olives are harvested later, at full ripeness, so the millings neatly dovetail into one another. Now we're up to eighteen thousand trees. I'm hoping we can buy a few more properties to start an orchard using a semi-dwarf olive tree from Spain. We can grow five times as many olives, and the trees mature in half the time as normal trees."

Jack leaned against the rock where she was sitting and asked, "So how many trees does it take to make a gallon of olive oil?"

Samantha tried not to notice that Jack was so close to her, that his shoulder brushed against hers. He smelled good, of shaving cream and Lifebuoy soap. *Why does he always smell so good?* "Well, if a tree is fully mature, then the rule of thumb is that one tree equals one gallon. Technically, one hundred pounds of olives equals one gallon of olive oil."

"What about the extra virgin or virgin olive oils? Or are they from different trees?'

Samantha covered her mouth with her hand and then burst into laughter. "Sorry! It's not a bad question. Whether an olive oil is considered extra virgin is decided by a panel of experts who are known for their 'nose.' They actually smell and taste for defects."

"Ah. Another area in which I have been woefully olive ignorant." He smiled. "So what would your grandfather think now?"

"He probably would've been pleased to see how we've tweaked his original plan. We still have a ways to go, though."

She pointed to the ridge. "Jack, if you look over there, you can see Mr. Malcolm's property." She knew this land with or without working eyesight.

"You mean *my* property," he corrected, mildly.

"See how the lines of olive trees stop suddenly? Then they start again at the other side of the property? Over to the far left, at the Mitchell property, the same thing happens. The line of olive trees stops abruptly then starts again back at the border of Running Deer."

"I can see it," he said.

"So you can see how important it would be for Running Deer to have those properties so that we can expand. They're very important pieces of land for our ranch. Almost like missing pieces of a pie."

"Samantha," Jack turned to her. "Let me say this one more time. For the *last* time. I am *not* selling."

Samantha frowned.

"I admire your persistence though. You would've made an excellent football player." Then his voice softened to a more serious tone. "About Running Deer. I do have one more question. When is enough, enough?"

Chapter Eight: New York

Jack tried calling Samantha's hotel room one more time before he had to hurry to meet Lucy. He was eager to hear how the plane ride went, still a little amazed that she went through with the trip to New York. He had half-expected her to bail at the last minute. He glanced at his watch and reached for the phone. This time, she answered.

"Did you make it?" Jack asked her.

"We're here!" she answered happily.

He grinned. "You sound...empowered!"

"A few months ago, this trip scared me to death. But Azure made it so easy. Anyone would have thought she flew on planes and strolled through a new city every day of the week. Jack, I have to admit, if it weren't for your bull-headed obstinacy—"

"Don't give me all the credit, Sam," he said, laughing. "You hung in there. You're the one who made this happen. You and Azure. That's what I call teamwork. I'm proud of both of you. Give Azure a Milk-Bone for me."

"I'd better go. This call must be expensive. They have special events planned for us each day. I'm supposed to meet someone from the magazine downstairs in a few minutes to get the schedule."

"Sam?"

"Yes?"

Jack hesitated, wanting to say something but unsure if he should. He settled on, "Enjoy yourself."

* * * *

A few days later, after a whirlwind of VIP treatment, Samantha and Azure flew back to California. After the airline shuttle dropped her at the cottage, she tossed her bags on the porch and went over to the farmhouse. Pete met her at the door as Lily lunged for her from his arms.

"You're back!" Pete said. "Kat's getting her hair cut. She should be back soon. So...worth the trip?"

Samantha pulled Lily close and kissed the violin curve of her neck. "Beyond great, Pete. Azure and I even walked up the stairs to the crown of the Statue of Liberty! 354 steps! Twenty-two stories high! I almost passed out. I wish you and Kat could've been there. It was *amazing!* I brought Lily a present from FAO Schwartz. You'll be astounded at the rave reviews we're starting to get. Tons of publicity. Wait until you hear this—one company offered to *buy* us! It was a lowball price, but still, think of where we were just a few years ago."

"How well I remember. Struggling to sell one bottle at a time at every street fair and farmer's market we could stake out."

She passed Lily back to Pete and went back to the cottage to unpack. Flipping on her clock radio, she was amused to hear the song *Leaving on a Jet Plane*. She emptied out her purse and found the prescription for sleeping pills from the doctor. She held the thin paper in her hand then crinkled it into a ball and tossed it in the wastebasket.

Just as she was shoving her empty suitcase to the back of her closet, the phone rang. A smile broke over her face when she heard Jack's voice on the receiver.

"Hey, Sam! Welcome back," Jack said. "Listen, that interview we did at CCAB is going to be on TV at seven o'clock tonight. Mind if I come over and watch it with you? "

"Really?" she said. "I would've missed it. Come over while I make dinner. We can watch it while we eat." As she hung up the phone, she realized that she had just offered to make dinner, and she had nothing in the refrigerator. Then she ran a hand through her hair and wondered if she had time for a shower to get rid of that stuck-in-an-airplane-all-day sticky smell. She decided the shower was more important. She could raid Kathleen's refrigerator for dinner ingredients.

Within the hour, Jack arrived at the cottage. "Welcome back!" he boomed as he opened the door. Azure jumped up to greet him. He bent down and stroked the dog's head. "You did good, girl," he said fondly. He tossed his coat on her sofa.

"The entire trip couldn't have gone any better," Samantha said, eager to fill him in on the details. Just as she got to the part about the carriage ride through Central Park, her phone rang.

"Bet that's for me," Jack said, sounding apologetic. "I'm sorry, Sam. I needed to firm up plans so I left your phone number with Lucy."

Samantha's jaw dropped open. *The nerve of this guy!* Samantha let him answer the phone and went to the kitchen to stir the eggs she had borrowed from Kathleen to make omelets, trying not to listen in on his conversation. Or, at least, trying to not look obvious about it.

"Hi, Luce! Oh, oh I see." He sounded disappointed. "Sure, I can understand if something important came up. But I'd really like to see you. I haven't seen you in a while. What about Saturday? Okay, I'll see you then." Hanging up the receiver, Jack exhaled, sounding discouraged. Then he flipped on the TV. "Sam, it's starting."

Samantha came over and sat down next to him. It wasn't a very long segment, but it thrilled her that Running Deer was mentioned, and complimented, more than a few times.

After it was over, Jack said, "Great job! And Azure, you were awesome. Better than Lassie." He rubbed Azure's tummy as she sprawled on her back appreciatively.

"You don't think I said too many 'uhs' and 'ums'?" Samantha asked, biting her lip.

"Not at all! You sounded more articulate than the interview lady. Besides," he said, stretching as he straightened up, "people are watching the dogs."

Samantha frowned. *So was Jack.*

After dinner, Jack helped Samantha wash and dry the dishes. The kitchen was so small that they kept bumping into each other. "Jack, can't you just stand in one place to dry the dishes?"

"I *am* standing in one place! You keep jabbing me with your elbow."

She flicked some bubbles from the sink at him. He grabbed her arms to stop her and held on.

Without thinking, she blurted out, "Why do you always smell like soap?" *What in the world made me say that? I am getting so much like Kat!*

Jack only laughed. "Must be a throwback to my football days. I used to scrub myself raw after a game. There's no worst smell on this planet than a football locker room after a game."

She crinkled her nose at that pungent image.

He slipped his arms around her waist and pulled her close, leaning toward her. As his lips gently grazed hers, featherlight, it took an instant for her brain to register what was happening and then she pushed him back. "*What* are you doing?" she gasped.

Jack released her, abruptly. "Am I that rusty?"

Her cheeks started to burn. "No. It's not that. Jack, I can't. I'm not—"

"Oh. Oh, I'm sorry," he said, sounding embarrassed. "It seemed like the right thing to do. I thought we had something special…I uh…I thought it was mutual."

"You must have misunderstood. I couldn't possibly…I'm only interested in…" She fumbled for words.

"Ah, I get it," he said flatly. "Mr. Malcolm's property."

Samantha didn't respond.

"I read you loud and clear. You're all business." He reached over and grabbed his coat, slipping it on. "But Sam, for the last time, I am *not* going to sell that property. Good night."

As she heard the sound of his footsteps crunch down the gravel driveway, she felt a pang of regret and almost went after him. But then she thought of Lucy and decided this was all for the best.

The next morning, Samantha arrived at her office to find Lena eagerly waiting for her at the door. "Miss Sam! You won't believe what just happened. You *won't* believe it! I just got off the phone with somebody from a television production company. They said that they saw your television interview about the dog school! They're making a documentary on health food and a tofu company had to drop out because a customer died after eating its tofu—what is tofu, anyway? It looks like whale blubber—"

"Lena! What did they want?"

"They want to substitute the tofu with Running Deer!"

Samantha gasped. "What did you tell them?"

"I said Miss Sam was very busy and would get back to them when she could. We don't want to sound desperate."

"Yes! Yes we do! Desperate is good! Desperate is wonderful! Quick, Lena! Get them on the phone."

"Oh no, Miss Sam! We can't! The phone rates don't go down until after nine tonight."

Samantha clenched her teeth. "Lena, just get them on the phone!"

After speaking to the production company to book the date and time for the camera crew and interviewer to arrive, Samantha called her sister to tell her the news. "Kat, I have good news and bad news. A production company asked if they could include Running Deer in a documentary they're doing on health foods! They're highlighting a granola company, a yogurt company, and us! They've already sold the documentary to PBS. It's supposed to air in late November. Can you *believe* what this will do for our Christmas season, Kat? Our business is going to skyrocket!" She almost shivered with delight. "But, Kat, here's the bad news: They're coming in two weeks. *Two weeks!* They want to film while we're harvesting and milling."

Samantha was waiting for a squeal of excitement, but Kathleen didn't react. Puzzled, she paused.

"Sam, something's wrong. I'm having really bad cramps." Softly, Kathleen added, "And I'm bleeding."

* * * *

As soon as she hung up with Samantha, Kathleen called the obstetrician's office. "Sounds like you're miscarrying," said the nurse. "Come in this afternoon for an ultrasound so we can try to find a fetal heartbeat."

"I figured as much." A fetal heartbeat. How clinical! *She's talking about my baby.* Kathleen wiped away some tears and blew her nose.

Minutes later, Samantha and Azure arrived at the farmhouse.

"Can't you find Pete?" Kathleen asked miserably, as soon as she saw her.

"Lena and I tried, but he's out in the orchards without his walkie-talkie," Samantha answered. "I'll stay with Lily if you need to go to the doctor's office."

117

"I want you to come with me. Maybe Nonna can watch Lily." She dialed Nonna's number and was relieved when she answered, assuring Samantha she'd be right over.

Samantha fixed Lily a snack and brought Kathleen some tea. "Kat, we can go as soon as Nonna comes."

An hour later, Nonna still hadn't arrived. Samantha called her apartment a number of times, but there was no answer. Kathleen saw worry flit across Samantha's face. Then, just as quickly, it passed. "I'll bet she's having trouble with that ancient car of hers," Samantha said, making light of the matter. "We'd better just go. Do you think you can drive to the doctor's office? It's not far. We can just bring Lily."

Kathleen went upstairs to get ready to go, angry with Pete and Nonna for being so unavailable. *Where are they when I need them?*

Dr. Utley confirmed that Kathleen was miscarrying but told her to go home. "We need to let nature take its course. Call me tomorrow and let me know how you're doing. Plan on bed rest for a while. It'll take time for your body to get back to normal, Kathleen. Call me if there seems to be anything unusual."

"Oh, like *this* isn't unusual enough?" Kathleen blurted out accusingly. Then she said the thing that frightened her the most, "You *know* how long it took to get pregnant with Lily. What if I can't ever have another baby?"

Dr. Utley didn't bat an eye. "Well, Kathleen, you *did* get pregnant with Lily," he said calmly. "And you will most likely be able to get pregnant again. Miscarriages just happen."

Men don't understand anything.

An hour later, back at home, she climbed into bed and pulled the covers over her head, angry and sad.

* * * *

Samantha gave Lily a snack and rocked her for a few minutes before tucking her in for a nap. Then she went downstairs to call Lena and see if Pete had shown up.

"No," Lena said. "I haven't seen him."

"Have you sent anyone to look for him?"

"Well, no. You didn't tell me to look for him. You just said to let you know when he showed up."

Just as Samantha was about to slam down the phone, Lena asked if she wanted her phone messages. Trying not to scream, Samantha said 'yes' in an icy tone. "You have a message from Alice Lawton at the bank. She wants you to call her immediately because there is a situation."

Another situation? I still haven't had any time to figure out what caused the first situation. Samantha memorized the phone number Lena gave her and quickly called the bank. "Is Alice Lawton available?"

"Miss Lawton the bank manager?" asked a young voice. "She's in a meeting."

"Is there someone with whom I could speak about Running Deer Ranch?"

"The petting zoo?"

"No!" Samantha said indignantly. "It's an olive oil ranch."

"Oh. Sorry. I'm new to the bank." There was murmuring in the background. "Actually, there's someone here right now who works for Running Deer Ranch."

"*What?* Who?"

"I can't give out that kind of information over the phone."

Samantha's jaw clenched. "Well, could I at least *speak* to that person? I'm one of the owners of the ranch. I'm concerned that someone is acting without authority."

"Well..." the young voice hesitated. "Just one minute."

Samantha heard mumbled whispers. Then a familiar voice asked, "Hello? Who is this?"

"Nonna?" Samantha asked, amazed. "I thought you were coming to the house hours ago!"

"Is this Sammy or Kat?"

"Sam. Nonna, why aren't you here?"

"I had to run an errand at the bank."

Samantha's heart missed a beat. "What kind of errand?"

"I'm just taking care of a few personal things. Nothing to worry about. I need to go and finish this up."

"Wait! Nonna, *wait*! Is Pete there with you?"

She heard the click of the phone hanging up.

Kathleen called to her from the upstairs bedroom. She and Azure went upstairs and found Kathleen locked in the bathroom, crying.

119

Through the bathroom door, Kathleen cried, "Oh, Sam, This is awful! It's like the worst period anyone could ever have. Can't you find Pete?"

"Not yet. I'll keep trying. He's out in the orchards. I've left a message with Lena; she'll give it to him if he shows up at the office. You know what it's like during harvest." She put her head against the bathroom door. "Dr. Utley said it would get worse before it gets better. I'll go find a heating pad. Can I get you anything else? Tea? Bayer aspirin? Anything to eat?"

Just then, Lily called out, awake in her crib from her nap.

"I'll take care of her, Kat. You just rest."

And so the rest of the afternoon and night wore on. Kathleen finally fell into an exhausted sleep by midnight. Samantha dropped into a restless sleep in a chair in her sister's bedroom, Azure lying devotedly by her feet, never leaving Samantha's side.

The next morning, a phone call woke them up. "Better now," Kathleen answered, yawning. "I'll be there later today." She put the phone back in the cradle on the night table. "That was the doctor's office. They want me to come in for a check," she told Samantha.

"Are you up for driving? In case we can't find Pete?"

"I can't *believe* we can't find him when I needed him." Slowly, Kathleen sat up in bed and cautiously swung her legs over the side. "I'm going to go take a shower."

As Samantha went down to start breakfast, she stopped by Lily's room and heard her playing in the crib. Samantha went in to pick her up.

"Oh, baby Lily, you are a breath of fresh air." She hugged her little niece and kissed her soft, silky cheeks. "But I am *so* glad you're not walking yet."

As soon as Samantha strapped Lily into her highchair and gave her Cheerios to eat, she called the bank and asked to speak to Alice Lawton.

"Speaking. Oh, hello, Miss Christiansen. You're going to have to come into the bank as soon as you can."

Samantha wondered if a person could actually detect her blood pressure rising. And how high could it rise before it caused a heart attack? She did not like Miss Lawton, she decided. "Couldn't you just explain to me what has happened to create a problem?"

"Right now I have a customer in my office, and this is not a conversation to have over the phone. Come in as soon as you can." Click.

Samantha slammed the phone back in the receiver. "Grrr! This is so frustrating!"

"What's so frustrating?" asked Kathleen, as she came downstairs in her robe.

As Samantha opened her mouth to answer, Pete's truck rumbled up the driveway. Pete hopped out of the car and came into the kitchen. The two sisters stared blankly at him while Lily called out for her father. "What's going on?" he said as he went over to pick up his daughter.

"Let me take Lily over to feed Spitfire and Azure, and I'll let the two of you talk," said Samantha.

An hour later, Pete stopped by the cottage to pick up Lily. "I'm sorry. I had no idea what was going on here."

"I know. It couldn't be helped. At least you're here now. Kat needs you." She poured two cups of tea and handed one to him. She sat down on the couch next to him, dreading her next task. "Pete, were you at the bank yesterday with Nonna?"

"No. I was out in the orchards. We're short some hands, and some of the pneumatic combs keep breaking down. Spent all night working on them. I couldn't leave until we got them working, not with ripe olives ready for harvesting." He put the tea cup down and brushed his hands against his blue jeans. "I can't get the dye from the olives off my hands." He exhaled, exhausted. "What was she doing at the bank?'

"I have no idea. Something's not right with Nonna or with our bank account." She tried to sound calmer than she felt. She swallowed hard, hating to ask. "Pete, do *you* know what's going on?"

He groaned, covering his face with his hands. "I should have told you about this when it first happened." He dropped his hands to his lap. "Nonna was a little short on cash a while back and asked me to float her."

Samantha leaned forward. "Go on."

"Problem was, I didn't have the cash. You know what a problem cash flow can be in a family business. Everything's in assets. But I knew a guy, who knew some guys, and I was able to set up a short-term loan for her."

"Why didn't you tell me about it?"

"I didn't even tell Kat. Nonna came to me for help. She's never asked me for anything. I wanted to help her out without involving the entire family."

Samantha took that in for a while, biting her lip. "But why would she have been short on cash? We worked out a budget for her when she decided to move to Shady Acres so she wouldn't worry."

"I have no idea why she needed the money."

"You never thought to ask her?"

"She's like you, Sam. Doesn't tell anybody anything. I figured that it was costing more to get settled into the new place than she had thought, and she didn't want to come running to you. She's been working so hard on cleaning out the farmhouse and getting Kat to sell stuff. Just seemed like she needed a little bit of help."

"How *much* help?"

"Well," he cleared his throat. "That's been an added complication. Originally, it was for $1,000. Then she thought she might need another $1,000. We had a re-payment schedule figured out with these guys, but I think Nonna might have missed a payment here and there. They keep bugging me for reminders."

Samantha nearly gasped. *A reminder! Like the one at the Award Ceremony a few months ago. The one I blamed on Jack.* "There's something funny going on with Running Deer's bank account. A few weeks ago, when I was at the Academy, you or Nonna wrote a check that bounced then deposited money and resubmitted the check again."

Pete stood up and reached over to pick up Lily from the floor. "I don't know anything about the bank or that check, Sam. I haven't written a check...well, ever. You told me not to touch anything with Running Deer while we had this outstanding loan. Do you want to get down there today? I could drop you at the bank on the way to Kat's doctor appointment."

"Yes, good idea." As Pete reached for the door handle, Samantha said, "Pete, I'm sorry about the miscarriage."

"Me, too." He sounded sad.

Later that morning, Samantha went to the bank to meet with Alice Lawton, a woman who took her banking responsibilities seriously. "I called you yesterday morning to let you know that the funds in Running Deer's account went below the minimum amount required. That's the second time it's happened this month. You can't let this account be overdrawn, not if you want this loan to remain in good standing." Miss Lawton clucked her tongue like a disapproving librarian.

Samantha was stunned. "That's impossible! I set up the account so that we always need two signatures to do anything on this account—pay bills or payroll. It *always* requires my signature, with either my grandmother's or my brother-in-law's."

"Well, see for yourself." She passed the withdrawal slips to Samantha.

This woman is getting on my last nerve. "There's a reason I have a guide dog," Samantha snapped. Azure thumped her tail.

"Oh. My apologies." Miss Lawton didn't seem at all sorry. "Let's see....yes, here it is...it says 'Anna Christiansen' and 'Samantha Christiansen'. There, does that help?"

"Look, if you'll give me a piece of paper and a pen, I'm going to sign my name. You tell me if it matches the signature that's on the slip." Samantha reached into her purse for a signature guide.

"What's that?" asked Miss Lawton.

Samantha spoke slowly, the way someone would speak to a kindergartener. "A tool to help me sign my name straight."

Miss Lawton held out the paper for Samantha and indicated where to sign. Then she examined the two signatures, side by side.

"It's the same, Miss Christiansen. They look identical."

"Look carefully at the 'S'. Is there a curl on the top of the 'S'?"

"Yes, there is. Why? Isn't that your signature?"

"Um, uh," Samantha stumbled for a moment.

Miss Lawton seized on her hesitation. "Forgery is a very serious offense." She started to cluck her tongue again.

"No, it's not a forgery," Samantha lied.

She transferred cash from her own savings account into Running Deer's account, to cover the missing money so that they could pay their vendors, make payroll, and stay above the minimum amount. The months of harvest were traditionally lean, but as soon as the Christmas season ended, they were usually in the black. Or sort of black. More like gray, she thought, biting her lip.

Afterwards, she headed to the bus stop, wondering why Kathleen had forged her name. *Again.* It made Samantha furious to think Kathleen was dipping into Running Deer money like it was her own savings account.

For the first time in over two months, Samantha waited for the bus, this time with Azure. Preoccupied with the banking problem, she climbed up the bus' steps. When she reached the top, Jimmy said, "Uh, Sam, what are you doing?"

"What does it look like I'm doing?" she answered, smiling. "Riding the bus."

"But, uh, you have a dog," he said, reluctance in his voice.

"A *guide* dog, Jimmy. Not any old dog."

"I'm sorry, Sam. I can't let dogs ride on the buses."

"Oh, you. Stop that teasing, Jimmy."

"Sorry, Sam. Nothing personal. Dogs aren't allowed on buses. It's not fair to the other riders."

Stunned and embarrassed, Samantha and Azure stepped back down off the bus. "Do you believe that, Azure? Thinking you're any old dog?" She leaned down and stroked Azure's head.

She tried to recall what the CCAB had taught the students to do in such a situation. Samantha wished she had paid more attention to that lecture about the new California Civil Code Sections. She was pretty sure it was now illegal to refuse to let her guide dog ride on public transportation. But...she wasn't positive. Even during the lecture, she knew that her strategy of taking Azure in public places would be to try to avoid confrontation.

The fatigue of the day hit her. She let out a discouraged sigh. She wished she had her sister's moxie. Kathleen would tell her to get back on that bus and take her to go see Jimmy's supervisor. Kathleen would have the California Civil Code Sections in her purse, highlighted with a yellow marker, ready to pounce. Samantha preferred to handle things quietly. Unfortunately, that meant she and Azure would be walking home today.

She thought of calling Jack to ask him how to handle this kind of thing. But then, with a thud, she remembered how they had last left things. With piercing awareness, she realized that somehow, over the past few months, she had started to count on Jack. He had become her friend.

An hour later, Samantha and Azure turned up the lane toward the ranch. She walked as slowly as she could past Jack's house without being obvious, hoping, without success, that she might run into him. He's probably out with Lucy, she decided, shaking off her regret.

As soon as she arrived at the farmhouse, she checked on Kathleen. Pete was in the kitchen, stirring macaroni and cheese, with Lily hanging on his hip like a chimpanzee. "Dr. Utley said she's okay, but it'll take some time to get back on her feet. She's in bed now. She doesn't want to talk to anyone," said Pete, yelping loudly in mock pain as Lily pulled tufts of his hair.

She knew she should have told Pete that his wife had been helping Nonna clean out the business account, but she just didn't have the heart. Not today, anyway. Not right after Kat's miscarriage. She decided to go down to the office to distract herself from the mounting problems she faced. She finished up the day's orders and stacked them in a pile so Lena could mail them off. Then she confirmed orders for print advertising space in foodservice trade magazines.

She frowned as she picked up the still yet un-proofed order for bottle labels. She couldn't ask Lena to proof it. Last time she did, Lena missed typos in the word "olive oil," spelling it "spoiled oil."

Next, boldly anticipating a spike in activity after the health food documentary aired in early December, Samantha decided to double the quantity of packaging materials ordered for the holiday period. "Oh, Azure, I hope that television show works out well. Otherwise, we are going to have *a lot* of excess inventory. And Running Deer will have yet *another* situation."

As Samantha realized she was talking to Azure like she were a person, it crossed her mind that Bob was right; she *had* turned into one of those dog ladies. Shaking her head, Samantha decided it was time to call it a day. She and Azure went back up over the hill to the cottage.

Even at home, her mind couldn't settle down. She brushed Spitfire, cleaned his hooves, and added two flakes of hay into his manger. Still restless, she cleaned the rooms in her cottage, nearly picked up the phone to call Jack, but stopped herself, dusted the room again until, finally, the phone rang. She lunged across the room to answer it. "Hello?" she asked, trying not to sound out of breath.

"Samantha!" It was Dr. Sommers. "I was just thinking about you and wondered how you and Azure were getting along."

"Oh, it's so good to hear your voice, Dr. Sommers." *So good.* She was surprised to hear from him. She curled up on the loveseat. "Azure's doing great. It's…taking me some time to get back into the swing of things. Things are…harder than I expected…but it's not Azure." Without meaning to, she spilled out the story of Kathleen's miscarriage, her worries about her grandmother, the bank situation, the trip to New York City, and the documentary.

"Sounds like a pretty full couple of weeks, Sam." He paused. "You probably haven't had any time to listen to the tapes I gave you."

"Actually, I have. I try to listen a little in the morning as I'm getting ready for work. It's sort of…calming. Soothing, actually. I keep finding myself…surprised by Jesus. I had an idea that he was sort of a…oh I don't know…kind of a Berkeley type. A tofu-and-Birkenstock guy. But he's not. He's very direct, very purposeful."

Dr. Sommers laughed. "I agree with you, Sam. I think most people don't have a clue about Jesus. Only what pictures or little songs they might have had in Sunday school years ago or others' perception of Him. Say, have you noticed how many times blindness comes up in the gospels?"

She tucked the receiver under her chin and twisted her hair into a ponytail. "I have."

"Jesus was no stranger to people's difficulties. Even ours." Then he added, "So... Jack lives nearby, doesn't he?"

"An interesting segue, Dr. Sommers, speaking of difficulties."

He chuckled. "Meaning?"

"We just don't seem to be able to have a very...easy friendship. We argue a lot."

"Maybe you're talking about important topics."

Samantha couldn't disagree; she and Jack did talk about important things. Now that she thought about it, she couldn't recall a single deep conversation she and Bob ever had. *But then again, Bob and I never argued.*

"Jack strikes me as the kind of guy who likes to fix things for people," continued Dr. Sommers. "Find a solution to every problem. He just may not know how to do it right. Or how to say it right."

Samantha fidgeted on the chair. "I can't seem to go more than a few days without getting upset with him." Then she surprised herself by admitting, "Now, though, I think he's upset with me. In fact, I know he is."

Dr. Sommers listened carefully. "Sam, for the first thirty-two years of marriage, my wife expected me to read her mind. It took years for her to understand that I wasn't that intelligent. It's been much better since she finally started to spell out the obvious to me."

"How long have you been married?"

"Uh, let's see. In six months it will be thirty-three years."

Samantha burst out laughing.

"What I'm saying is that you might need to be more direct with a guy like Jack. Like clubbing him on the back of the skull with a two-by-four."

"Don't you think I'm direct?" Samantha asked curiously.

"Well," Dr. Sommers hesitated. "Well, I haven't known you very long, but I would say you're a private person who doesn't share her thoughts easily."

"Really? Oh…maybe I'm not. My sister says I will end up exploding one day from stuffing all of my opinions." Samantha sighed. "Right now Jack is mad because I want to buy his property to expand my business. But I'm really not mad about that." *Not anymore. I was mad about the property, but I've gotten over that.*

"So what *are* you mad about?

She hesitated, not sure she wanted to divulge this information to anyone, but something about Dr. Sommers' non-judgmental manner always reassured her. "It's just that…I know he's…interested in me…but he's also dating someone else. I really don't want to start anything up with someone who plays the field."

"But Sam, I don't think he plays football anymore."

Samantha laughed. "Not *that* kind of field! I meant, a womanizer."

"Jack?" He sounded skeptical.

"Yes! He calls this woman when I'm with him, makes plans with her, and sometimes he leaves suddenly to go meet with her. Talk about red flags! It may work for this Lucy lady, but not for me. I do *not* need that in my life. My life is complicated enough."

"Lucy?" He coughed into the phone, covering up a laugh. "Is *that* the other woman you're talking about?"

"Yes. He's not even secretive about her," she said accusingly. "He acts like dating two women at once is no big deal!*" Call me a square, but that's not for me.*

"Oh Sam. Sam, Sam, Sam. You *need* to have a talk with Jack. You need to have him tell you who Lucy is."

* * * *

An hour later, Jack heard a timid knock on his door. When he opened it, he was shocked to see Samantha standing there, a big basket in her arms, Azure by her side. He didn't really think he would be seeing much of her anymore, not after he made a fool of himself in her kitchen.

But I'm not going to let that happen again. No way. Even if she is beautiful and smart and her eyes…they were like a weathervane for her feelings, those eyes. They could change so fast, from soft and warm to stormy mad. Jack! He caught himself. *Get hold of yourself, man! Where is your pride? This woman is wired for one thing: ambition.*

"Well, well, well. It's my determined little neighbor, paying a call," he said crisply. "Did you bring your contractor? Stopping by to check out the floor plan?"

"Of course not!" she answered earnestly. "Besides, I was planning on tearing down the house and planting olive trees."

He crossed his arms and tried not to notice how cute Samantha looked when she was being earnest. "Exactly why Mr. Malcolm didn't want to sell it to you. He built this house for his bride years ago. It may be showing its age a little, but it's a wonderful old place. He handcrafted all of the interior woodwork himself."

"He built this house for his bride?" she repeated. She scratched her head. "How did I not know that? All I had ever noticed about Mr. Malcolm was his annoying throat clearing habit that sounded like he was coughing up fur balls."

"Never even asked him, did you?" Jack accused. "He made me promise not to *ever* sell to you. He told me that when you put in the processing facility, it turned this little neighborhood into a veritable highway."

"I would *hardly* call four or five extra cars a day a veritable highway," Samantha said huffily. "Well, maybe a couple of dozen cars on weekends. And a lot of trucks do rumble through." She frowned and started talking to herself again. "Actually, there has been quite a lot of traffic since we built the processing facility." She caught herself and looked at him defensively. "It is zoned for agricultural use, you know."

He almost laughed at her. Almost. "Well, good-bye." He closed the door.

He stood behind the door, feeling like a crazed adolescent, but he wanted to see what she would do. The door bell rang again. He grinned. After a long pause, he opened the door again.

She smiled broadly. "I brought you a welcome-to-the-neighborhood gift." She handed him a basket of homemade almond nut muffins, still warm from the oven.

Sounding colder than he felt, he asked, "Any chance that they're laced with strychnine?"

"No!" she said indignantly. Then, brightening, she added, "but I did make them with olive oil. People don't realize that you can bake with olive oil."

"Ah," said Jack, peeking into the basket. "Well, thank you for the baking tip. Good-bye." He closed the door on her again and stayed put, a smile tugging on his lips. *Watch it, ol' boy; she's after something. Don't be a sucker. She only wants my property.* His smile faded.

She rang the doorbell again and waited patiently. Finally, Jack opened the door.

"Jack, I wasn't entirely truthful with you the other day," she said quickly, as if she expected him to close the door on her again.

Interested, he leaned against the door jamb and waited for her to elaborate.

"You interrupted me when I said I wasn't interested, and you thought I was going to say that I was only interested in this property. Well, the truth is that I realized a while ago that you weren't going to part with this property. Jack, the truth is…" she jutted out her chin, "well, the truth is that *you* haven't been truthful with me."

He was completely confused. "*What* are you talking about?"

"What I was going to say the other day was that I'm not interested in getting involved with a…" she raised her arms in the air "…with the kind of guy who plays the field."

"Plays the field?" He put a hand to his chest. "M*e?* What have I possibly done to give you that impression?"

She drew an audible breath. "Jack, who is Lucy?"

"Lucy? I've told you about her. I must have mentioned her a dozen times."

"You have! But you have never said *who* she was."

He scratched his head. "But I *must* have told you. I'm sure I did. At least, I meant to. I *should* have." *Could that be what this is all about?* Then he erupted into laughter. "Is that why you pushed me away when I tried to kiss you the other night? You think I'm *dating* another woman?" He nearly doubled over, laughing so hard.

Samantha remained stoic.

He covered his hands with his face, trying to recover. "Oh, Sam, I am *really* bad with details, aren't I?" He took his hands off of his face. *How could I be such an idiot?!* He took a deep breath. "She's not a woman, Sam. Lucy is my fourteen-year-old daughter." By the look on her face, he knew that Samantha was working the numbers in her mind. In a serious voice, he added, "And no, my wife was not her mother."

Chapter Nine: Enough

\Kathleen spent the next day in bed. She wasn't able to sleep, but she didn't have any energy, either. Her feet seemed caught in quicksand; just moving them took extra effort.

Late in the afternoon, Samantha came up to her room to try and talk, but Kathleen was in no mood for conversation. "Sam, leave me alone. I need rest." She glanced at her sister. "And that's my blouse you've got on."

"No, it's not. You've borrowed it so often you think it's yours." Samantha sat cross-legged at the foot of her bed, leaning against the bedframe. "Kathleen, I know you're not feeling well, but there are a few questions I need to ask you."

"Not now." Kathleen didn't mean to snap at Samantha, but she couldn't care less about the business today. Besides, her mind felt sluggish.

Samantha sighed. "Kat, we still have a business to run. I've been trying to get caught up and found this order for the labels on your desk. I thought you were going to proof it and send it off weeks ago." She handed the order to Kathleen.

Kathleen pulled the covers up over her head, letting the order slip to the floor. "Proof it yourself." She knew that was a low blow, but she didn't care.

"Well that's a little hard to do when it's not in Braille," Samantha snapped. "Why didn't you just ask Nonna to proof it?"

Kathleen sighed. She hated it when Samantha acted all stiff and stern like a company president. "She's hasn't been around."

"Look, I do feel sad about the miscarriage. I *really* do. But I have to get some things figured out."

"Like what?"

"First of all, why did you write a check out of Running Deer's account while I was at CCAB? A check that bounced? And then, why did you make a deposit to cover it? Where did that cash come from?"

Uh oh. How did Sam catch that? Kathleen pulled herself up in bed, stuffing a pillow behind her back, resigned to the interrogation. "I finally got a check from the consignment shop that has been selling Nonna's junk. I mean...antiques."

Samantha pressed her fingers to her temples. Kathleen knew that meant she was *trying* to be patient. "Why would you make a deposit on the business account? Now it looks like income. We'll have to pay taxes on it."

"I was just covering Nonna. She needed the money."

"Then why did *she* write a check from the business account?"

"She didn't say. She just needed a little extra cash, and you weren't around, so I wrote your name on the check. And then again on the deposit slip."

"Why would you *do* that?"

Exasperated, Kathleen tossed her head back and clunked it against the headboard. Rubbing her head, she said, "See? *That's* why I don't tell you things. You get upset about the smallest things."

"And now you've done it again. Just this week. Kathleen—*why* did you forge my signature on those withdrawal slips that Nonna has been taking to the bank?" Samantha asked in very clear, measured tones.

"Because she couldn't get any cash *without* your signature." *Isn't that obvious?!*

She sighed. This conversation was robbing her of her last ounce of energy. "You were in New York, and she needed money. We couldn't wait for Pete to come home...so I just made a decision and signed a couple of slips. Lena showed me where you kept the checkbook."

Samantha jumped off the bed, hands planted firmly on her hips. "You are *not* to touch that account! You know how we all feel about your money management skills. You have none. That's why we all agreed to take your name off of the account in the first place. *You* agreed to that! You admitted you couldn't be trusted!"

Kathleen pulled a pillow over her head. "Sam, I don't feel well. Right now I just don't care about this stupid olive oil business. Leave me alone."

"Only if you promise me you will never, ever, ever sign my name again. On anything! I'm not kidding, Kat. I don't know why Nonna needs money, but you must not let her tap into the business account. You're jeopardizing this company."

"Oh, *give* me a break! You said we shouldn't break the loan covenants. One or two little bounced checks would hardly take down a company."

"A bounced check jeopardizes the good standing of our loan! This sends a red flag to the bank that we have no money to make those loan payments. If we can't make our loan payments, *that* could take down this company. I *told* you there were loan requirements. I explained it all before I left for the Academy. You may not care about Running Deer, but I do. So does Pete."

Kathleen pulled the pillow off of her head. "Fine! I promise. Now leave me alone."

Exasperated, Samantha turned to leave and said loudly to Azure, "I just can't worry about it right now. I have too many other things to worry about. *Somebody* has to run this company. Right?"

Azure shook her head, flapping her ears, almost like she was consoling Samantha. Disgusted by Samantha's noticeable lack of sympathy, Kathleen threw a pillow at the door behind her.

* * * *

Saturday morning dawned with a hint of fall perfuming the air. *Probably one of our last warm days,* Samantha thought, walking outside and inhaling deeply. She was just about to head up to the area where workers were harvesting olives when she heard someone with a recognizable limp approaching her, gravel crunching beneath feet.

"Hi, Jack," she said, a smile spreading uncontrollably across her face. "You have good timing."

"Another one of my sterling qualities," he said cheerfully.

"Along with everlasting smugness," Samantha said, still smiling. "I've been trying for two weeks to get up to the orchards and check on the harvest. I *finally* have a free morning."

She walked over to the truck and gave Jack the keys. "Here. Let's drive around the ranch. I'll show you the orchards. The olives are getting harvested and processed at the mill. It's fascinating to watch if you like machinery."

Jack jingled the keys in his hands. "Sam, I can't."

"Can't what?"

"Drive."

Samantha was floored. Was that why he rode the public bus? Or bicycled everywhere? Or why he never drove a CCAB van? "Can't? Or don't?"

"I don't drive. Period."

"But why not?"

Jack handed her back the keys. "It's personal."

A fuzzy image started to take shape in Samantha's mind, slowly, like Nonna's television set with a tube that took forever to warm up. Softly, she asked, "Does this have something to do with your wife's car accident?"

He didn't respond.

It seemed there was more Jack wanted to say. She waited until a horrifying thought popped into her head and out of her mouth. "Oh, Jack. Don't tell me you were the driver."

Jack walked over to the horse corral and leaned his back against the railing, hands in his pocket.

Samantha went over to him, leaned against the corral next to him, waiting patiently. She could tell he was arranging his thoughts.

Finally, he spoke. "We'd been to a party. Another car ran a red light and T-boned right into us, plowing into Ellen's side. Killed her instantly. She wasn't wearing her seatbelt. The police determined it was the other driver's fault. The guy's in jail, five to seven years, for gross vehicular manslaughter while intoxicated and felony drunken driving. His blood alcohol was three times the legal limit."

Jack took a deep breath. "He was my best friend on the team. We'd been roommates for years. I visit him once a month at the prison." Jack kicked the ground for a while, absently. "I don't blame him. I should have been able to prevent the accident. Maybe I could have if I hadn't been drinking myself."

"Is that why you don't drink?" She noticed he didn't have wine at dinner the other night.

"I was, uh, rather alcohol-dominated. I have since discovered that I'm an all-or-nothing kind of guy."

She wasn't sure she should ask him any more questions, but she was interested in knowing more, so she decided to risk it. "So you quit playing football after that?"

"The accident re-injured my knee and ended my career." He turned and faced the corral. Spitfire had come over to them and pushed his head over the railing, wanting a pat.

Samantha stroked Spitfire's long nose. "How did you end up here?"

"I bicycled a lot to rehabilitate my knee. I was trying to figure out what to do with the rest of my life. So one day, a friend and I were bicycling all over the valley and just happened to ride past the CCAB facility. I've always loved dogs so I decided to take a look. Next thing I knew, I was hired. I love it, too. I feel I'm making a difference. When I was playing football, it was all about me. I hardly thought about anyone else, even Ellen." He was quiet after that.

Ellen. It was the first time he had said her name aloud. Samantha felt oddly embarrassed now that she had seen him with his guard down. She sensed he had said all that he wanted to say. Respecting his privacy, she put the keys back in the truck. "Well, how about a walk then?"

* * * *

They hiked up the trail to the orchard where the workers were harvesting olives, using pneumatic combs so as to not bruise the fruit. Jack walked up and down the rows of evenly spaced, carefully tended olive trees as Samantha spoke to Pete. He was grateful for some breathing room; telling her about Ellen's accident was unexpected. Uncomfortable, too. It dug up painful memories he liked to keep buried. He liked it better when he was helping other people with their lives. It felt safer.

"Thanks for waiting," Samantha said. "I just had to talk to Pete about a few things. I haven't seen much of him lately. We've got a problem with the County."

"What kind of problem?"

"After the olives are processed and the oil is extracted, there's waste to manage. Only ten percent of the olive pressing comes out as oil. The chemicals leached from the olives and pits can be toxic to the ground and water. We're planning to turn it into compost, but the County wants us to add more ingredients to it to round it out." Clearly annoyed, she shook her head. "Never mind. Everything with the County gets complicated. Want to see the new mill?"

"Sure."

"We have to hike back down to the facility."

As they went inside, Samantha pointed to the interior windows that separated the offices from the milling facility. "You'll have to put on some protective clothing to go in to the mill. It will be loud. Cold, too. We keep the temperature cool to protect the fruit and the aromas and to reduce oxidation."

"What fruit do you keep talking about?" asked Jack.

"Olives! They're actually a fruit. The olives are processed as quickly as possible—usually within twenty-four hours. That's why we wanted this facility so close to the orchards. The olives are brought in ripe from the fields. First the olives are cleaned and ground into a paste—milled— to extract the oil. Pits and all. Speed is necessary so the olive paste doesn't warm up. Heat can ruin the flavor. After the oil is extracted, it's put into two large stainless steel tanks and kept below 65 degrees and then we bottle as orders come in."

He was impressed with her knowledge. And her brains. It reminded him of how articulate she was during the interview back at the Academy and that speech he heard her give at that Award Ceremony. *She knows her stuff.* "Looks like a good year?"

"Best ever."

As they walked into the processing facility, the noise was deafening. Afterwards, Samantha couldn't stop smiling.

"Why do you look so satisfied?" Jack asked, amused.

"Oh, if you could have only seen us a year ago! Our old mill made the most horrible sound. And that was when it worked...which wasn't often. Whenever I hear the sound of that well-run machinery, I can't hold back a grin."

137

Letting his gaze slide away, Jack was startled to realize he wished he had known her a year ago. He hadn't really had any feelings for a woman since Ellen had died. Well-meaning friends had tried to set him up, and he'd even obliged them once or twice, but he never wanted to go out on a second date. *And here I am, wishing I knew Sam a year ago.*

But he wasn't sure if she felt the same way about him. In fact, he wasn't at all sure *how* she felt about him. It stunned him that she had shown up at his door with that basket a while ago. He had left her house thinking he wouldn't be seeing her again. Even worse, he had a feeling she wouldn't have even noticed his absence. He, on the other hand, had felt like he was stepping around a crater, a gigantic empty hole. He couldn't concentrate, couldn't sleep. Practically couldn't eat. Like a stupid love-sick puppy, he thought, disgusted.

Following her into the office, he watched Samantha pull out bottles of different olive oils, recognizing them by their shape. She took out dipping bowls and placed one in front of each olive oil. Deftly, she flipped the bottles and filled the small bowls with a few tablespoons in each. "Well, you've done this a few times, huh?"

She nodded. "Taste from mellow to spicy, just as in wine tasting. Try this first; it's a Spanish olive oil. Probably typical of what you're accustomed to," she advised, handing Jack a small plastic cup with a teaspoonful of the Spanish olive oil.

"Smooth," he said, after tasting.

"Exactly! Very light. And now for the Tuscan variety." She poured the Tuscan olive oil into another small plastic container and put it in the palm of her hand to warm it. "Follow my example," she said. "Cover the top of the cup as you swirl it to capture the aromatics. Now smell. Recognize anything?"

Jack inhaled deeply. "Fresh cut grass?"

"Yes! That's from the chlorophyll. Now...swallow it, and see if it makes you cough."

He started sputtering as the oil hit the back of his throat.

"Perfect! It should. It has a peppery flavor, too, doesn't it? Spicy."

He coughed. "Feels like I have bees in my throat."

As they headed back down to the cottage, Jack thought about trying to hold her hand but then he thought better of it. He was still smarting a little from how she yelped when he tried to kiss her.

Scattering his thoughts like buckshot, Samantha asked, "So what do you think?"

"About who?"

She gave him a strange look. "About olives."

Oh. His cheeks grew warm. "The mill is amazing. Massive granite wheels! Can't imagine what it took to lug them into place. I had no idea of what went into a bottle of olive oil."

They stopped for a moment on top of the ridge that overlooked the farmhouse and the cottage. They sat perched on a rock, basking in the sunshine, leaning on their elbows, quiet and content. Jack was grateful she dropped the subject about Ellen. That was another thing he liked about Sam. She seemed to know when to ask a question and when to leave it alone. Jack glanced over at her, trying not to think about how desperately he wanted to kiss her. "So do they love it as much as you love it?"

She sat upright. "Who? Pete and Kathleen? Do they love it? I think so." She raised an eyebrow. "What would make you ask such a thing?"

"They leave the running of the business to you."

"We each have a division of labor. Pete puts as much sweat and blood into Running Deer as any Christiansen. And Kat, when she's focused, has an amazing creative flair. She's the reason we've won those awards."

"Seems like you have to hold the whole thing together."

Samantha stood and crossed her arms, gripping her elbows. "Well, lately it's been...there's a lot of pressure on us...for different reasons."

"I can tell. You look worried when you talk about the ranch. You bit your lip and crossed your arms while you were talking to the foreman. Kinda like you had a headache." *Actually, standing just like she is now.*

She dropped her arms to her sides. "Lately it has been a headache."

He stood up to face her. "Sometimes I just wonder if it's too important to you."

"What do you mean?"

"I asked you a while back: When is enough, enough? You didn't answer."

She stiffened her back. "Success doesn't just happen, Jack. It takes years of planning and hard work. You can't ever get to a place where you coast. Not in this business. You need to carve your niche." She crossed her arms again.

He frowned. He wasn't trying to upset her, especially because it had only been a few days since their last argument. He really wanted to understand what made her tick. Why was the business so important to her? "Your grandfather was happy to let it coast. Sounds like he was happy to grow the olives and sell the produce."

Her arms flew up in the air. "And Running Deer was nearly tapped out when he died! I don't know what my grandmother would've done, except for selling the property. Changing direction and creating a brand of olive oil is what saved this ranch."

Dang, she's got her hackles up. "I'm just saying that it's hard to keep a balance when all you think about is being a success. I've been on top of that game, Sam. It's not all it's cracked up to be."

"You can't compare playing professional football to running a family business," she said, bristling with irritation.

Calmly, he sat back down on the rock. "I'm not so sure I agree. I played football because I was very good at it. I was drafted two years into college. But success was the worst thing that ever happened to me. It messed me up. And when it all fell apart, I discovered what was really important in life."

He stood, facing her, and put his hands on her shoulders. "You're good at what you do, Sam. But it seems just a little too important to you. You don't make time for anything else besides work. How much more olive oil does the world need?"

Samantha flinched, shrugging off his hands. Her eyes narrowed. "You sound just like my parents."

Jack plowed on, oblivious. "Look, Sam, I respect what you have done with the ranch. All that I am saying is that I hope you'll make time for other things in your life. Other people, too."

After they got back down to the cottage, Jack glanced at his watch. "Great Scott! I'm late. How about if I pick you up for church tomorrow? I'd like to try your little church. 9 a.m.?" And off he jogged without waiting for her answer.

When Jack came to pick Samantha up in the morning, he could tell she was angry. Her mouth had a tight, pinched look. He knew the anger was directed at him, but he had no idea why. On the walk down to the church, he tried to coax it out of her. "Sam, I can't read your mind. Tell me what I did to upset you."

She remained silent.

"Okay, then, I'll try guessing. Was it because I said the world had enough olive oil? Because that might not have come out right. I didn't mean it like it sounded."

"No." She picked up her pace.

Jack lengthened his strides to match hers. "Was it because you thought I wanted you to give up the olive business? Because that's not what I was trying to say. That didn't come out right, either."

"Just drop it."

"Was it because of my basic personality?"

"Now you're close," Samantha said, as they went into church.

During the service, Jack asked, a little warily, "Still mad at me?"

Samantha sighed. "Always a little mad, I think."

He grinned. At least he was on her mind. *Always. She said "always."* He was making progress.

* * * *

Every employee of Running Deer was pressed into service to prepare the ranch for the filming of the documentary. When the day arrived, the camera crew drove up the gravel driveway at daybreak to set up for a full day. The weather cooperated perfectly. The soft light of autumn only highlighted the silvery skirts of the olive leaves, rippling softly in the gentle breeze. The crew didn't finish until long after dark.

Samantha returned to her cottage after 10 p.m. *What a day! A long, exhausting, wonderful day.* She had just finished brushing and flossing her teeth when the phone rang. She hurried to answer the phone by her night table.

"Sam?"

Her heart speeded up when she heard Jack's gentle voice. Samantha climbed into bed, tired but happily satisfied with the day. "Hey."

"Hey yourself. How did it go?" asked Jack.

"Amazing! Now I'm glad we had that day-long interview back at CCAB because I knew what to expect. They were very professional and knew just what they were looking for. Can you imagine, Jack? Fifteen *hours* of shooting for a fifteen-minute interview."

"Why did it take so long?"

"The camera crew had to set up outdoors, look for good lighting, no shadows, just the right view of the olive trees. And Pete kept blowing his lines. He hates to be in front of a camera. He had to do a ton of re-takes. It was actually kind of funny. Well, not so much for Pete." She couldn't help but grin at the memory of Pete's humiliation.

"When will it be aired?"

"Early December." She smiled with satisfaction. "Our Christmas sales are going to benefit. I'm *so* glad we have the new press in place. What a difference! The oil even tastes better."

"Was Kathleen able to participate?"

"No. She wasn't up to it." Kathleen seemed worse lately, tired and short-tempered. Samantha started chewing the inside of her mouth, worried about her sister.

"Sam? I have to ask you a favor. Could you take Friday off and go somewhere with me?"

Oh no. She leaned her head wearily on her hand, thinking of her lengthy to-do list.

"It's important, Sam," Jack said, sensing her hesitation. "I'd really like you to come. Something has come up that I have to take care of that day. I'm taking the day off of work."

"What's so important?"

"I'll explain when I see you. I'll pick you up at eight. Okay? I'm glad the filming went well. Night."

* * * *

Early Thursday morning, Samantha went over to give Kathleen a recap on yesterday's interview. Pete was downstairs in the kitchen, feeding Lily. "Is Kat upstairs?"

"Still sleeping. Better not wake her."

Something in his voice made Samantha stop short. "Is she okay?"

"She's…she didn't sleep well last night so she's trying to catch up this morning."

"The doctor told her to expect to feel a little depressed as her body gets back to normal. But maybe this is more than a little." She frowned. "What does Nonna think?"

"I haven't seen Nonna in days," Pete answered.

"I haven't either." She had called Nonna a couple of times every day to find out why she was at the bank, but she was never home.

"I thought Nonna was going to come and take care of Lily, but I ended up having to drop Lily with Lena the last few days. I called Nonna a couple of times, but there wasn't any answer, and she hasn't called back. It's not like her to go off the radar like this, especially when she knows we need her."

A lot of things about Nonna weren't typical lately, Samantha thought, bothered. "I'll take Lily today so you can get up to the harvest."

"Thanks, Sam. You're the best. But I'm going to have to find somebody else to help soon with Lily. I can't keep begging Lena, and Nonna…well, guess it's good she's finding things to do in the retirement home."

Samantha called the doctor for Kathleen and made an appointment. Then she called Nonna, but there was no answer. As Samantha put the phone back in the cradle, her portending heart started to race.

* * * *

The next morning, Jack tied his tie in the mirror and felt as if it was cutting off his air supply. He had always hated ties. He pulled it apart and tied it again, keeping it as loose as he dared, but he knew the problem wasn't the tie. The problem was his anxiety over how this day would play out. But after the long conversation he had with Dr. Sommers the other night—when Sam was so mad at him and he couldn't really figure out why—he was sure this was the right thing to do. Full disclosure, Dr. Sommers recommended after listening to Jack. "Why was she mad at you this time?" he had asked Jack.

"I suggested that the olive farm had become too important to her."

"Oh," Dr. Sommers said in a flat tone.

"I care about Sam," Jack defended. "It concerns me to see her so wrapped up in the olive farm. Her family kind of takes advantage of her, it seems, and they expect her to handle the whole thing." He drizzled to a stop after realizing Dr. Sommers wasn't responding.

"Jack, you've got to stop telling her what she should do or should not do."

"But…I was just trying to help."

"She's an independent woman. That's probably one of the reasons you're attracted to her. She wants to figure things out for herself." He paused. "And by the way, have you thought of telling her a little more about yourself?"

No, he hadn't.

That was the point when Dr. Sommers told him it was high time for full disclosure.

Jack hung up from that call, amazed. It hadn't occurred to him that the communication problem he felt with Samantha was because of him. Be more open? It pained him to be more open. It even made his stomach hurt. But he had a lot of confidence in Dr. Sommers' advice. *After all, the guy's a sage. He's been married for sixty or seventy years. He must know something about women by now.* He locked the door behind him and hurried to Samantha's cottage.

"So what's up with this mysterious errand?" she asked him as she gulped down her last sip of coffee.

Jack was already slipping on Azure's harness. "I told you about Matt, right? The guy who slammed into our car the night that Ellen was killed? Matt is up for a parole hearing, and I'm going to testify on his behalf. I'd like you to meet him." *And*

I'd like him to meet you. He held out her coat to her, trying to hurry her along. He didn't want to be late.

They took a ferry to San Francisco from Santa Galena to get to the county courthouse. Jack was relieved when he saw that the proceedings hadn't begun yet. Matt had just been seated at the parolee's table, and the parole board wasn't present yet. Jack guided Samantha over to meet Matt.

Although Matt was handcuffed, standing between two armed guards, Jack enveloped him in a big hug. Then Jack turned to Samantha. "Matt, this is Samantha Christiansen. And her guide dog, Azure."

"Hi Matt," Samantha said.

"Pleased to meet you," Matt answered.

Automatically, Samantha lifted her chin a notch to meet Matt's voice. Jack whispered, "He's nearly 6'5". And that's just his belt size."

"Oh. You're bigger than Jack!" she said, eyes wide.

Matt laughed. "I'll say. Jack was the runt on the team. He barely tipped the scale at 250 pounds." Then Matt grew serious. "So, little buddy, think there's any chance that today might fall into my favor?"

Jack tried not to pay any attention to the square knot in the pit of his stomach. "Sure hope so, pal. I've been praying for that."

"Good." Matt turned to Samantha. "Every little bit helps."

* * * *

Afterwards, Samantha and Jack stopped for dinner at a little outdoor seafood stand near the ferry building. After they gave their order, they found an empty picnic table.

"You did a wonderful job testifying," Samantha said. "I can't believe the parole board ruled in Matt's favor. Shortening his sentence by two years! I think it was because of your testimony. You should have been an attorney. Blessed with the art of persuasion."

"No, thanks," he said, laughing. "I'll stick with dogs. They don't have as much to say as lawyers."

Samantha tilted her head. "Jack, was it hard to forgive Matt?"

"Matt blamed himself so much that I couldn't help but forgive him. Did I tell you he pled guilty? Didn't even plea bargain to get a reduced sentence. Just admitted guilt to the judge."

Samantha was amazed at how at ease Jack was talking about this, after seeming so uncomfortable about it the other day. "Do you mind if I ask you about Ellen?"

He hesitated. "You can ask me anything."

Samantha caught his hesitation. She wondered if she shouldn't ask anything else but then she could hear Kat's voice in her head, "Well, he said you could ask him anything! So what are you waiting for?" Softly, she asked, "What was she like?"

He crossed his arms, weighing his words before answering. "Well, she was gorgeous. She loved to party and have a good time. She had a flair for the dramatic." His voice trailed off.

Chin propped on her clasped hands, Samantha said, "She sounds a little like Kat."

"I've thought that, too, even now, with her—"

Just then, they were interrupted by a young boy who recognized Jack and wanted his autograph. Disappointed that their conversation had been broken off, she excused herself to go to the restroom.

In the bathroom, she overheard two young women talking to each other over neighboring toilet stalls. "Did you see Jack Shaw? I can't believe he's with that dog lady." Her voice carried a hint of disgust.

"She's not a dog lady. She's blind. It's one of those seeing eye dogs."

"Seriously? Then what is a guy like Jack Shaw doing with a blind chick? I mean, she's cute, but ...ya know? He could have anyone."

"Maybe she's his sister."

Samantha combed her hair and put on fresh lipstick, waiting patiently for the young women to emerge from the stalls. Their conversation abruptly stopped when they saw her.

"I'm not his sister." She smiled benignly at them. "Guess Jack Shaw realizes the blind chick is worth it." She opened the

146

bathroom door and said, "Let's go, Azure." And she left the bathroom, glowing with smugness.

By the time she returned to the picnic table, Jack had picked up their crab sandwiches. He handed her a few napkins and paused. "Now why do you look like the cat that just swallowed a canary?"

"Oh, nothing." Her mouth crinkled into a grin, thinking of those two girls in the restroom. "So…tell me something I don't know about football."

"Sam, you know nothing about football," he said before taking a bite of his sandwich.

"I know one thing! I know that the football is made out of pigskin."

Jack groaned. "No, it's not. It's just what it's called."

"Oh," she said, crestfallen. "Then I know absolutely nothing about football."

During dinner he patiently tried to explain the game to her.

"And you really enjoyed bashing into other players?" she asked.

"It's not called *bashing*. It's called blocking. Remember, the point of the game is to get the ball to the end zone." He paused. "The opposite team's end zone," he clarified.

Samantha nodded earnestly. "Jack, are you recognized often when you're out in public?"

He seemed surprised by the question. "Less and less."

"When you were out with Ellen, did people come up to you like they did to us tonight and ask for your autograph?"

He cleared his throat. "Yes."

"Did Ellen ever think it made her feel invisible?"

Jack was quiet for a moment. "Are you about done with your sandwich?" His voice sounded tight.

She gave a quick nod, worried she might have asked the wrong question.

"Then let's head over to the ferry."

* * * *

As they waited for the ferry, they sat down on a bench, smelling the salt air, listening to the lonely call of seagulls.

147

Jack leaned back, his arms outstretched on the top of the bench. "I want to tell you about Ellen."

"Jack, you don't need to explain anything," Samantha interrupted. "I'm sorry if I sounded like I was prying."

Jack shifted in his seat. "I don't think you're prying." He crossed one leg over the other, rubbing his stiff knee. "I met Ellen when I was a rookie player. We met at a party and were crazy about each other, right off. At first, our marriage was pretty much blue skies and gentle breezes. But as my career took off, I was gone a lot. I was away for training camp and most of the season and busy with team obligations when I was home. Seemed as though the more attention I got as a ball player, the more invisible she felt."

He cleared his throat, trying to get the words out. "I thought it would help if we had a child. I really wanted to have kids, maybe more than Ellen did. We started trying but didn't have any luck. So we went to a special doctor and he found that Ellen had some…female…problems. And then…" he hesitated. "And then she found out about Lucy. I had met Lucy's mom a couple of years before I knew Ellen. I paid child support, thinking that was the decent thing to do. But, uh, I had never told Ellen about her. Came close to telling her once or twice but…" *It was easier to ignore it,* he finished silently.

Samantha's eyes went wide. "How *did* she find out?"

"Lucy's mom called the house one day, asking for an increase in child support. Ellen took the call." Jack kept shifting his weight, clearly uneasy.

Azure stood up and stretched then settled down again for a long nap. Jack had almost forgotten she was there. He used the interruption to stand up. He turned to face Samantha, hands shoved safely in his pockets. He wondered what she was thinking. Her face showed interest. But not judgment.

"Ellen sent Lucy's mother a check. She, uh, never told me she knew about Lucy. The accident happened about six months later."

"But how…?" Samantha started, confused.

"After Ellen's death, I found her diary. In a strange way, the diary became the catalyst for me to face up to myself. It wasn't just that the accident cost me my marriage and my profession; it also made me realize what a phony I was. On the outside, everything looked incredible. But the truth was that I was a very self-centered jerk." Earnestly, he added, "I know that's true because that's what Ellen called me in the journal."

"Why didn't Ellen tell you that she knew about Lucy?"

"I don't know. I just don't know."

"You must know, Jack," Samantha said softly.

He dropped his chin to his chest and sighed. "Yeah, I probably do." He exhaled. "I think she was afraid to." He crossed his arms against his chest. "She had been getting panicky that she would never be able to get pregnant and wanted me to quit football so that I would be home more, and I wasn't going to let *that* happen. Things between us were going from bad to worse. And then the accident happened," he managed. *Oh, man, this was hard to talk about.* His mouth had gone dry as a desert. "And the coroner's report said that Ellen was six weeks' pregnant."

Samantha didn't say a word, didn't even move.

"In Ellen's diary," Jack continued, his voice cracking, "she wrote that she wondered why I didn't have the guts to be a father to Lucy. She wondered how Lucy felt, growing up thinking she didn't even matter to her father."

He winced. "Those words haunted me. I just had never thought about Lucy in that way. Lucy's mother lived up near here, so I moved to the area to try and get to know her before it was too late. That was when she was eleven. Not a great age to suddenly appear in a girl's life."

"A better age than never," Samantha said gently.

"Maybe, but Lucy was not happy with my sudden appearance. Still isn't. She sees me as an inconvenience."

"And her mother?"

"She's married to a fireman over in Napa, and they have three little kids. Lucy gets lost in the shuffle." Jack turned to face Samantha. "There's a lot in my past that I'm not proud of." He wondered what she was thinking; she had been carefully listening to him, but he couldn't read her expression. He wouldn't blame her if she was calculating how quickly the ferry would dock and if she could make a run for it.

149

Samantha shifted on the bench and turned to him. Then she said something so unexpected, so incredibly kind, simple and comforting. It touched him deeply. "Actually, Jack, I was just thinking that there's a lot in your present that you *can* be proud of."

* * * *

As the ferry pulled into the dock, they walked over to go inside and sit down. The ferry was almost deserted, just a few business people returning home, reading newspapers, or sleeping.

Samantha sat there quietly, thinking about Ellen and Jack and Lucy. Samantha was amazed that Jack was being so open with her, as though he wanted her to know everything about him. Almost as if he didn't want her thinking he was a better man than he was. She wasn't sure she could ever be that vulnerable to anyone, not even to Kathleen.

She couldn't deny she was staggered by Jack's story; she wasn't even sure how she should react. But a part of her felt in awe of him, too. Not many men would have faced their mistakes and tried to make amends the way Jack did—moving to live near Lucy, working at CCAB. It was almost hard to believe he was the same person.

Azure draped her head over Samantha's knees. As Samantha stroked Azure's ears, she asked, "Is that when you found your faith?"

"That was a terrible time for me. I felt horribly guilty about Ellen, Matt was in the middle of his sentencing, and I was testifying on his behalf, and I was recovering from knee surgery."

He stood up again, bent over and massaged his knee. Samantha had a hunch that a long day of sitting and walking was taking its toll on his leg but doubted he would complain. Jack didn't seem to be a complainer.

"So I just started going back to church, the way I was raised. Each time I went, I felt a little…better. Like the burden was lighter. I started to realize that I had let God into certain parts of my life, but kept Him out of areas I didn't want Him to mess with. Kind of like I had done with Ellen. By doing that, I missed a full relationship with God. Just like with Ellen, too.

Somehow...I don't even know if I could say it was a specific day or a moment...somehow, I just felt connected to God. I knew I was forgiven. I was finally able to let it go and have a fresh start. It wasn't really like a lightning bolt. It was a process."

They rode home on the bus in a thoughtful and companionable silence. As they walked down the lane towards Samantha's cottage, she said, "Jack, do you realize that for the first time, we have spent an entire day together in which you have not tried to re-arrange or improve my life? Today, you just let me be a part of your life."

"Kind of a messy life, Sam."

"Everybody has things they've made a mess of."

"Not you. I doubt you've even had a parking ticket."

"True. But that's not such a remarkable accomplishment when you've never driven a car."

Jack laughed. "Ah, blind humor." Solemnly, he asked, "Sam, does knowing all of this about me change anything? Because now is the time to tell me."

Now she understood why he wanted her to accompany him today and why he was so open with her.

"Yes. In fact it does." She took his hand and wove her fingers between his. "I like you better."

Chapter Ten: Lucy

Early the next morning, Kathleen heard someone rummaging down in the kitchen, the clink of dishes as they were being stacked in the dishwasher and then the comforting sound of a percolating coffee pot. She thought it might be Pete but then dismissed the thought. Pete hadn't washed a dish in years. She decided it must be Sam; she felt relieved that Lily could be taken care of today. Kathleen rolled over and tried to sleep until a gentle knock on her door woke her out of that hazy dream state—half-asleep, half-awake.

"Kat, you've got to get out of bed. You're starting to stink." Samantha placed a cup of hot coffee on the nightstand next to Kathleen's bed.

"Where have you been anyway?" Kathleen lifted her head up and dropped it back on the pillow. "And where's Nonna? I thought I could count on the two of you. I can't take care of Lily right now. Yesterday wiped me out."

"I was just gone for one day. I'm back now." Samantha sat on the bed next to her. In a softer tone, she asked, "So how are you?"

"Just great," Kathleen answered, scowling at her sister, crawling deeper under the covers.

As Samantha leaned back on the headboard, her hand brushed against a mound of used, crumpled tissues near the pillows. Her brows furrowed together. "Kat, how are you really?"

"I'm just... sad," Kathleen started, her voice trailing off. She sat up in the bed and reached for a tissue, getting ready to bare her soul to her sister.

"Kat, I finally asked Nonna why she had withdrawn money, and she couldn't remember. She had no idea what I was talking about. Do you know why she needed the money?"

"You've seen Nonna? Where has she been?"

"I spoke to her on the phone. And that took some work. She's hard to track down lately," Samantha said, eyebrows furrowed in worry. "So do you have any idea why she needed the money?"

Kathleen looked at her, amazed. "I don't know. I never asked. She just needed it." She slid back down into the bed and rolled away from Samantha, facing the wall.

"Kat, you have to make yourself get up and get going."

She pulled a pillow over her head. In a muffled voice she said, "The doctor said to rest."

"The miscarriage caused a mild depression; you're going to have to plow your way through it."

"Then give me time to do it," Kathleen said. *You think I want to be like this? Being depressed feels terrible!*

Samantha sighed and swung her legs over the side of the bed, getting ready to leave.

"Sam?" Kathleen asked, pulling the pillow away from her face. "Remember when you asked me if I thought God existed?"

"I remember."

"If God is out there, why does He let stuff like this happen? Why can't God act...like God?"

Samantha crossed her arms and lifted her face to the ceiling, as though the answer would drop down from the heavens into her lap. "Well, using that logic, if you blame God for allowing you to have a miscarriage, why is it you never thought to credit Him for giving you Lily? And Pete?"

Why do I bother? "You know what, Sam?" Kathleen snapped. "Why don't we talk about this when you have a miscarriage someday because you really can't understand what I'm going through, can you? And by the way, don't ever consider going into psychology. You'd be a terrible counselor." *Oh, what is wrong with me? How could I say those things to my sister?*

Samantha quietly got up to leave the room. "Kat, you're going to feel better soon. This depression isn't going to last. You're going to feel good again. Try to sleep. I'll take care of Lily."

As Samantha's hand turned the doorknob, Kathleen lifted her head and mumbled, "Sam, I'm sorry."

* * * *

153

Samantha waited for Lily to wake up and then took her over to the cottage. As she was walking across the driveway, Lily in her arms, Pete drove up and wearily got out of the truck.

"Pete, *where* have you been? No one can ever get hold of you!"

"Working nearly twenty hours a day at the processing facility to fill all of those orders you created through your brilliant marketing plan!" Pete barked, completely spent.

"*My* marketing plan?" she roared. "You were the one who had to have the new state-of-the-art press!"

"That was only because I wanted to make a *better* olive oil. Not because I wanted to supply the *world* with olive oil!" he shouted in exasperation.

"But how do we pay for the press if we aren't expanding production and selling more product?" she shouted back, equally exasperated. Distressed by their angry voices, Lily started to cry. Samantha turned on her heels and marched into the cottage.

After Lily calmed down and was content to play in the playpen, happily occupied for a few minutes, Samantha used the lull to call Dr. Sommers and ask him about Kathleen's question. That question bothered her. And her answer to Kathleen seemed woefully inadequate.

"Ah, the dilemma of the sovereignty of God," said Dr. Sommers after hearing Samantha's story. "It's a difficult concept. It has so much to do with the free will that God has given man. Volumes have been written about it. Hmmm...I might recommend a book to you. It's called *The Problem with Pain* by C.S. Lewis."

Samantha wrote down his suggestion as quickly as he spoke.

"Sam, there's something that you and your sister need to know," continued Dr. Sommers. "God does care even about a miscarriage. It doesn't escape His notice. 'Are not two sparrows sold for a penny? Yet not one of them will fall to the ground apart from the will of your Father. And even the very hairs of your head are all numbered. So don't be afraid; you are worth more than many sparrows,' Jesus said, in Matthew 10."

Samantha quickly scribbled down that reference, too.

Later that day, Jack walked up to Samantha's cottage with Lucy. After introducing them, Samantha shooed him away.

"Are you sure about this, Sam?" Jack didn't sound sure. "Maybe I should stay."

"Positive. It's just a few hours." She thought asking Lucy to babysit was a brilliant idea. "It's a win-win, Jack," she told him on the phone last night. "I need help, and I want to get to know Lucy." She was curious about Lucy. Very curious.

"But Lucy isn't always...easy to like," Jack replied. "And her moods are unpredictable. Sometimes...actually, most of the time, she just seems mad."

Samantha reassured him that it was worth a try.

* * * *

"Look, nothing personal, but I don't want to be here," Lucy announced after Jack abandoned her. "Jack *made* me come. He said you needed help with some kid."

"I do. This is my niece, Lily. My sister lives in the big farmhouse over there and isn't feeling well. I take care of Lily as much as I can so that my sister can rest. Your dad said you're good with kids and might be willing to help me. I hope he told you I want to pay you."

"Well, just for the record, I hate kids." *And I do not want to be here.*

"Oh."

Lucy felt pleasure when she saw the hurt look on Samantha's face. With thinly veiled hostility, she asked, "So you're the latest girlfriend?"

"No, we're just friends."

Sure you are, sister. Lucy raised an eyebrow. "He told me you were his girlfriend."

Samantha looked genuinely surprised. "He did? He hasn't told me that."

Lucy saw Samantha's fingers graze the open dial of her wristwatch. A crooked little smile broke out on her face. *Good! I'm getting to her. She's wondering how much longer she's stuck with me.* "I hope you know that he has a girl in every port."

Samantha's eyebrows shot up. "Wow. Sounds like a busy sailor."

Lucy walked around the cottage, looking at Samantha's pastel drawings on the walls. "My mom was one of those girls of his, you know."

"Yes, he told me."

Lucy spun around to face Samantha. "Did he also tell you that he suddenly decided to make an appearance after twelve years just cuz he read his dead wife's diary and feels guilty?"

Samantha nodded. "Yes. He did tell me something about that."

"I hate him."

"Because he didn't show up for twelve years?"

"Nope. Because he did." Lucy nearly spat it out.

Samantha inhaled sharply. "Let's try something else," she suggested. Her face brightened. "Lucy, do you like horses?"

"I've never ridden," she said dismissively. Lucy looked out the window longingly at the horse corral. She had always wanted to ride a horse, but her mother said it was too expensive a hobby. *She sure doesn't seem to have a problem spending money on things she wants. Peroxide for her hair. Jungle red nail polish.*

"Well, let's go try."

Aha! "I thought you said you were blind." *She's faking! Bet she's trying to get Jack's sympathy.*

"Being blind doesn't mean I'm incompetent," Samantha said.

Lucy thought Samantha's face just took on a tight, pinched look, as if she was starting to get a headache. She found that people often got that look around her, especially her teachers. Her stepfather, too.

"I have a horse named Spitfire that I got when I was— well, just about your age. Don't worry; he doesn't have much spit or fire left in him. Come on; let's go to the barn."

With Lily buckled safely in her stroller and out of harm's way, Samantha introduced Lucy to Spitfire and showed her how to put on the saddle and bridle. She led the horse out to the corral and taught Lucy how to exercise him on the lunge line. Once warmed up, she helped Lucy climb up on the horse's back while he was still on the lunge line. "Ready now? Put your foot in my hands, and I'll help you get up on him."

Lucy looked down at Samantha's clasped hands. "But I'll crush him."

"Don't be silly!" said Samantha. "He's a big, strong quarterhorse. A work horse."

"Well, I'm a big, strong girl. Just look at me." She slapped her bottom with her hands.

Samantha grimaced. "Lucy, that's kind of hard for me to do."

"Oh, right. I keep forgetting. You don't act blind. I mean, like, your eyes even track my eyes. On TV, blind people are always staring off into space."

"I know. Funny part of retinitis pigmentosa. The brain still knows to tell the eyes to look about four inches above someone's mouth. But...I am blind. So tell me what you mean."

Sure. Make me say it. Why not just cut out my heart with a dull kitchen knife? "Picture someone who is five foot two and weighs one hundred and sixty pounds. Short and wide."

"How tall is your mom?"

"Tiny. Petite. Size two. Life's little cosmic joke. I got my height from my mom and my width from Jack."

Samantha smiled at her. "Real women have curves, Lucy."

Lucy rolled her eyes. "Yeah, right. Well, there are curves, and there are lumps."

Samantha tightened the girth on the saddle. "I was pretty lumpy myself when I was fourteen."

"*Right,*" Lucy snapped. "Bet you could've been a model when you were young." *She is gorgeous. And dressed like she stepped out of a magazine. Everything even matches! If she were really blind, then her clothes would end up all mixed up and her hair would look like it's been in a wind machine.*

Samantha tried hard to stifle a grin but couldn't help it. "I remember how thirty seemed so ancient when I was fourteen."

"Oh. Sorry. I just meant, your eyes are incredible. You don't even need eyeliner, huh?" Lucy peered at Samantha's ponytail. "And...how do you get your hair so straight? My friend Becky and I tried rolling our hair in orange juice cans, but we couldn't sleep."

Samantha smiled. "It's just naturally straight. And my eyes don't work, Lucy. They're just window dressing. What I meant is that I think I understand what it's like to be fourteen and not be like everybody else."

Spitfire turned around and snorted at them, impatient. "Cool it, Spitfire. Don't interrupt." Samantha pushed his head away. "When I was about your age, maybe a little younger, I started losing my vision. I have a genetic disorder that is destroying my sight. I can hardly see anything anymore. Like I'm looking down two straws."

Lucy looked over at the farmhouse. Jack had told her Samantha was a twin. He said they looked eerily similar, but they weren't identical. "Does your sister have it, too?"

"No. She's not a carrier."

"So she got off easy, huh? Doesn't it fry you that she got the good eyes?"

Samantha's eyebrows shot up. "Well, I'd be lying if I didn't admit to having indulged in a few pity parties."

"So that's why you're not married, huh?"

"Because I'm blind? No, that's not why. Lots of blind people get married."

"Then why aren't you—"

"We'd better get you up on Spitfire before he falls asleep!" Samantha interrupted, cutting her off.

* * * *

A few hours later, Jack returned on his bicycle. He found Samantha standing with Lily in her arms over by the corral. "Excuse me, ma'am. I must be lost. I thought this was Running Deer Ranch, but I must be mistaken. I dropped off a cranky fourteen-year-old, but all that I see is a girl with a grin spread ear-to-ear."

Lucy was cantering a weary looking Spitfire around the corral. "Hey Jack! This ol' horse wanted to quit on me, but I wouldn't let him!"

"You look great on him, Luce!" Jack called out with admiration. "Like you've been riding forever! Don't let him quit on you!"

"She's a natural rider, too. Look at how quiet her hands are," Samantha said. "You can't teach that; she just 'got' it."

158

"How could you tell that her hands are quiet?" he asked.

"Spitfire has a sensitive mouth, so if Lucy was pulling on the bit too much, he would be jerking his head. I would've heard him."

Jack watched Lucy ride for a while. He was shocked. He'd never seen Lucy without a scowl on her face. She almost looked...nearly happy. "Did you get any work done at all? Lucy was supposed to be here to help you, but it looks like you've helped her."

"Let's just say the day's work was to bond."

Jack stroked Samantha's hair. Without thinking, she leaned in against him. He put his arm around her and kissed her gently on the top of her head. Something had changed between them from the day at Matt's parole hearing; something had been sealed.

"Say, what's this about a girl in every port?" Samantha teased.

Jack laughed. "Did she tell you that? Why does everyone assume I'm such a Casanova?"

As they were saying goodbye, Lucy stunned him by saying to Samantha, "I guess I could come back now and then, after school on my bike, since you need so much help with that baby. I don't live so far away."

"Really?" Samantha seemed pleased. "I'd like that, Lucy. I could use your help. But...I know you don't like kids."

"This one isn't too bad. She doesn't cry much. It's the yapping and the crying that I hate."

The next day, Jack came up to the cottage in the morning in time to get Samantha for church just as Pete came over to hand off Lily to her.

"Join us, Pete?" asked Jack. He wasn't sure what made him ask; Pete just looked so forlorn.

Pete shook his head. "No, I'd better get some work done." He raked a hand through his hair. "On second thought, maybe I should. Can't hurt right now. Give me a second to change, and I'll be right out."

"I did *not* expect that," said Samantha, eyes wide.

"Isn't Kathleen improving?" Jack asked, concerned.

"Not yet. Maybe next week. The doctor said it takes about a month for all of the hormones to get back to normal." Then Samantha cocked her head. "Jack, why don't you ever call her 'Kat'? Everyone else does."

"Can't," he said, shaking his head. "Hate cats."

* * * *

That week, Lucy biked over after school each afternoon to watch Lily so that Samantha could go down to the office to get some work done. She told Samantha that she needed the money, but the truth was she liked being around her, talking to her girl-to-girl. Samantha actually listened to her. She didn't obsess about Lucy's appearance like her mom did.

Lucy had never been around a woman who was as pretty as Samantha but didn't seem to care about it. And Samantha didn't seem uncomfortable around Lucy like Jack did. Jack bugged her. He tried too hard. She knew it seemed mean, but the harder he tried to make her like him, the more pleasure she took in disliking him.

"I like your pink cottage," Lucy said once Samantha returned back to the cottage one day.

"Thank you. I love it. I call it Mise-En-Place. It means—"

"Everything in its place. I know, I know. I take French at school. My teacher is completely neurotic. Every now and then she is seized with a spasmodic fit of reform and screams 'mise-en-place' at us to start class. You should see her. You wouldn't believe her hair! It defies gravity. Completely vertical. My friend Becky and I think she's trying to cover her bald spots."

Samantha burst out laughing. That was another thing Lucy liked about Samantha. She thought Lucy was funny. It was easier being around Jack when Sam was with them. Last weekend, they walked through the farmer's market. Lucy found that she didn't get mad at Jack during the entire afternoon. Not once. Sam had a way of bringing out the best in them.

Lucy's thoughts drifted to the guy who came up to her when Samantha and Jack went to buy ice cream cones. Lucy had taken Azure to get some water from a drinking fountain.

"That your dog?" asked a guy with long curly hair tucked behind his ears.

160

Beneath his wire granny glasses were bright blue eyes, fringed with thick black lashes, Lucy noticed immediately. He wore a bright orange and red tie-dye shirt and ripped blue jeans. On his feet was a beat-up pair of Birkenstocks. "Um, no. She's a guide dog. You know, for a blind person." *Stupid! I sound so stupid.*

"Cool." He held out his hand to her. "Name's Chance."

"Oh. I'm, Lu-Lucy." She shook his hand and felt an electric shock. *Was it possible to fall in love on contact?*

Chance moved in a little closer, spiking Lucy's self-consciousness. "So, then, Lu- Lucy, assuming you're not blind, whose dog is it?"

Lucy tried to give a sophisticated laugh at his joke about her name, but it came out as a snort, mortifying her. She decided not to talk anymore; her voice couldn't be trusted under the circumstances. Instead, she pointed into the ice cream store at Jack and Samantha.

Chance followed her point and peered into the store. "That lady was on TV, wasn't she?"

Lucy nodded.

"Thought I recognized her." Chance turned back to Lucy with a cat-in-the-cream smile, revealing perfectly straightened white teeth. "So, Lu-Lucy, how'd you like to hang out together sometime?"

Lucy tried not to faint right there on the spot. She glanced in the ice cream store to see if Jack had noticed Chance talking to her. Knowing Jack, he would chase Chance off. Fortunately, Jack was preoccupied with trying samples of every ice cream flavor. Samantha, Lucy noticed, had chosen vanilla. Lucy quickly sprawled her phone number onto a piece of paper and thrust it at Chance. He grinned, kissed the paper, and tucked it in his shirt pocket. As he walked away from her, he flashed the peace sign at her. Lucy's heart was thumping. This kind of thing happened to other girls, never to her. She realized she was holding her breath.

Lily called out, snapping Lucy back to the present. Samantha bent down to pluck her from the playpen, but Lily reached out for Lucy.

"She's a smart kid," Lucy said as she hoisted Lily onto her hip. "We watched a new TV show today. Called *Sesame Street*. Kinda cute but I bet it won't last." She pulled Lily's hand away from trying to pull her big hoop earrings. "She even started to walk today."

"What?" Samantha said, slumping her shoulders. "Kathleen is missing so much."

"Just a couple of steps then she trips. But she got up and tried again."

"Want to stay for dinner?" Samantha asked.

"Only if you're serving grapefruit." She passed Lily over to Samantha.

Samantha looked puzzled.

"My mom has me on another stupid diet. This one is 'The Grapefruit Diet.' Last week was 'The Rice Diet'. She watches a lot of day-time TV," Lucy rued. To her, that explained everything about her mother.

Samantha laughed.

"I'm not kidding! My mom is obsessed with my size. She tapes pictures of Twiggy on my mirror. She's that model whose knees look like Olive Oyl on the *Popeye* cartoons."

"Why would your mother want you to look like Twiggy?"

"She thinks I'm going to be just like Jack if I'm not careful."

"Would that be so bad?"

This woman really is blind! "Jack is huge!"

"I didn't mean his size, Lucy. I meant his personality. His sense of humor. His way with people. Especially his way with animals. Have you ever seen your dad with dogs? He's amazing. When I've noticed you with Azure and Spitfire and even with Lily, you remind me of your dad."

"You think I'm like Jack?" Lucy grabbed her own throat in a mock strangle.

"I think you're a lot like him. Except for liking my cottage. He says it makes him feel like subscribing to *Good Housekeeping*. That's where you're very different."

"*Right.* Like Jack has an inner feminine side." Lucy picked up her book sack and headed to the door then paused,

162

something on her mind. *Should I tell her?* "Sam, I, uh, met a guy a while ago."

"Oh?"

"I sorta like him." Lucy put back down her book sack. "Actually, I think he sorta likes me, too."

"I'm not surprised." Samantha put the tea kettle on and pulled out two mugs, preparing for a chat. "So tell me about him."

* * * *

On Saturday morning, Lucy surprised Samantha by showing up unannounced, "Because she happened to be biking nearby," she said. Samantha was grateful for her help; Kathleen was only up for a few hours each day and then went back to bed, leaving Lily to Samantha's care, and Pete was working long days out in the processing facility.

Lucy fiddled with Samantha's clock radio, tuning it to a rock-n-roll channel. "Here it is! Sam, come and listen!" She turned the volume up as loud as she could. "This is the song I was telling you about. *Space Oddity* by David Bowie."

Samantha sat down and listened with Lily on her lap. When it was finished, Lucy explained, "It's about an astronaut guy named Major Tom who goes into space and looks back at the earth and decides he's going to just float off into space. It is *so* cool! Chance loves that song. He says David Bowie is going to be as big as the Beatles."

"Sort of a haunting song, isn't it?" Samantha said. She noticed how many references Lucy had been making lately to Chance, her new boyfriend. Chance seemed to be very knowledgeable about pop culture. And he and Lucy were spending quite a bit of time together. *I wonder if Jack knows? Oh, but I do not want to get in the middle of this.* Samantha went back to her adding machine to tally up the month of October's figures for Running Deer as Lucy played with Lily on the floor.

"So what kind of music did you like when you were young?" Lucy asked.

"My sister was crazy about Elvis Presley. We both liked the Kingston Trio and Buddy Holly. Oh, and Woody Guthrie and Pete Seeger."

"I have absolutely no idea who you're talking about. Except for Elvis. Everybody knows Elvis."

"No kidding. Even Nonna." Samantha tried to type in some numbers at the adding machine.

"Sam? Why do you have a television when you can't see anything?" asked Lucy.

"Because I can still hear," Samantha answered distractedly. She frowned. "You know what I wish I had? An accountant."

"So how do blind people pick out the right color clothes to wear each day?"

Samantha flicked the switch to turn off the adding machine. "We create tricks. Let me think...well, for example, I use small safety pins attached to the labels to help me figure out what color a shirt or skirt is. One for blue, two for green. Plus I try to keep everything simple."

"Like what else?"

"Well," Samantha paused, thinking, "like my hair. I keep it long because it's easier to manage. I can throw it in a ponytail or a braid or barrette if I'm in a hurry. There are a lot of tricks you learn to make life more manageable so you can be more self-reliant."

"Like what?"

"Well...suppose I drop my keys, and I'm not sure where they fell. I squat down and divide the area around me in a big circle—an invisible circle—then I spread my hand on the ground around each quarter circle, so that I know I've covered that area, until I find my keys." She clicked her fingers. "Works every time."

"What else? Like how do you know how to eat a plate of food without making a mess?"

"I pretend that the plate is like a clock and figure out where the food is by where it is positioned on the plate. For example, salad at three o'clock, chicken at six o'clock, cantaloupe at nine o'clock. Peas can be tricky, though," she added with a wink.

"What about soup cans? How can you tell which is which?"

"I put rubber bands around the cans. One for chicken noodle, two for tomato soup, three for cream of mushroom."

Samantha went over to Lucy and Lily and sat on the floor with them, throwing in the towel on the work she was trying to get done. "There are lots of ways to make life easier for blind people. For example, my cottage doesn't have any furniture with sharp corners. Coffee table, bed, sofas—everything has rounded corners. That's why I don't like going to your dad's house—I'm always banging my shins on something."

"But how do you do things like grocery shop?"

"I can ask a clerk at the store to help me find things, or I'll go with Kat or Nonna. But don't underestimate smell and touch. They are incredible resources. Most blind people would say that those senses have really sharpened since they lost their vision. Have you ever heard of echo-location?" She thought for a minute to find an example. Then she called out Azure's name, and Azure came bouncing over to her, licking her face. "Hear her tags jingle? That's one example of how you can locate things through sound."

Lucy scratched Azure's ears. "Isn't that what bats use? I think my science teacher said they're blind, and they use echo-location to find their prey."

"Yes! Exactly!" She smiled at her. "And then there's the sense of smell, too. I can even identify people I know by their smell."

"No way. What do I smell like?"

Samantha took a deep breath. "Like Breck shampoo."

Lucy gasped. "That's exactly what I use!"

Later that day, Samantha and Azure, Lucy and Lily went downtown to a department store to get a new winter jacket for Lily and got sidetracked, via Lucy's navigational skills, into the teen clothing department. Just as they entered a store, Lucy called out, "Oh my gosh! There's Chance!" She turned to Samantha. "Let's go. He's been wanting to meet you."

A young guy ambled over to Lucy, kissing her loudly right in front of Samantha.

"Sam, I want you to meet Chance." She turned to Chance and whispered, "I can't believe we bumped into you!"

Samantha held out her hand. "Your name is Chance?"

165

"Yeah."

"Your parents named you Chance?" Samantha asked again, unable to fathom that.

"Yeah," he answered. "Cool dog." He patted Azure on the head. "Bet she's valuable, huh?"

"Very," Samantha answered.

"How much do you think?" Chance asked.

"Pardon me? Did you really ask how much do I think she's worth?" Samantha asked.

"Yeah. How much?"

"Uh...um...I couldn't put a dollar amount on a guide dog," Samantha said. "What makes you ask such a thing?"

"No reason. Look, I gotta split. My friend is waiting for me." Chance kissed Lucy goodbye, a wet and noisy kiss, Samantha noticed, before he ambled away.

"Lucy, how old is Chance?"

"I don't know. He dropped out of school. He says he doesn't need government programs trying to indoctrinate him."

"He was smoking, wasn't he?"

"Yep! Camel Unfiltered. He says it's a man's smoke. It's the only cigarette he'll smoke. He wears tinted granny classes and love beads and tie-dyed shirts." She sighed. "He is *so* cool."

"What exactly does he do all day?"

"Works at a car repair shop. But just for now. He has big plans to travel across the country in his friend's Volkswagen bus."

"Doing what?"

"He's in a rock band. No Name."

"Their band doesn't have a name?"

Lucy snorted. "The name of the band *is* No Name. Chance says it represents the meaninglessness of society."

While Lucy changed into an outfit, Samantha mulled over meeting Chance. Besides his odd name and the fact that he sounded older than Lucy, much older, in fact, it also bothered her that she thought she recognized his voice but couldn't quite place where she might have met him.

Later, in a stuffy little dressing room, Lucy asked Samantha, "How do I look? Does this top make me look bulky? God forbid that I would look bulky."

"You know what a better question is? How do you feel?" Samantha asked.

Lucy hit her forehead with her palm. "I'm sorry! I keep forgetting that you're blind."

"It's got nothing to do with being blind. How you feel about yourself is much more important than worrying about what you look like. Or what you *think* you should look like."

"Sheesh, Sam. Were you *ever* fourteen?" Lucy asked, turning around to face the mirror, fidgeting with the outfit.

Samantha laughed. "Yes! But my grandmother always warned us not to let others determine how we felt about ourselves."

Lucy turned to face Samantha. "No kidding? That same old lady I've met a couple of times at your cottage when I babysat Lily?"

"Yes. She's very wise. And she's not *that* old. Why? Does that surprise you?"

"Sort of. Whenever I've seen her, she just has kind of an empty look in her eyes."

Samantha drew back, startled by Lucy's observation.

"And she can't remember my name, no matter how many times I tell her."

"Well, she's still adjusting to a move." Samantha tried not to bristle by Lucy's blunt opinion of her grandmother. "Stop kicking, Lily!" A shoe flew off Lily's foot, which interested Azure, inspiring her to lick Lily's toes, causing Lily to squeal loudly. All three, plus the dog, were cramped in the tiny dressing room.

We need to get out of here, thought Samantha, claustrophobia starting to overwhelm her. Samantha re-tied Lily's shoe. "Okay, so let's try this again. How does this shirt make you feel?"

Lucy turned back to the mirror. "Good, I guess. The color makes me happy."

"Perfect! Let's buy it and surprise your dad. He's planning to meet us at the grocery store so we can shop for dinner."

167

"Let's just go to a restaurant. There's a Mexican place Jack says is good."

"Oh, I can't," Samantha said. "I tried to go there recently, but they told me they don't like dogs in their restaurant."

"What?!" Lucy roared. "That's outrageous! Do you mean to tell me you can't ever go to that restaurant again?"

"I can. It just means that I need to be prepared for a confrontation." An unpleasant one. She stood up to go.

"Wait until I tell Chance! He'll organize a protest at City Hall. Maybe a sit-in! He loves that kind of thing."

Samantha tried to dodge that bullet. "No! I...want to handle those things in my own way." *And what way is that,* she could hear Kathleen ask her. *Doing nothing? Like you've done with the bus?* Samantha frowned. "Want to wear the blouse out?"

"Sure!" Lucy said, as her focus riveted back to her appearance. "Hey, Sam?" she added bashfully, touching the mirror with her hand. "What do you *think* I look like?

Samantha smiled, remembering just what it felt like to be an insecure fourteen-year-old. "Why, Lucy, I don't *think;* I *know*. You're beautiful."

Lucy was still for a long moment, then dug in her book sack searching for a tissue, claiming she had a cold and needed to blow her nose.

Chapter Eleven: **Nonna**

"Lucy said she hates me a little less since you're in my life," Jack said one evening while he and Samantha were having dinner at her cottage.

"She doesn't really hate you, Jack," Samantha said knowingly. "She just wants to make things hard for you. I think she wants to make you prove that you're going to stick around."

"Is that the way fourteen-year-old girls think?" he asked, sounding perplexed.

She nodded. "Even thirty-year-old girls."

"So, to translate this into a language that I actually understand, the best offense is a good defense?"

"That's one way to look at it." Samantha took a sip of iced water, trying not to laugh. "To quote Lucy's father: 'Don't quit on her'."

"Never. I like a challenge." He reached for the last piece of bread in the basket. "She said she thinks you're cool."

"She said that? That just shows how smart she is. She's absolutely right. I *am* cool. Blind chicks can be cool." Samantha was not immune to a person thinking she was cool, even a fourteen-year-old person. *Actually,* she realized, *Lucy might be the first person to ever describe me as cool. Serious, responsible, level-headed, but never cool.*

"Very cool," Jack agreed, as he leaned over to kiss her. "Has she told you about Chance?"

Samantha gave a slow nod. "I even met him once, at the mall."

"What did you think?"

Samantha frowned. "Hopefully he's a passing phase. Um, might be a good idea if you could meet him, though."

"I've tried. Lucy keeps hedging. I think she's worried I'll try to intimidate Chance." He took a bite of food and swallowed. "She's right. I will. I mean, what kind of name is Chance? High risk." He took another bite. "Lucy told me she's worried about my weight."

"See? She doesn't hate you. If she did, she'd be plying you with bacon so you'd have an early heart attack." Samantha took a bite of her salad. "By the way, Jack, what *is* your cholesterol level?"

"Don't know. Never had it taken. Never plan to."

"Why not?"

"I'm afraid of needles."

Samantha's eyebrows shot up. "So you could get out on a football field, smash into other unusually large men until the umpires blew their whistles to break it up, but you're afraid of a tiny needle piercing your skin?"

"Referees. Umpires go with baseball. And yes, I am."

"You are *such* a big baby." She went into the kitchen to refill the bread basket.

Jack turned to face her in the kitchen. "Lucy is paying more attention to what she eats. Last weekend, she had a salad and asked for the dressing on the side. First time I've ever seen her be careful about what she eats. So I told her I'd help and try to eat better, too."

Samantha sat back down and smiled as Jack helped himself to another serving of bread.

"No butter?" he asked with disappointment.

"No butter. Olive oil." She poured an emerald green olive oil into a small dipping bowl. "Try this. This is called 'olio nuovo'—'new oil.' It's the first-of-the-season olive oil this year. Fresh from the mill. Olio Nuovo is even honored in festivals in Italy."

Jack dipped his bread in the green, spicy olive oil. "Hey! This *is* good!" He dipped it in again.

"I told you! You'll never use butter again."

"Tuscan Ketchup," he said with a grin.

She smiled, surprised that he even remembered that Italians called olive oil 'Tuscan Ketchup.' "Fourteen-year-old girls are rather complicated creatures. I'm not surprised my parents shipped us off when we were about that age."

Jack chewed the bread thoughtfully. "I think that might be the first time I've ever heard you mention your parents."

"Really? Well, I guess they're not a big part of Kat's and my life. They live in Papua New Guinea and they're very...dedicated to their work."

"How did you end up here, living with your grandparents?"

"Kat and I were born in Papua New Guinea, but I started to have vision problems around age ten. They felt it would be best if I came back here to get some Orientation & Mobility skills. Kat didn't want me to go without her so they sent us both."

Jack filled his plate up with the rest of the salad and emptied the jar of Bacos on top. "Sounds like you didn't want to leave."

"It was devastating. It was an idyllic childhood—Kat and I spent hours playing games with local kids with so many places to explore. And the wildlife! Just *amazing*."

"Hard adjustment?" he asked, hitting the bottom of the salad dressing bottle with the palm of his hand to get the last little bit of dressing on to his plate.

"Coming here? Very hard. Even though Kat and I spoke English, we didn't understand anything about being typical American teenagers. We were clueless whenever someone at school talked about television, or movies, or the latest clothes, or pop music. But...at least we had each other." She refilled her glass of iced water.

He took a bite of salad. "When did you last see your parents?"

"Whenever they have a furlough. Every five years. They were here for Kat's wedding. So...I guess three times in the last seventeen years." Samantha frowned. "Hmmm...they must be due for another visit soon."

He put down the salad dressing bottle. "You *must* be kidding! You've only seen your parents three times in seventeen years? For how long?"

"A couple of weeks. Their furlough lasts a few months, but first they go to Sydney or Hong Kong for medical and dental check-ups, then they come back to Running Deer for a visit, then they travel around to churches that support them for more fund raising."

"But you must call. My folks call me and my brothers every Sunday evening like clockwork."

"Really? That's so sweet, Jack," she tilted her head at him, imagining what his two parents, whom she'd never met, might look like as they called all four of their grown sons every Sunday evening. She smiled, picturing a kind, portly couple, holding a phone between them.

"We've never called each other unless it's a dire emergency," she explained. "Too expensive. They believe in living just like the locals live. I think they take a strange pride in being out of step with the modern world." She grinned. "Sometimes, even common customs! Once, my dad was in the United States on furlough and gave a talk at a church, *barefoot!* That's what they do in PNG, so that's what he did here. Kat and I were *mortified.*" She shook her head, half-laughing, remembering that day. "I guess you could call them Jesus Freaks."

"Ouch," said Jack.

"What? Is something wrong with your salad?"

"Just don't like that term 'Jesus Freak'."

"Oh. Sorry. Well, anyway...we've always just used the old fashioned method of communication. Kat and I take turns sending off a monthly letter. At least, we try to send a monthly letter." Samantha wrinkled her forehead. *Whose turn was it?* She couldn't remember.

Jack went into the kitchen to get a third helping of soup. From there he asked, "What kind of work did your parents do in Papua New Guinea?"

"Well, the tribes of PNG are so isolated from each other—because of the terrain—that they speak completely separate languages. Over eight hundred tribal languages. My parents' work is to translate the New Testament into native languages."

Jack came back to the table and sat down, spreading his napkin on his lap. "Doesn't sound like such trivial work."

"No, it isn't. And it's a difficult life in PNG. There are no creature comforts. It's actually quite a noble life that my parents chose. That's the problem..." her voice trailed off.

Jack put his fork down. "What's the problem?"

A warning bell rang in her head. *Do I really want to tell this to Jack?* "The problem is that Kat and I always seemed to have to compete with God for our parents' attention. And naturally, God always won."

Jack covered her hand with his large, calloused hand. "Ever think that might be the obstacle that keeps you from giving yourself wholeheartedly to God?"

Samantha tensed up.

"Well, a child's first impression of God is based on parents."

Samantha started to bristle. *I knew I shouldn't have told him.* She stood up to clear her dishes.

He followed her into the kitchen. "I'm just saying that it's something to think about."

Samantha put her dishes in the sink and started filling it up with warm water, trying to look distracted and disinterested. "What's the obstacle?" she said as she squeezed soap from the bottle into the sink. "My parents?"

"No," he answered. "Forgiving them."

The next afternoon, Samantha listened for Lucy's bike on the gravel driveway so she could get down to the office. Today, she thought she might take Lucy and Lily with her.

She was starting to think that Lucy wasn't coming when Nonna's car pulled up to the house. Lucy hopped out of the passenger side. Samantha held Lily on her hip as she went to meet the car. "Hi! How did you two find each other? Lucy, where's your bike?"

"Lucy bumped into me downtown so I gave her a lift. Is your sister home? I'd like a cup of tea," said Nonna.

"Nonna, Kat still won't get out of bed. Go up and see her. She could use some cheering up. Maybe you can talk her into a shower."

Nonna went into the farmhouse as Samantha turned to Lucy.

"Want to go down to the office with me?" Samantha asked.

Lucy hesitated, waiting until Nonna went into the farmhouse. "Look, Sam. Your Nonna is nuts."

Samantha stopped short. "What do you mean?"

"I saw her at a stoplight in that big ol' car of hers. She didn't move her car. Other cars kept honking their horns at her, but she just sat there. Didn't budge. Like she was in a twilight zone. You know, doo-doo-doo-doo." She sang out the first few notes of *Twilight Zone*.

"Maybe something is wrong with her car."

"No, nothing is wrong with her car. I locked my bike up and hopped in the passenger side and told her to drive."

"What happened then?"

"She just drove like nothing ever happened. Weird, huh?"

As Samantha let that comment sink in, an electric current shot through the pit of her stomach.

* * * *

Later that week, the documentary that featured Running Deer aired. The next morning, the phone was ringing non-stop with orders.

"This is amazing!" Samantha said to Pete at the office. "They warned me about this. They told me to get prepared because we're going to get slammed. They said another company hadn't anticipated a spike in sales and nearly collapsed! But," she added confidently, "we will be ready."

"Miss Sam, *how* are we going to fulfill all of these orders?" asked Lena with a frantic look on her face while the phone continued to ring.

"Call the temporary agency. Tell them we need as many people that they can spare."

"What kind of qualifications do you want?"

"Anyone with a pulse."

That afternoon, the bottles ordered for the Tuscan olive oil were delivered. As Samantha signed off on the order, she held one of the bottles in her hands. "Isn't it a beautiful shape, Lena?" she asked, running her hands along its lines. "Very distinctive. We'll need to get these bottles cleaned and ready for labeling so that we can get those orders fulfilled. They arrived just in time."

"I like how the customer will be able to see the color of the olive oil in it," said Lena.

Samantha froze. "What do you mean?"

"The green color of the oil will look so pretty."

"Lena?" A horrible realization welled up within Samantha. "Isn't the bottle colored?" *Please tell me it's colored. Please!*

"No, Miss Sam. It's clear."

Samantha sat down in her chair to catch her breath. "Go find Pete in the processing facility. Tell him I need to see him. *Now.*"

As Pete came in to Samantha's office, he took one look at the bottle and said, "Oh no. She didn't. Please tell me she didn't order *that* bottle."

"How did this happen?"

He sunk into the chair facing her. "You gave Kathleen the job of picking out bottles while you were at CCAB. One evening at dinner, she showed me this bottle. She said that she felt we really needed to use a truly Italian bottle for this Tuscan oil. She said she was going to talk to the vendor about ordering them. I *told* her that it would only create more problems. I tried to talk her out of it. I swear I did! But then I got busy with the delivery of the new mill and forgot all about it."

"Pete, do you *realize* what this means? Our Tuscan olive oil, *our liquid gold*, in a clear bottle? It'll go rancid. Light is the *enemy* of olive oil."

Pete put his head in his hands. "I know. I know."

"How could Kathleen have possibly made this kind of a decision?"

Pete squirmed uneasily in the chair, like a trapped animal. "She never liked the bottles you picked out last year. She didn't think they were unique enough. She told me she thought boxing the bottle would make it distinctive."

"If she had only told me months ago, we could've at least gotten a box designed for it! But now...in the middle of harvest..."

"I'm sure she planned to tell you...certainly she would have told you...but then the miscarriage happened...well, she wanted it to be noticed on the shelves and perceived as a premium product."

"It *is* a premium product! The seal for the extra virgin oil won't even be seen if it's in a box. You *know* how important that seal is! If I can't get these bottles returned, we are going to have to pay a fortune to the ad agency and the printer to come up with a box for the bottles. For *these* orders." She banged her fist down on the desk on top of the large stack of waiting-to-be-fulfilled orders.

"It *is* a beautiful bottle, don't you think?" Pete said, trying to mollify Samantha.

She flashed him a look of anger and picked up the phone to call the bottle vendor who was sorry to inform her that the bottles were a special order and couldn't be returned. He added meekly that Kathleen had ordered five years' worth to get a special price.

Immediately after hanging up on the bottle vendor, Samantha called the advertising agency that Running Deer used for print ads and gave them a rush project for a box design that she knew would considerably bump up the agency's revenue for the year. At least someone will be making a profit this year, she rued, sinking into her chair and banging her head against her folded arms.

* * * *

"Are bottles really all that important?" asked Jack, as Samantha complained to him about Kathleen's bottle order that evening on the phone.

"All that important?! *Jack!* Haven't you ever noticed what olive oil bottles look like in a grocery store?"

"Nope." *Who notices bottles?*

"The bottles *are* the packaging. They sell the product. Olive oil bottles are very eye-catching, elegant, and stylized. They're not like wine bottles. The bottles are meant to project what the company is trying to say about its product. And they're always, *always* made of a colored glass to help deflect sunlight from turning the oil rancid. Ultra violet light can ruin the product," Samantha added miserably.

"But Kathleen must know that."

"Oh, she knew. She *wanted* to box it so that it would seem to be even more of a stand-out on the shelves. She felt that it had to be a truly Tuscan bottle. So she ordered five years' worth."

Jack whistled in amazement. "So now what?"

"So...the bottles can't be returned and the advertising agency is delighted to help us. For a rush fee. And I know this sounds petty, but what really makes me mad is that I can't even yell at Kat because it would only worsen her depression." She exhaled, trying to calm down. "Oh well, what's done is done. Knowing my sister's luck, we'll end up winning an award for packaging creativity." Samantha took a deep breath. "Okay. I'm done complaining. Tell me about your day."

He stood up and looked around his house for a dog, careful not to trip over the phone wire. "My day? Let's see. Tonight I brought home a dog in training that is close to being class-ready. The instructors try to take the dogs home once or twice so we can see how their house manners are." He spotted the dog in the kitchen, paws on the counter. "Down!" he scolded.

"How is this dog doing?"

The lop-eared yellow lab had a disarming grin as it galloped into the living room to greet Jack. Jack put a hand out to catch his collar and calm him down. "He could moonlight as a Hoover vacuum! He picks up everything that isn't nailed down. I even found a dollar bill glued to the roof of his mouth. He gives me this grin and tries to look stupid, but he knows exactly what he's doing. We have a little more work to do with him." Despite his complaints, he stroked the dog's head affectionately.

Samantha smiled. "I thought Lucy might come by today."

"Nope. Lucy was at CCAB this afternoon. She bicycled over to have me sign her report card," said Jack, bothered.

"That bad?"

"Terrible. The teacher added a note saying that, 'Lucy is a bright girl but does not pay enough attention to details'. Details like due dates for projects or homework assignments." He paused for a moment. "Too bad they don't give a grade for vivid imaginations. Last week she called me at work to excuse her from Spanish class. She had a substitute teacher whom she swore she had seen on a wanted poster at the Post Office."

Samantha burst out laughing. "Did you excuse her?"

"Nope. I told her to get back to Spanish class." He paused. "The other day I noticed that she smelled like cigarette smoke. Have you ever noticed?"

"Well, um, yes. The last time I was with her." Samantha wasn't sure if she wanted to get in the middle of Jack and his daughter, but she had a feeling she was already involved. "Chance smokes." *And who knows what all he smokes?* she wondered but didn't say. "Has she had problems in school before?"

Jack exhaled. "She's never been a great student, but I think this Chance guy is a bad influence. He told her that report cards are a right wing conspiracy to impose conformity on the masses."

"What?" Samantha sounded amused. "How did her mother react to her report card?"

"I think she's afraid to show her mom. Her mother seems to have a lot of…expectations for her." *That's putting it mildly.*

"Maybe it was a positive sign that she showed the report card to you. Maybe she's starting to think of you as a parent."

"Nice thought, but I think it was really more of a tactical decision on her part. She needed a parent to sign it before she could return it, and I'm sure she thought I would be a pushover. Once I had told her that I hadn't done well in school, either," he said.

He had regretted sharing that information with Lucy as soon as the words left his mouth. *It's just that she can be so hard to talk to.* He found himself babbling about all kinds of things, just to try and keep Lucy from looking so bored when she was with him. Lately, he preferred to be with Lucy when Samantha was with them. *Lucy just seems softer around Samantha.*

"Didn't you like school?"

"Hated it. Too hard to sit still all day. School always made me feel bad, too. Like I could never measure up." He gave a short laugh. "And I couldn't either. The only way I got into college was with a football scholarship. The day I got drafted into the NFL was the happiest day of my life. I had a bona fide excuse to be done with school."

"Lucy *is* a lot like you. I mean, details *tend* to get overlooked by you, too."

"I know. Big time," he said wretchedly.

"Sometimes when I'm with you, I feel like I've missed the first chapter of a book. Or the first scene in a movie."

Jack frowned. It wasn't the first time he had been told something like that.

"Curiously, though, when I was at CCAB for that month, you didn't miss a thing."

"That's because I'm so focused there. It's when I'm trying to juggle a bunch of things that stuff falls through the cracks."

"Stuff like telling me you had a daughter."

"Yup," he admitted.

Samantha smiled. "Just like you, Lucy is going to do well in life. You've been incredibly successful in your adult life, from football fallback—"

"Quarterback," he interrupted. "And the term is fullback."

"—to guide dog instructor. How someone does in school doesn't always indicate how they're going to do in life."

He thought about that for a moment and then said, "Actually, I learned more from football than I ever did in school."

"How so?"

"I learned to be patient. You need a surprisingly large amount of patience in football. The team is large, there's offensive and defensive and specialty teams, and everyone spends a lot of time warming the bench. Especially so when you're second string. But I think that's how I learned to have patience for my students at CCAB."

He paused, wondering where that dog had gone. "Hold on a second, Sam." He put down the phone and went to the bathroom, finding the dog drinking out of the toilet. Jack jerked him out, closed the bathroom door, and picked up the phone. "Learned about discipline, too. Football is an extremely demanding sport." Then he added, "Bet you were the type of student who sat in the front row of the class and raised your hand to every question the teacher asked."

Samantha grinned. "Something like that. Actually, I used to get so sick with anxiety about timed math tests that were taken on Wednesday that I started worrying on Monday and couldn't sleep for two nights. I was a champion worrier even then."

"Why were math tests such a big deal?"

"I *don't* know. Oh, yes, I do. That single sheet of paper represented my life, and if I failed, then I would fail at life."

"Hmmm. Your folks must have put a lot of pressure on you."

"No, not really. Not about school, anyway. I put pressure on myself. Excelling in school was the only thing my parents seemed to notice as remarkable about me."

"Sam, you're going to have to let it go with your parents."

"Let *what* go?"

"Wanting more from them." Jack paused, searching for the right words. "They may not have more to give you. But God can be enough."

Samantha didn't answer. He knew her well enough by now to know she was squirming, that this was getting too personal for her.

As he expected, she changed the subject. "Jack, don't underestimate Lucy. She's a very special girl. She's a lot like you. And just like you, she's going to do well in life."

Now Jack was silent. He hadn't expected a compliment like that.

"Still there?" Samantha asked.

"Yes. Still here." He swallowed and took a deep breath. *Do not say it, Jack. Do not, do not, do not say it.* "Sam? I'm falling in love with you." He slapped his hand against his forehead. *I said it.* "Are you still there?" he asked apprehensively, after he didn't hear any response. He couldn't even hear her breath. *Oh no, what have I done? Is it possible to retract that statement?*

After an eternity, she spoke. "But you've only known me a couple of months!" she protested, half-laughing, half-serious.

He brightened, remembering that Dr. Sommers recommended full disclosure. *Might as well just admit it.* "That's all the time I need."

"Jack. Be serious."

"I am being serious."

"Sometimes I don't even know why you bother with me. I'm stubborn, I take life too seriously, I take myself too seriously, I've been accused of being a workaholic, I'm defensive, Kat thinks I'm too boring and predictable, and I get angry, but I don't express it well—"

"Yup," he agreed pleasantly. "I've been on the wrong end of that once or twice."

"—and you are I are *complete* opposites."

"I've noticed that. But that's a good thing."

"And then there's my blindness, too."

"You forgot a few qualities, Sam. You're brave and smart and strong and beautiful. Funny, too, though you don't mean to be, which makes it funnier. And you try so hard to not be dependent on anyone, yet you don't even realize that your entire family is very dependent on you."

Samantha didn't respond.

"Still there?" he asked.

He heard her exhale, as if she had been holding her breath.

"Yes. Still here. Okay, let's talk about my blindness. I realize you're more aware of problems blind people have than most, but it's hard enough, even for me."

"Are you bothered that I have a bum knee?" He patted his knee, which made the dog think Jack wanted him up on his lap. Jack pushed the dog down, telling him, "Hey buddy, four on the floor."

"Jack, I'm *serious*."

"So am I. Everyone has limitations or flaws of some kind, Sam. I sure do."

"I'm talking about a practical, day-to-day basis. Being visually impaired is difficult, Jack. With other senses, you can still retain some independence. Losing vision means a great reliance on others. Blindness is part of my package."

Jack became solemn and earnest. "I understand what you're saying, Sam. What I want you to understand is that I don't see your blindness. I only see you." He paused. "Do you remember that night at the Academy when I told you having a guide dog might not be for you?"

"Of course I remember."

"That was the night I saw the *real* you. You were willing to face your fears and do what you needed to do. I was impressed. Really impressed. That was the moment I started falling for you. Haven't stopped since." He saw the dog gallop upstairs, as if a steak dinner was waiting for him on the top step, right off the grill. *Why didn't I put that dog on tie-down?* "Look, I'd better go. I'll talk to you tomorrow."

* * * *

Samantha held the phone for a long time after Jack said goodnight, a little stunned. Terrified, too. Jack's profession of love astounded her. How could he be so open, so vulnerable? She put her head in her hands. *And I didn't even respond to him in a meaningful way; I sounded like a blathering idiot.* But she couldn't respond; she wasn't ready to. Besides, words like those were too hard for Samantha to speak. She had never told a man she loved him. *Actually, the truth is that I don't think I've ever truly been in love.* Still, she thought, mystified by this entire relationship, Jack had a way of listening and understanding things that she didn't even say.

* * * *

The next day, Samantha was in her office, with the door shut tightly because of the noise from the mill, when Lena told her she had a phone call from someone who sounded drunk.

Curious, Samantha picked up the phone and broke into a smile when she heard a familiar and lovely accent.

"Bon jour, Zamanza!"

"Etienne? Etienne Number Five?"

"Oui! It iz me! My daughter and I watched the televizion show on your company ze ozzer day! And ever zince I have been wondering how you and ze Azure are doing?"

"We're doing very well, Etienne. In fact, I can't believe that I ever got along *without* Azure. Remember how nervous I felt on that first day back at California Canine Academy for the Blind?"

"Oui! I remember."

"And how are you, Etienne? How is Oriole?"

"Ze iz magnifique!"

Samantha couldn't help but laugh as she heard the contagious enthusiasm in Etienne's voice.

"Zo, Zamanza, do you zink zat having Azure haz given you balanz in your life?"

"Excuse me?" Samantha had forgotten how trying to understand Etienne felt like trying to package fog.

"When you were at ze Academy, it zeemed az if you had no balance. Work, work, work. I have been hoping zat you have more balance now. Remember ze French mantra?: Tout est question d'equilbre," she said. "Everything iz a matter of balance."

Samantha ran her hand along her bulletin board, hunting for that Braille note that Etienne had given her when she was still at CCAB. She had tacked it up when she first came back from the Academy. Now she couldn't find it. "Hmmm. I must say, Etienne Number Five, you always make me think."

"Oui! Iz good, no?"

"Yes, Etienne. It's very good."

"I must go now, Zamanza. Off to my yoga. Iz good to hear your voice. Oh, and Zamanza? I zink zat your rezeptionizt iz not zo good at anzering ze phone. No? Au Revoir!"

"Thank you so much for calling. Good bye, Etienne!"

For a long while after Samantha put down the phone, she pondered Etienne's phone call. She picked up the two tickets to the symphony that the bottle vendor had dropped off to her that morning. Knowing she loved the symphony, he gave her tickets a few times a year. Kathleen and Samantha usually made a girls' night out of it. This year, because Running Deer had placed such a large order with him and because he felt badly about the clear glass bottle fiasco, he had bought her two box seats.

"Sam?" asked Jack when he called later that evening. "I've been thinking. We need to have some fun. And since I can't talk you into going to a football game with me and my buddies—"

Samantha rolled her eyes, thinking of how much fun *that* would be for her.

"—let's take off on Sunday afternoon and go to the beach so we can surf."

"Surf? You want to *surf*? In *November*?"

183

"Why not? It still warms up in the afternoon. And the waves are great!"

"But the weatherman said it's supposed to turn cold this weekend! Really, *really* cold!"

"Weathermen are always wrong."

"I'm wary of the ocean, Jack. I never like to venture more than ankle deep and that's on a perfectly hot day in August."

"I thought you liked the ocean."

"I do. From a distance. And I've never surfed in my life!"

"I'll teach you! I have some wetsuits we can wear."

"Jack, it would take two of me to fit into one of your wetsuits. No, thank you," she said, laughing. "Besides, I'm sure Pete needs me to take care of Lily."

"I already checked it out with Lucy. She agreed to babysit." He paused. "Well, I didn't give her a choice. She was planning to head to Berkeley with this Chance guy to march in a protest against Vietnam so I needed a good reason to keep her here."

"March in an anti-war protest? She's only fourteen!"

"Exactly my point. In Berkeley of all places! That's why we need a reason to make her skip it."

Samantha was reluctant to say 'yes,' but suddenly heard Etienne's voice echo 'balanz?' in her head. "Okay. I'll go to the beach with you, but I *don't* want to surf. You surf, and I'll bring along some work to do."

"Fine," he grumbled.

"And in exchange, Jack, you have to do something fun next weekend with me. Something *I* consider fun."

"Something *you* think is fun? Like what?" he asked, sounding doubtful.

"*Yes*, Jack, I *can* be fun," she said firmly. "A vendor gave me tickets to the San Francisco Symphony in Davies Hall. It should be a wonderful program! Kathleen isn't up to going. I even thought of going alone, but somehow, the symphony should be a shared experience. And now *we* can go!" She was delighted.

There was complete silence on the other end of the phone.

"Jack? Are you there?"

"Yes," he answered in a flat, dull voice. Jack sounded markedly less excited.

"Oh, Jack, cheer up! It'll be *fun!*"

The weather ended up turning cold on Sunday, as predicted, but Jack insisted that he was hardy enough to handle the brisk ocean temperature. Samantha sat bundled up next to Azure on the beach, protected from the wind by a rocky cliff, glad she had anticipated it to be bitterly cold and had dressed accordingly. She hoped Jack wasn't going to freeze to death on his surfboard like a popsicle in his black wet suit.

She brought a new tape recorder she wanted to learn how to use so she could dictate work assignments for Lena. As she held the tape recorder in her hand, she pondered the fact that she should probably let Lena go and hire a more capable assistant. *But there is something so doggedly loyal about Lena. She has seen us through much leaner days. No,* Samantha resolved, *I can never fire her.* But she would keep trying to find ways to help Lena become more self-sufficient and productive.

After a long while, Samantha heard angry barking coming from the direction of the ocean. Even Azure sat up in alarm. Soon afterwards, Jack came trudging up the beach, dragging his surfboard. She handed him some towels and blankets to warm up. "What was that noise? It sounded like a dog fight."

"Oh, I bumped into a seal," he answered in a dejected voice.

"What?" Samantha asked, wide-eyed, jaw dropped open. "Do you mean to tell me that you had the entire ocean to surf in, and you *bumped* into a seal?" She started to giggle. "How could you *not* avoid a seal?!"

"There's a lot of kelp out there. It was hard to see him," he said defensively.

She doubled over in helpless laughter.

"I'm glad *someone* is amused," he said. "The seal certainly wasn't."

"Maybe in your wetsuit, he thought you were a potential suitor!" She couldn't stop laughing.

"Sam, it's really *not* that funny," Jack said in an injured tone.

"It reminds me of when Kat was sixteen and just learning to drive!" Giggles kept bubbling up as she tried to talk. "No matter how nearly empty a parking lot was, she always managed to back into someone's car!" Then she started laughing all over again. "You're absolutely right, Jack. This *was* fun!"

The next Friday night, Jack and Samantha and Azure went to the San Francisco Symphony. It was the first time she had heard the newly appointed conductor Seiji Ozawa conduct. Samantha smiled to herself, enjoying the thrill of being in the heart of San Francisco, sharing the excited buzz of the symphony hall, surrounded by likeminded music enthusiasts. Even Azure, head resting on Samantha's feet, seemed enchanted by the melodious sounds. Samantha decided that sitting in a darkened symphony hall, soaking in glorious sounds, was one more experience to add to her list of times in which she completely forgot she was blind.

Actually, there were a number of times recently that she was completely unaware of being blind. *Life just doesn't get better than this,* she thought, satisfied. "Jack?" she whispered. "Oh Jack, I'm so glad we came. Isn't it *wonderful?*" She paused, waiting for him to agree. But he didn't respond. She leaned closer to him and realized why. He was lightly snoring.

Chapter Twelve: **Sweepstakes**

On Sunday afternoon, Nonna drove Samantha to the store to buy groceries for the week. Pushing the cart down the cereal aisle, Nonna noted, "Seems as though we haven't done this in a while, have we?"

"No. We haven't spent much time together at all lately," answered Samantha. Grocery shopping used to be a Sunday afternoon routine before Nonna moved to Shady Acres.

"That's what happens when boyfriends come around," Nonna, a teasing smile in her voice. "Grandmothers become second fiddle. Maybe not even in the orchestra."

Samantha laughed, enjoying the relaxed afternoon with Nonna. Maybe her grandmother *had* just been stressed from the move, she decided. Maybe things will get back to normal now.

In the check-out line, Samantha was fishing cash out of her wallet to pay for the groceries when the checker groaned loudly. "What's wrong?" she asked, alarmed.

"Is that old lady with you?" he asked.

"Yes. Why?" Samantha turned curiously toward Nonna who had been helping to bag the groceries.

"She didn't use any bags. She just loaded everything back into the cart." With a weary sigh, sounding like he had worked one shift too many, he pulled out some bags to load up the groceries.

Samantha's concern for her grandmother spiked up again, higher this time.

* * * *

Later that evening, Jack and Lucy arrived for dinner. "Sam, this is incredible!" said Jack as he took a bite. "How did you get the chicken to taste like this? Mine usually ends up tasting…tasteless. But then again I don't cook. I heat up frozen TV dinners."

Samantha smiled and filled a glass of milk for Lucy.

"Hey Jack, have you ever seen the dials on Sam's oven?" asked Lucy, pointing to the kitchen. "They're specially designed for blind people so they don't burn themselves."

He smiled. "I have noticed that, Luce," Jack answered.

"Sam said she wants to hire me as her apprentice some day," said Lucy proudly. "Right, Sam?"

Samantha nodded at her in agreement. "I do. I think she would do a better job than Lena." Her smile faded. "Even now."

"Don't I get any credit for introducing the two of you?" asked Jack.

Ignoring Jack, with her mouth full of food, Lucy asked, "Sam? What's the deal with that creepy mask on the wall?" She had wondered about that thing. *It seems so out of place from Sam's girly stuff.*

"It's a Trophy Head," said Samantha matter-of-factly. "In Papua New Guinea, many of the tribes had spirithouses in the center of the village, and they would bury a Trophy Head under each post."

"A wooden head like that?"

"Oh no," laughed Samantha. "A *human* head. At least, they used to use human heads. Not so much anymore. The spirithouses had to be replaced frequently because of fire or termites so they required many heads." She smoothed her napkin in her lap. "But in the last few decades, headhunting raids have been frowned upon by western influence so they substituted wooden carved head for real ones."

Jack leaned back in his chair as Lucy finished chewing her chicken, a thoughtful expression on her face.

"Well, that's just a *replica*, you know," Samantha said reassuringly.

Jack put down his fork.

"Um…do either of you know anything at all about Papua New Guinea?" asked Samantha.

"I know that it's near Australia, and it's the size of California," volunteered Lucy. "We studied it last year in geography. My teacher was a complete pothead, totally whacked out, but I think I remember a few things."

Amused, Samantha asked Jack, "How do teachers have the steely self-esteem to endure their teenaged critics?"

Chin to his chest, Jack didn't respond to her question. Lucy noticed that he wasn't eating.

"What else do you remember?" Samantha asked Lucy, cutting up her green beans.

"Let's see. It's the second largest island in the world, and the wild life is abundant and diverse." Lucy took a bite of her chicken.

"No kidding," said Samantha, remembering fondly. "Spiders the size of dinner plates."

Jack put his head in his hands.

"It's a land of contrasts," explained Samantha. "There's a spine of mountains that run the length of the island from north to south, called the 'highlands,' with snowcapped mountaintops and insular valleys. Then, in the lowlands and along the coastline, are swamps and tropical rain forests. The tribes are isolated by the rugged territory even from each other. When European explorers arrived searching for gold, they found Stone Age cultures—completely cut off from the modern world."

"Isn't that the place where they do that whole body tattooing?" asked Lucy, nonchalantly. "Man, Jack, you look pale." She recognized that glazed look in his eyes. Her little brother got it right before he barfed.

"Yes! Good memory, Lucy!" Samantha said. Oblivious to Jack's discomfort, Samantha plowed on. "Your teacher was better than you think. Probably seems strange to westerners, but personal decorations are a major art form for the Papua New Guineans, and the basis of their primitive art is religion. It's a way to express their beliefs. They tattoo their body and do something called 'scarification.' There's one tribe that believes that the crocodile is the creator of all things. So during initiation rites, boys have patterns cut into their backs to produce raised skin like a crocodile." She took a bite of salad.

Abruptly, Jack stood up. "Excuse me for a moment. I need some fresh air." And he rushed out of the cottage.

Samantha looked at Lucy, eyebrows raised. "What's the matter with him?"

"Bet he's gonna hurl. He's sort of squeamish. Could you pass the bread, please?"

When Jack came back in, Samantha asked him if he was okay. He assured her he was but asked if they could *please* change the subject. Lucy rolled her eyes and mouthed the word "big baby" at him. He gave her a playful shove.

"I just don't know where Nonna could be going all day. And why she needed money," Samantha said, looking worried.

"Sounds to me like she's at the race track," said Lucy nonchalantly.

"Lucy!" cautioned Jack.

"Well, think about it. She's short of cash, she's always disappearing. I think she's puttin' money on the ponies."

Samantha was silent.

"Well, follow her then if you don't believe me," said Lucy, devouring a large piece of roasted chicken with admirable gusto.

"That just doesn't seem right," said Samantha. "I know you've only met her as an elderly woman, but she's a wonderful person. I owe her...*everything*. She was the one person in my life who had so much confidence in my abilities. I wouldn't have tried half the things I've done in my life if it weren't for my grandmother. I just couldn't start *spying* on her."

Lucy shrugged. "Heck, then I'll spy on her."

"Lucy, you need to stay out of this," Jack said sternly. "And just what do *you* know about putting money on the ponies anyway?"

Lucy didn't pay any attention to Jack's warning. She informed Samantha that she and Chance spent the next few days following Nonna around town after school. "It wasn't hard, Sam; she drives so slow in that big ol' Buick Riviera. Who *drives* those old dinosaurs anymore? Just ol' cottontops. And she always goes to the same places: this Western Union telegraph office, the bank, and to Vinny's Pool Hall at the edge of town."

Samantha was incredulous. "She goes to a pool hall? My *grandmother* goes to a pool hall?"

"Yeah. Don't worry. I didn't go in. Chance followed her in, but I stayed in his car. But I *told* you, Sam! She's running the ponies."

☐

Samantha, Azure, Lucy and Lily took the bus and went over to Nonna's. Samantha wanted to ask her grandmother some questions about these strange errands. They passed the mailman as they headed toward her apartment. "Lucy, would you save the mailman a trip and go get Nonna's mail for her?" Samantha plucked Lily out of her stroller and hoisted her on her hip to climb the stairs to her grandmother's door while Lucy ran off to talk to the mailman.

"Samantha!" Nonna said, as she opened the door. "Lily! What a nice surprise!"

"Hi!" She gave her a hug and said, "I brought Jack's daughter, Lucy. She'll be up in a moment. Remember Lucy?" she prompted.

"The round girl with red hair?"

Samantha froze, stunned. "Lucy has *red* hair?"

"Flaming carrot red."

"Straight or curly?"

"Curly. Frizzy, in fact. And she has dark brown eyes, as dark as coffee beans, and her face is covered with freckles."

What?! Why has Jack never mentioned that Lucy has red hair? Well—that's Jack. Not exactly a detail guy. Then Samantha asked, "Does she look much like Jack?"

Nonna seemed to understand the layer beneath Samantha's question. She went over to the sofa and patted it so that Samantha and Lily came to sit down near her. "Only in their size. Jack is, well, rather a portly fellow."

Samantha nodded knowingly.

"And he does have dark brown eyes like Lucy's. He has a darker complexion than Lucy. She's pretty fair. Jack has strong eyebrows that frame his eyes. And he has a cleft in his chin like Rock Hudson. His smile lights up a room. I can't really picture him *not* smiling. And he wears his hair very close clipped in that popular way young men do when they have a receding hairline."

Samantha grinned.

"And when he thinks no one is watching, he looks at you...completely besotted."

Samantha shook her head. "Nonna, no one says besotted anymore."

"Really? Well, that's a shame. It's such a good word. Still, he does look besotted."

Samantha laughed, cheeks flaming. "I wonder what's keeping Lucy? She went to get your mail—"

Just then, Lucy burst through the door. "Hey there!" she called out happily.

She reminds me so much of Jack! Even the way she enters a room. "Any mail?" Samantha asked her.

"Uh, just this." Lucy handed Nonna a magazine.

"Thank you, Lucy. Here, sit down," Nonna said, standing up to make room for her on the sofa.

"Smells like gingerbread," Lucy said, sniffing the air.

"It is. Your sister's favorite," Nonna said to Samantha.

Actually, it's my favorite, Samantha thought. *Kat hates the taste of ginger.*

"I made it this afternoon and thought I'd bring it over tomorrow, but you could take it home with you now. Is Kat improving?"

"Not yet," said Samantha.

"She'll get better soon. She's done it before."

"What? *When?*"

"When you spent that summer at that...um..." Nonna stopped, searching for the word.

"School for the Blind?" Samantha supplied.

"Yes. That's it! Well, Kat had the blues that summer. Took her a while, but she got over it when you returned home."

Samantha was floored. "Why didn't I know about that?"

"We didn't want to worry you. You needed to get those skills. Kat just had to learn to live without you. She's always been too dependent on you."

On me? I thought I was the one who was dependent on Kathleen.

"Sheesh, Sam, you and your sister sure looked alike as kids!" said Lucy, holding up a picture frame. "I can't tell who is who!"

"Sam always dressed in pink. She's always loved the color pink," said Nonna. "That's why her cottage is decorated in pink." She went to get the gingerbread in the kitchen.

"Well, it's not really *decorated* in pink, Nonna," Samantha objected loudly. "There might be a few pink *accents* here and there."

"Nah, it's *really* pink," Lucy corrected.

Samantha sat there silently, thinking about her grandmother. About how much support her grandmother had given her through the years. *Here I am, spying on her like a common burglar. I just can't ask Nonna about where she's been going lately. If Nonna wants to drive around town to odd places, that's her business.* As Samantha stood up to tell Lucy that they should leave, the phone rang.

"I'll get it, Nonna." Samantha picked up the receiver and said, "Hello?"

"Hello again, Mrs. Christiansen! It's me. Just wanted you to know that we've had a little glitch in getting the prize money to you."

Samantha thought about hanging up, but the fact that the man seemed to know her grandmother's name alarmed her. "Oh?" asked Samantha, keeping her words to a minimum while still encouraging the man to talk.

"I need to collect another advance fee from you to cover the federal taxes on this prize money."

Samantha felt a jolt. "How much?"

"Only $1,000. The last fee was to cover state taxes, but the Feds want their cut, too." He clucked his tongue. "Such a crime."

She took the phone over to the window, out of hearing range from the kitchen, as her heart started to pound.

"So here's what I want you to do," the man continued. "Get a money order from your bank for $1,000, payable to cash, then go to Western Union and get a mailing envelope. I'll call back to confirm that you got these things and then I'll give you instructions as to where to send it. I'll call you back within a few hours, Mrs. Christiansen, and by this evening, you'll be a millionaire! Guaranteed!"

"Really?" Samantha asked, eyes narrowed with suspicion.

Then the man told her, "Congratulations again, Mrs. Christiansen! God bless you!"

The nerve of that guy! Samantha hung up the phone and stood there silently, wondering what to do next. Briefly, she thought of just asking Nonna about the phone call. Then she remembered how confused and agitated Nonna had become when she had tried to talk to her about the bounced checks. Somewhere in the back of her mind, she realized her grandmother was losing her ability to handle finances, but she never imagined that someone would try to take advantage of her.

Nonna brought the gingerbread to her, wrapped up in many layers of tin foil, and asked, "Who was on the phone?"

"Wrong number." She hugged Nonna goodbye, tucked the gingerbread into her purse, and decided that she and Lucy would make a pit stop at the police station on the way home.

A policeman listened to Samantha's story and seemed to know exactly what was going on. "It's the Sweepstakes scam. The last couple of years, ever since magazines started up those sweepstakes, we've had a slough of scammers. We get complaints about them all of the time. Con-artists who prey on elderly victims."

Samantha felt hopeful. "Then you can do something, can't you?"

"These guys are incredibly shifty," the policeman answered. "They use false identification to pick up the money. By the time we get a phone number or an address, they've moved on. I'll take all of the information you can give me and fill out the report, but I just wouldn't hold out for any hope of nailing these guys or of getting any money back."

"What do you mean? She *didn't* wire any money to him."

"This time. But what about last time? Did they use that advanced fee scheme?"

Samantha felt an alarm bell go off in her head. She nodded.

"Chances are she's been conned before. These guys keep selling their list to other cons, so the same gullible people keep getting hit up."

Lucy tapped Samantha's elbow. "There's something else you should know, Sam. The mailman told me he's worried about your grandmother. He said she's been getting these kinds of things for a while now. More and more each week." Lucy pulled out her book sack and dumped the contents on the counter. Dozens of sweepstakes cards and envelopes and packages, all promising: "You've won! Call this number to claim your prize!"

Samantha picked up the pile of papers with a sinking feeling.

"And I know you don't like me snooping," Lucy said, "but when you were on the telephone, I noticed a bunch of yellow receipts to Western Union stuffed in a tea cup on the top of a bookshelf."

Suddenly, Samantha's chest hurt. She thought her heart might explode.

"Are you mad at me for taking them?" Lucy asked, sounding worried. "Maybe I should have just told you at the apartment, but it just didn't seem like your Nonna's train was on the tracks today." She hesitated. "She didn't wrap up the gingerbread, Sam. That package in your purse is a bottle of dish soap. I watched her wrap it."

Samantha nodded slowly, as the knowledge that her grandmother wasn't well and wasn't going to get better settled in to stay. "No, Lucy. You were smart to pick them up."

The police officer added one more piece of advice. "Ma'am, the best thing you can do right now is to protect your grandmother. Get her phone number changed, divert her mail to a P.O. Box, freeze her bank accounts. This is going to be a headache."

"Yes, I can see that," Samantha said irritably, annoyed that he didn't seem to feel the gravity of this information in the same way she did.

"Do you have the power of attorney?" he asked.

Samantha sighed. "No."

"You'd better get it. Soon."

At the bank, Samantha discovered even worse news. As she reviewed a current month's bank statement from her grandmother, she found that several marketing companies had accessed her grandmother's checking account number and were making unauthorized withdrawals from her account. *No wonder Nonna hasn't had any money.*

Samantha froze the accounts, changed Nonna's phone number, got a P.O. Box so that her mail could be filtered, and called Pete to come down to the bank so they could make a double signature authorization to get Nonna's name off of Running Deer's accounts. Pete drove Samantha, Azure, Lucy, and Lily back to Running Deer. It was small comfort, but at least her grandmother could no longer spend money she didn't have.

"That explains why she had no money in the first place and had to ask Pete for a loan," Samantha said to Jack back at her cottage that evening when he dropped by to pick up Lucy.

"But where did she get money?" asked Jack.

"I have *no* idea. I checked Running Deer's accounts, and there haven't been any withdrawals in the last few weeks that I haven't authorized."

"What about those creeps she meets at the pool hall?" asked Lucy. "Think she could be dealing with loan sharks?"

"What creeps?" asked Jack warily. "Lucy, what have you been up to?"

Momentarily distracted, Samantha realized that was the second time she had heard Jack talk to Lucy like a father talked to a daughter. There had been a shift between them, she realized, not really sure what had changed or why.

* * * *

Thanksgiving morning dawned dull and brooding. The sky turned bruised, dark and blue, as Samantha slid the turkey into the oven. She struggled with fitting the turkey into the roasting pan, as if it felt as reluctant about Thanksgiving as she did.

Holidays were Kathleen's domain. Normally, Kathleen made Thanksgiving into a lavish and enormous feast, inviting as many friends as could be squeezed around the groaning farm table. This year, the responsibility for the event wordlessly shifted to Samantha, so she decided to simplify everything. Except for the turkey. The house had to have the all-day-long roasting turkey smell in it, if it was really going to feel like Thanksgiving, she told Pete, after he suggested getting cold cuts from the deli.

Samantha hoped that the aroma from the turkey would coax Kathleen to the table. She decided everything else could be store-bought. The only guests would be Nonna and Jack; Lucy was expected at her stepfather's family. "It won't be up to Kat's usual standards, but we'll still have a celebration," Samantha said consolingly to Pete as she handed him the shopping list.

After Samantha had set the table, she took lunch to Kathleen and found her sitting on the couch, leaning against a mountain of pillows, watching *On the Beach.*

"Why on earth would you watch a movie about a nuclear bomb killing everyone in the world when you *already* feel depressed?" Samantha turned the dial off on the television and sat down on the sofa.

"It came on after the news. Did you know that California is due for a major earthquake any day now, and the entire state might fall into the ocean?"

"Oh, Kat, you've got to be careful of what you fill your mind with. You're only making it worse."

Kathleen curled into a ball, tucking her head down.

"Can you smell the turkey?" Samantha asked hopefully.

"Uh huh," Kathleen mumbled.

"Doesn't it smell good?"

"Uh huh."

"Nonna should be here soon. Jack promised to come early, but he seems to be from a notoriously late species. We'll eat at four o'clock. Sound good?"

Kathleen lifted her head. Her voice, slow and drifting, murmured, "I'm just not up to it today, Sam."

She sounded so sad and forlorn that Samantha felt a great tenderness toward her. "Tell me how you're feeling."

Kathleen sighed and put her head on her knees. "I feel like I'm in the ocean, and I keep trying to swim to shore, but I just can't reach it. The tide keeps pushing me back. I'm just exhausted from trying."

"You just need time to get back to feeling like yourself."

Kathleen didn't respond.

"Have you tried reading those books I got you?"

"No." They were still on a pile on the coffee table, positioned exactly as Samantha had left them.

"In the *Bible* there's a story about a prophet named Elijah. Queen Jezebel threatened to kill him, so he ran like a rabbit out to the desert, feeling very depressed. He even begged God to let him die."

"So?" Kathleen asked, not sounding at all interested.

"So what do you think God did?"

"In the Old Testament? Probably smote him."

A good sign! Kat hasn't completely lost her sense of humor. "Just the opposite. God sent an angel to take care of him and to give him food and water. He was very, very gentle with Elijah. Like…God understood depression."

"What's your point?"

"Maybe that your miscarriage did matter to God, and how you're doing now matters to God." She brushed Kathleen's hair off of her face, like a mother soothing a child. "What have you got to lose by at least trying to find out more about God? Thinking there is an impersonal and random Universe out there doesn't do much for you when you're down and out." Softly, she added, "Wouldn't really hurt to check it out, would it?"

Kathleen didn't answer.

"Kat, you know why I think you're depressed? I think it's because the miscarriage was something you couldn't control. It just happened. And I don't think you know how to handle things you can't control." As soon as she said it, she knew it was the wrong thing to say. It might be true, but it was still bad timing.

"And you do?" Kathleen spat out, before stomping upstairs, angry.

Samantha wanted to shout a retort: "Yes, as a matter of fact, I do! I've had a little more experience dealing with things I can't control! Like, for example, *blindness!*" But she didn't say it. She knew it would be futile. Just then, Samantha heard a car pull up on the gravel driveway. It didn't sound like Pete's truck or Nonna's Buick, and Jack didn't have a car. She went to the door to see who had arrived.

Two police officers were at the front door. "Ma'am, could you come outside with us for a moment?" Samantha followed the police officers out to their squad car. In the back of the squad car was Nonna. "She's been driving around one particular city block for hours. Finally, we pulled her over. She doesn't know where she is. Her driver's license in her purse showed this address."

As if a large cloud had passed in front of the sun, Samantha sensed her life would never be quite the same. "Thank you, officers. I'll take care of her. Where *is* her car?"

"7th and Vine." He handed her the keys. "But it's time she stops driving."

Samantha leaned into the backseat of the squad car.

"Sammy?" asked Nonna, sounding bewildered and frightened and small and old.

Gently, Samantha said, "I really need your help to get ready for Thanksgiving dinner."

When Pete and Lily came back from the supermarket and her grandmother was safely napping upstairs, Samantha asked, "Pete, what are the chances that Nonna has continued to borrow money from those two hoodlum friends of yours?"

"They're *not* my friends!" Pete said defensively. "I just knew a guy who was able to borrow money from them quickly. It worked out fine for this guy so—"

"I'm *not* trying to make you feel guilty. I just wondered if you have any idea how much money she owes them? Or how to find them?"

"No. I've been so hard to reach in the last month. That must have been when they started working directly with her. Did you check her phone bill?"

"I checked it, but they must call her from a payphone."

"Look, Sam, I'm sorry. I really blew it. I've been so busy with the harvest and with Kat, the whole thing has slipped my mind. I guess I just got distracted."

Just got distracted. Those words stung Samantha like a bee. *That's exactly how I would describe myself over the last few months. Distracted*

She finished preparing the dinner, fighting a wave of overwhelming discouragement as she realized how fragile her family had become.

Unexpectedly, Jack showed up right on time, his arms full of brightly colored chrysanthemums, two pies from his favorite bakery, and a quart of vanilla ice cream, because he insisted that 'pie-and-ice-cream' was one word. Trotting behind him was Lucy. "Hope you don't mind a straggler," Jack said, as Lucy squeezed past him.

"Hi, Sam! I wanted to go with Chance to Santa Cruz. But then my stupid mother said I had to go to my even stupider stepfather's parents' house for dinner, and I think that their house smells like *mothballs*, so I begged and begged, and my stepdad said, '*Fine!* If you're just going to sit there and mope all afternoon then *go* with Chance.' And then Mom said to him, 'Don't yell at her on Thanksgiving! Besides your parents' house *does* smell like mothballs.' And then *they* got in a big argument about his decrepit ol' parents. So I called Chance, but he had already split. So I called Jack, and he said I could come here, and my mom and stepdad were still arguing so they agreed to let me come here," Lucy said smugly. "I brought some little kid games to play with Lily. Oh, and I brought my latest Bob Dylan LP for you to listen to."

Jack groaned. "Oh, no! I don't want to listen to Bob Dylan whine on Thanksgiving."

Samantha had never been so glad to greet any two people in her life. She surprised them by engulfing them both in a huge, heartfelt hug.

After resting, Nonna had gone up into the attic to sift through a few boxes. When it was time to sit down at the dinner table, Jack went up to fetch her. Afterwards, he quietly handed a folder of musty papers to Samantha in the kitchen. "They're old stock certificates," he whispered to her. "I just happened to notice them. They had been thrown on top of a box of junk like she had found them and forgotten about them. They were covered in dust." He picked up the platter with the turkey on it to carry into the dining room. "But it might be worth checking them out."

As they sat around the dinner table for the meal, Pete tried his best to put on a good front but he was exhausted. Kathleen finally came downstairs but sat like a stone in the chair.

"Eat something, Kat. Don't just move your food around your plate," Pete whispered in a worried voice.

Oh, Pete, leave her alone. Just being here is taking every ounce of energy Kat can muster. She doesn't even pay much attention to Lily. Samantha passed the potatoes to her grandmother as her worry for her family continued to spike. *Nonna seems passive and withdrawn.*

Jack and Lucy, however, were consuming the meal with enthusiasm and kept up a light stream of chatter about everything under the sun. After Jack's pies and ice cream were served with steaming hot coffee, the dark skies, groaning with heavy clouds, finally started to pour.

"Here it comes," said Pete, raking a hand through his hair. "We aren't done with the harvest yet. Ugh, think of the mud."

Jack said, "Glad I brought an umbrella. Lucy and I are on kitchen clean-up duty then we'll get on home."

"No, don't go," urged Samantha. "We can go to my cottage. *It's a Wonderful Life* is supposed to be on tonight."

Lucy sighed. "Another nail in the coffin of my cool factor," she muttered.

"I can run you home later, Jack," Pete offered.

"Jack, why don't you ever drive your car?" asked Kathleen.

Samantha inhaled sharply. *Kathleen finally shows interest in someone and asks a question. And it has to be that question!*

"Jack doesn't even *own* a car," volunteered Lucy.

"Why ever not?" persisted Kathleen.

"Good luck finding the answer on that," Lucy said reproachfully. "I've asked him *hundreds* of times. It's *such* a pain to walk or take buses. Or *bicycle* everywhere. It's *mortifyingly embarrassing.*"

Everyone looked at Jack to respond, but he was uncharacteristically speechless. He didn't seem to know what to say.

"I can answer that," Samantha said.

"Sam," Jack protested, biting off a warning.

Samantha reached over and put her hand on his forearm to reassure him. "It's one of the reasons why he's such a good guide dog instructor. He tries to live in the same manner that his students have to live so he can understand what it's really like to be visually impaired."

Everyone was silent.

"Bet you didn't know that part of an instructor's training at California Canine Academy for the Blind is to be blindfolded for two solid weeks. Day and night," Samantha added, trying to divert attention from Kathleen's original question.

"Sweet!" said Lucy. "Jack, you never told me that. Man, what a great opportunity to play some practical jokes on those instructors."

"Actually, Luce," Jack said, "Mr. Collins even went under the blindfold with a class. A couple of students rearranged the furniture in his dorm room."

Even Kathleen chuckled a little at that image. Everyone stood to start clearing the table. As he walked behind her, carrying dishes into the kitchen, Jack leaned over and kissed Samantha in the hollow of her neck. Samantha remained behind to blow out the candles at the table. She heard Jack laughing in the kitchen with Lucy as they organized an assembly line to rinse dishes and stack them in the dishwasher.

Listening to Jack's voice, such a deep, gentle voice, tipped Samantha over the edge. Tears flooded her eyes. She knew she had grown fond of Jack, and she truly admired him for the choices he made with his life. But today, with a sudden stab that pierced her heart, she realized all Jack had come to mean to her.

Chapter Thirteen: **The Dognapping**

The day after Thanksgiving, Jack sat down on the floor of his living room to brush Azure. The fire in the fireplace crackled softly, a steady warmth built. He glanced up at Samantha, seated on the couch, deep in thought, chin propped on her hands.

"I hate doing this," Samantha complained. "I'm taking control of Nonna's life. I have spent this entire morning trying to dismantle her freedom."

"You're just trying to protect her until you can figure out what's wrong with her. It's all in her best interests, Sam. You've made a doctor's appointment for her, haven't you?"

She rubbed her temples. "Monday. I need to take care of that on Monday."

"Have you covered every single thing you can think of? Sealed up every hole?"

She shrugged her shoulders. "I think so. Everything that I know to do. I've changed her phone number, changed her bank accounts, gotten her a P.O. Box so that we can filter her mail, and removed her signature off of Running Deer's accounts."

"Any luck with those stock certificates?"

"I gave the folder to Pete. We think they might have been stocks that Gramps had bought years ago, but most likely they have either no value or they might be duplicates. Nonna had always kept track of those things, so if they had been lost, she might have already had them replaced."

"Still, someone should check them out," Jack advised.

"Pete said he would take care of it. He has a friend who is a stockbroker."

Jack rolled his eyes. *Isn't that how this mess got started in the first place?*

"Can you think of anything else I might be missing?"

"Maybe talk to the people at the retirement facility so they're paying attention in case those thugs come around."

Samantha's chin snapped up. "What do you mean?"

"Well, if the money has suddenly dried up for those guys, what are they going to do? They want to get paid back. Nonna might be at some risk."

She dropped her forehead into her palm. "Pete is trying to find them now."

"Any idea how much she owes them?" he asked as he stood up and stretched.

She winced. "Over $15,000."

"Wow. Wow. Wow."

"I'm glad my grandfather isn't here to see what she's done to their life work."

"Have you thought of asking her about the money? Or the sweepstakes?"

Samantha lifted her head. "I tried to ask once, but she got very anxious and upset. It was like a fog settled over her. I just didn't have the heart to accuse her. She doesn't know what she's done."

"Any idea how we're going to pay them back?"

She leaned back on the couch. "Kat can sell more stuff to the antique dealer if she ever gets out of bed. I'm hoping the people she loaned money from might let us work out a re-payment schedule, but I'm not sure how to get in touch with them. I know the company can't take on any debt. If we do, we'll run into trouble with covenants I made with the bank." Then she looked up at him and smiled. "Jack, you said 'we.' You said: 'how are *we* going to pay them back'?"

He shrugged. "I could help. I've got a few bucks tucked away."

"No, Jack. This is not your problem."

He sat down next to her on the couch. "Su problema es mi problema."

"Thank you anyway but no." She reached over and stroked his cheek, a gossamer touch. She appreciated how much he wanted to help her. "You're *such* a good guy."

He took her hand and kissed its palm. "Sam, will you let me pray about this?"

She yanked her hand back like she had touched fire. "Pray about this? About money? Jack, you're not supposed to pray about that kind of thing."

He nearly laughed at her but caught himself. "What *are* you supposed to pray about?"

"Well, big things, like hurricanes and famines."

Jack couldn't hold back a grin. "So we're not supposed to bother God about little details?"

"I guess," she said feebly, not really certain of the right answer.

"Scripture says to pray about everything."

"Everything? I really don't think the God of the universe needs to pick out the shoes I'm going to wear tomorrow."

Jack burst out laughing. "God knows about it anyway. Part of that omniscience thing He's got going on."

"But—"

Serious now, he said, "Sam, prayer is meant to be an ongoing conversation with God. About everything that matters to you. There's nothing that can shock God's ears."

Samantha shifted uneasily on the sofa as Jack took her hands in his and bowed his head. Her hands were trembling, he noticed, which made him realize how vulnerable she was right now.

"Lord, you are faithful to guide and instruct if we only ask. Please give Samantha the wisdom she needs to solve this problem. Protect Nonna from those who would do her harm. And please, heal Kathleen's mind, body and spirit, restoring her to full health. Amen." When Jack finished, he said softly, "See? Not so hard." He brushed some loose strands of hair off her forehead.

Samantha's eyes glistened with tears. "Jack, how can you be so sure? You're so sure about everything. About your faith, even about me. How are you able to be like that? How do you know for sure?"

Jack saw the anguish in her beautiful face. He pulled her close to him, wrapping his arms around her, wanting to hold her and comfort her.

"I wish I had your faith," she said. "I really do. I just don't understand how God could take everything away from my grandmother. She has spent her entire life doing good and helping others and loving God. How could He let this happen to her? Kat asked me once: 'Why doesn't God act like God?'"

Jack placed his chin on top of her head. "It's the illness that is doing this to her, Sam. God is taking care of her. Look at how you *accidentally* answered the phone call from that con-artist the other day at her apartment. Or how Lucy *accidentally* picked up the mail and noticed the sweepstakes. In just a week, you've been able to shut down those scammers. God keeps surrounding her with people who love her, who are trying to protect her and help her. That's God's work, Sam. It's the illness that is stealing her mind from her."

Nestled in next to Jack, with his arms protectively around her, she said, "I hope you're right."

"I know I am," he said. He leaned down close to her face, kissing her forehead then his lips brushed hers lightly. He knew he wasn't just falling in love with her anymore. He loved her, plain as day.

* * * *

A few days later, Samantha and Lucy were picking up a few things at the one grocery store in town that allowed Azure to accompany Samantha. Lily insisted on sitting in the back part of the cart; with Azure trotting alongside, they took up an entire width of an aisle. "Lucy, what would you think of working for Running Deer during Christmas vacation?"

Lucy hesitated. "Uh, I might be going someplace."

"Oh," Samantha said. "I didn't realize your family had vacation plans."

Lucy was touched by how disappointed Samantha looked. "Well, uh, it's not with them." She wasn't sure if she should confide in Samantha, but she was about to pop with news that she couldn't even tell her friend Becky. Becky would squeal to her mother then her mother would call Lucy's mother, then Lucy would get grounded.

So far, Samantha had been really cool about stuff. She hadn't gone blabbing to Jack about anything or anyone, like, for example, Chance. She knew that for a solid gold fact, cuz if Samantha had, Jack would've started badgering her with questions, thinking it was his fatherly duty. She leaned over to whisper to Samantha, "Chance thinks his band might have a gig or two in L.A. He wants to head down there for a while and catch that scene."

"What scene?" Samantha asked.

"Just see what blows in that town. He says he doesn't dig it around here any more." She threw a bag of Ruffles Potato Chips into the cart. "So he wants me to come with him."

Lily threw the Ruffles bag right over the side of the cart and giggled. "Lily! Don't throw things overboard!" Lucy picked up the potato chips and put them back in the cart. Lily started to cry so Samantha tore open a box of animal crackers and handed it to Lily to keep her happy while they finished shopping.

"What doesn't Chance like about it here?" Samantha asked.

"He just says there's not enough action going on."

"Um, what exactly does he mean by action?"

Lucy looked sharply at Samantha. When she saw Samantha's face full of worry, she instantly regretted confiding in her. "I haven't decided if I'll go or not yet. Probably not. No big deal."

* * * *

Samantha suddenly had an evanescent feeling of what parenthood must feel like. She tried to remain calm and not feel troubled about Lucy's developing relationship with Chance. She had promised herself to not get in the middle of Lucy, Jack, and Lucy's overly looks-conscious mother. But she knew Chance was trouble, and she knew Lucy was crazy about him. She couldn't quite understand what spell Chance had cast over Lucy and why she had fallen victim to it.

More than a little upset, Samantha tried to focus on the one thing she could control: her shopping list. "This is so frustrating!" she said, scowling. "Why do stores move things around so much? Just as soon as I get an idea of where things are, they re-arrange them."

"Is it hard to be blind?" Lucy asked Samantha, pushing the cart behind her.

Samantha knew Lucy was trying to smooth things over between them. "To be honest, yes. But trying to pretend I wasn't going blind was even harder. I put a lot of energy into the wrong things and missed out on a lot of the right things."

"Like what?"

"Like Azure."

Lucy snorted. "Too bad they don't provide service dogs for teenage blimps."

"*Stop* calling yourself a blimp. Stop *thinking* of yourself like that," Samantha said in a firm tone. "Those are junk thoughts. So you're not a size two. *So what?*! You have a beautiful, healthy body. You need to appreciate what you have."

Lucy's voice switched to a resonant sting that Samantha hadn't heard since the first day she had met her. "Try living with a mother who bribes me by paying me ten bucks for every pound I lose."

Samantha stopped and turned to Lucy. "Maybe your mom will change when she sees that you're happier with yourself."

"And how does that happen? Like *I Dream of Jeannie?* I just blink? Or *Bewitched?* I just snap my fingers and I'm forty pounds lighter?" To accentuate her sarcasm, Lucy snapped her fingers.

"Have you ever thought that maybe the way you've been made is also what makes you unique? Your body is God's idea. He assembled your package."

"Ugh. Then His style and design team needs work." But her voice had softened.

"No, it *doesn't*." Samantha tousled Lucy's hair. "But I do understand what you mean. For a long time, I felt like Kathleen got all of the breaks, and I was sort of leftover DNA. Sort of damaged goods."

"You really don't feel that way now?"

"No, I really don't," she answered sincerely. "From what I'm discovering about God, He doesn't make accidents." She stopped pushing the cart as an insight dawned on her. *Of course! How had I missed that? Lucy has been raised as though she was an accident. No wonder she has such a poor self-image. No wonder she's falling for the first guy who gives her the time of day even if he is a loser.* "Lucy, you were *not* an accident."

"*Right.* Tell that to a mother who was eighteen at the time and caught the eye of a professional football player."

"Those circumstances don't change the fact that it was God who brought you into this world."

"Oh, *sheesh,* you're starting to sound like Jack," Lucy said, back to bitter.

"Well, getting to know your dad has kind of woken up my faith. My faith has been sort of…dormant. Neglected." *Nearly DOA.* "That's one of the things I like about your dad. He challenges the things that *I* think are so important and makes me think about things that are a lot more important. At first it really irritated me. Really, *really* irritated me. But now I love that about him."

They turned the aisle to the produce section. Samantha picked up a grapefruit and smelled it before putting it in a bag.

"Sam? I didn't mean it when I said that Jack had a girl in every port."

Samantha grinned at her. "I know you didn't. I know he doesn't."

"So…you love him?"

"*What?*" Startled, Samantha dropped the grapefruit which got Lily giggling.

"Well, you just said you love the way he challenges you."

"I meant that I appreciated that quality." Now Samantha was obviously flustered. Her cheeks started burning. She felt her watch. "Could you watch Lily a minute? I just want to check on Nonna and Kat at the house."

She found a grocery clerk who took her to the office to let her use the phone. "Hi, Nonna. Everything okay? I should be home soon. No, Nonna, you need to stay put. What errand is so important? Can't you just wait?" Samantha frowned. "Nonna, you need to wait for me to come home. Remember, we shouldn't leave Kat alone. You just wait there until I get back. Wait," she added firmly.

The truth is I don't want to leave Nonna unsupervised. "We'd better hurry," she told Lucy. "Nonna is itchy to go somewhere. *Not* a good sign." She was glad she had asked Lena to pick them up. Lena always arrived early so they wouldn't have to wait long for her.

They checked out quickly, postponing the rest of the list for another day. As they waited outside for Lena, Samantha realized she had left her checkbook on the counter. "I'll get it," Lucy said. "Here, you take my book sack." She went into the store, Lily on her hip, to fetch Samantha's checkbook.

Suddenly, a Volkswagen bus sidled up next to Samantha and slowed. The car door opened, and a man jumped out, grabbing Azure's leash.

"Let go of the dog," he ordered.

Samantha froze. That voice! She recognized that voice. Azure growled. Samantha swung the bag of groceries at him, missing but scattering groceries all over the sidewalk.

"Let go of that dog!" the man shouted, yanking on the leash.

But Samantha wouldn't let go of Azure's harness. She refused to release it as the man struggled with her. She would not let go. She heard Lucy's voice as she came out of the store, screaming at the man to stop. For a split second, he froze then pushed Samantha *and* Azure into the opening of the van, jumped in the front seat, and the car sped off.

Heart pounding like a jackhammer, Samantha sat up slowly, recognizing the voice of the man who grabbed her. It was the same voice of the guy who approached her at the Award Ceremony last August. Like a jolt of electricity, she realized where else she had heard that voice—at the mall with Lucy. The voice belonged to Chance.

* * * *

The smell in the Volkswagen bus was a sour mélange of unwashed bodies, stale beer, and musty tobacco. "Well that's just *brilliant*," scolded the driver of the getaway van. "That's just *great*. Now we've got a *hostage*. We're *kidnappers*. We kidnapped a *blind* lady. That's just *great*." He sounded disgusted.

"She wouldn't let go of that mutt!" Then Chance's voice brightened. "At least we don't have to worry about her identifying us." He laughed hilariously at his own dumb joke.

If she were a cussing woman, Samantha thought, this would be the moment to indulge herself.

"Okay, lady, look, no one's going to get hurt," the driver said to her. "We're just trying to collect a little cash from that grandmother of yours. She owes us a chunk of change, and she keeps forgettin' to pay us."

Samantha's mind started to spin. So *these* were the guys who loaned money to Nonna! *Jack was right,* Samantha realized. *They want their money back.* Trying to sound calm, she said, "I know that my grandmother owes you money. We can work something out. But isn't it a little perilous to kidnap a guide dog? *And* a blind woman? Think about it. It's not worth the risk. You could spend *years* in jail. How old are you anyway? You sound young. Obviously inexperienced. Do you really want to spend the rest of your life in jail?" *Or should I say juvenile hall?*

"I'm old enough," the driver said, insulted.

"This is a new line of work for us," Chance said. "We'll get better at it. Besides you are free to go. Say the word, and we'll stop the van. You can walk away." He turned his face toward Samantha in the back. "But the dog stays here."

"I don't go anywhere without this dog. We are a *package*," said Samantha, who still held on tightly to Azure's harness. "If you just let us both go now, I'll figure out a way to pay you back, and I won't go to the police. You have my word."

"Well, thank you for that," said Chance, "but it was your grandmother's promise to repay us that caused this little pickle in the first place. See, we loaned her money that we had to borrow from Vinny. And Vinny is not a nice guy like us. To be honest, we don't even like dealing with Vinny. He don't believe in giving extensions like we have done to that no good husband of yours."

"My husband?"

"Yeah. The one who set us up with your grandmother and then stopped answering our phone calls."

"You have me confused with my sister."

"What sister?" asked the driver.

"I said 'mister'," Samantha corrected, quickly realizing that they had no idea who was whom. "You should have dealt with my mister."

"Well, we would've if we could find him," said Chance. "And then your grandmother changed her phone number and conveniently *forgot* to give us the new one. So we been having trouble getting hold of you people."

"With Vinny breathin' down our neck," filled in the driver, "Chance got a great idea after seeing you on that TV show. You said that this dog is priceless. And you and this mutt was easy to spot around town. Easier to find than that husband of yours."

They meant Pete! Samantha realized. Since harvest began, Pete had been working in the orchards and was hardly ever in town.

"So we got to brainstorming a way to get our money back from that wily Grandma," Chance continued. "*And* maybe get a little extra to tide us over. Sort of like compounded interest."

Suspicion mounting, Samantha asked, "What does that mean?"

"We're gonna get that dog school place to pay us to get the dog back. And you, too, now, thanks to my brilliant colleague," the driver added.

She heard Chance take a drag on a cigarette, unroll the window, and flick it out.

"Hold on, Nate. I might be able to salvage this," Chance said. "Maybe we can get this here lady to clean out her bank account while we're waiting on the dog school." He grabbed her purse and started fishing for her wallet.

"Good thinking, Chance," Nate said.

Chance dumped the purse's contents on the seat and cursed. "There's no checkbook!"

That's because Lucy has it. "You see, when you're blind, you can't write on checks," she lied. "I mean, how could I write a straight line?"

Nate exhaled loudly. "We shoulda thought of that."

It was at that moment that Samantha knew for sure she was not working with the brightest lights in the harbor. Her anxiety level started markedly dropping. She would be able to figure a way out of this. She knew she could.

"Just great," said Chance sounding disgusted. "Look, we gotta move fast. Let's call the dog school and tell them to drop the money at a specific place." He turned to Samantha. "So how much is that dog actually worth?"

"About $500.00," Samantha answered.

"Wait a minute," said Chance, his voice thick with disappointment, "On that T.V. show, you said it was *priceless*. You said it was *invaluable*."

Samantha's stomach started churning. Chance had been planning this for a while. Her heart broke for Lucy. "So you were just using Lucy? All along?"

Chance snorted a short laugh. "You know the saying. All is fair in love and war." He shifted completely around in the seat to face her. "So exactly how *much* is priceless?"

Samantha turned to face Chance, narrowing her eyes in a way she hoped was menacing. "I meant that you couldn't put a price tag on her. You know how people feel about their dogs. I'm kind of a dog lady."

Chance took that in for a while. "Well, now that we got you, too, we're gonna ask them for at least $20,000. That way we can pay Vinny and have a little extra to float our band for a while in L.A. until we land a record contract. Nate, pull over by that telephone booth. Write this down. Tell them that we need the money in cash by…say five p.m. today…or else."

"Or else what, Chance?"

"Just or else. Let them worry about the 'else'."

"Um, Chance, are you thinking that I'm making the call?"

"Sure," said Chance. "You need the experience."

"But, uh, couldn't I be nailed as a kidnapper?" Nate asked.

Chance sighed, exasperated. "Look, it's a pay phone. No one is going to trace us. We're not *going* to get caught, now are we?" He turned back to Samantha. "Do you know the phone number to the dog school?"

"Yes, I do." She gave them Running Deer's number, grateful for the very first time that Lena answered the phone with an annoying sing-songy "Hello-o-o!" despite the many times Samantha had coached her to identify the company.

"It's a pleasure to work with you," Nate said, writing down the number. "You are a very sensible hostage." He snorted a laugh. "Not that I have much comparison. You're my first."

"I just want to get my dog and me home as soon as possible," responded Samantha in all truthfulness.

213

Nate jumped out of the car to make the phone call. Samantha shot up a silent prayer that Lena would get the message to Pete. She had a fleeting worry that Lena might just put it on top of Samantha's desk, waiting for her to deal with it when she returned. *If I ever return*, she rued.

As soon as Nate returned, they drove out of town to the drop site to wait. Nervously, Chance fiddled with the radio, stumbling on a news station. "In late breaking news, a helpless blind woman and her guide dog were kidnapped today from a local grocery store," exclaimed the announcer in dramatic tones. "A store clerk noticed the blind woman fighting with the kidnapper. He reported that the kidnapper was wearing his auto mechanic's uniform with the name 'Chance' embroidered over his shirt pocket."

Chance swore under his breath.

Sounding worried, Nate added, "That can't be good."

All that Samantha thought about was that the stupid newscaster had called her "helpless."

When they got to the drop site on a dirt road near the outskirts of town, they waited anxiously in the car. "I told her not to come with any cops," said Nate, cracking his knuckles nervously.

Precisely at five, nearly dark, Samantha heard the sound of a car driving up and parking. "It's the dog school van. See any cops?" asked Chance.

"Nope," answered Nate, turning around and looking through the back windows.

"Okay," Chance said, his voice tight and drawn. "It's showtime. Watch the driver carefully. We'll wait until he drops the sack of money and gets back in the van. Then I'll run out and get it. Then we floor it out of here. We gotta do this right, or we're in a heap o' trouble."

As Chance got out of the car to retrieve the sack of money, Samantha could sense how intently Nate was concentrating on watching him. Timing was everything, and she knew this was her moment. Silently, she wiggled over to the van door, carefully unlocked it, then in one swift move, slid it open, and jumped out, pulling Azure, tumbling down into a ditch on the side of the road.

"Hey!" yelled Nate as he realized what she had done.

The CCAB van started its engine and drove toward the Volkswagen bus. She heard Chance scramble back into the van, yelling, "Never mind about them! Let's get out of here!"

The CCAB van went screeching after the kidnappers, leaving Samantha and Azure alone in the ditch to fend for themselves. Samantha sighed, brushed the dirt off of herself, then said, "So, Azure, what do we do now?"

They climbed up the ditch to the drop site, starting out in the direction that Nate, Chance, and the CCAB van headed, hoping to get to the highway. She planned to flag someone down and hitchhike home. The sky, threatening rain all day, opened up and began to pour. Samantha groaned. "Azure, could this day possibly get any worse?" she asked out loud.

She had an odd feeling that it would.

Chapter Fourteen: Homecoming

Picked up by a Good Samaritan who dropped her and Azure off at the police station, Samantha was relieved to find out from the police officers that Lucy and Lily were fine. She called the farmhouse at Running Deer, but there was no answer. She filled out reports and gave the police as much information as she could about the two kidnappers, which, she realized, was quite a lot.

"May I go now?" she asked wearily. "I'd like to get home and get dry." Her clothes were soaked through, and a sad, soggy Azure smelled like the wet dog she was. She thought longingly of a hot shower.

As an officer offered to drive them home, a call came in over the dispatcher that someone from CCAB had located the kidnappers and had them trapped in their Volkswagen bus. "Yes, yes, tell him that we've got her. She's here safe and sound," the officer relayed to the dispatcher. "Yes, yes, the dog, too."

"That must be the same person who met us at the drop site!" said Samantha. "I assumed it was an undercover police officer driving the van."

"Nope. We only got involved after the grocery store manager called us to report the kidnapping. We never knew anything about a drop site or a ransom." He gathered up the reports he had worked on with Samantha and stacked them together. "Want to stay? There's an officer on his way to make the arrests."

"No, but please give the driver a thank you for me. I should get home to my family. They're probably worried to death." Samantha had tried calling the farmhouse a few more times and tried Jack's home phone, but no one picked up at either location. She frowned. *At least, I think they might be worried.* "And my dog doesn't like to miss her dinnertime. She stares at me accusingly until I feed her."

"Uh, ma'am, I hope you don't mind my asking, but if you're blind, how do you know if she's staring at you?" asked the officer.

"Trust me. I know."

As the police car drove up the driveway to Running Deer, Samantha asked the officer if there were any lights on in the farmhouse.

"No ma'am. Dark as a pocket."

Where is everybody? "Thank you for the ride. Thank you for your help."

"Tomorrow we'll need you to come down to identify those two goons. I'll give you a call and drive up to get you."

Samantha breathed in the jasmine scent by her cottage door, grateful for the safety of her home, even if no one was there to welcome her. She tried Jack again, but there was no answer at his house. She dried Azure off, fed her and Spitfire, threw together a sandwich for herself, and took a long, hot shower. Samantha felt a little sorry for herself with such an underwhelming homecoming. When the phone rang, she rushed to answer it.

"Miss Christiansen? Alice Lawton here. Bank manager. I just heard on the news that you've been found. I'm very glad to hear that. Congratulations on getting out of a terrible situation. A terrible plight." She clucked her tongue in that disapproving way. "Imagine kidnapping a guide dog. What kind of a human being could do such a thing?"

"They were just stupid kids," Samantha answered. "And they've been caught." She got the impression that Alice Lawton hadn't called to congratulate her. "Is something wrong?"

She sounded hesitant, rare for Miss Lawton. "I have to let you know some serious news. I'm sorry to have to tell you this. I'm afraid your covenants have been broken. It's bank policy to call in that loan. You have ten business days to settle the account. I was able to get you that, at least."

This shock hit her like a hammer. "*What? Why?* How did this happen?"

"Your grandmother withdrew cash from an account that had been…well…inactive."

217

"How? How could that *possibly* have happened? I had taken her signature off of the business accounts. You helped me do it."

"This wasn't a business account. It was a second mortgage loan that your grandfather had opened nearly ten years ago but never actually used. Your grandmother's name is on the account. So is yours. Your grandfather had added your name to it before he died. That's why this has become a conflict. You were the one who broke the covenants. Not your grandmother. *You* were not supposed to have any other loans."

Samantha gripped her elbows, hugging herself to stifle a sudden chill. "I forgot," she said finally, forcing the words past the knot in her throat. "I forgot all about that loan." Her grandfather had set it up one year during a drought. She remembered the argument—her grandmother had insisted that drought was good for olives, and her grandfather told her she was crazy. Nonna was right. It was a bumper crop that year, and they didn't need that second mortgage, after all. But her grandfather never closed the loan. Heat ran down the back of her neck as she realized the enormity of the situation.

"Well, the account falls under our residential loans not commercial loans. And, it was a new loan officer who worked with your grandmother. That's why we didn't catch the problem until the loan had been activated. Believe me, Miss Christiansen, if I could've caught it ahead of time, I would've warned you."

A tight sensation in her stomach crescendoed. "How much? How much did she take?"

"The full amount of the loan. $50,000."

She felt her heart skip a beat. "Is there any way to stop payment?"

"I'm afraid not. She had the money wired out so it's already gone."

"Where did the money go? Where did she send it?" *Please, please. Not to some vague Western Union address.*

"To a title company. A local one."

A title company? For property? Perplexed, Samantha asked, "How much money do you need by Friday?"

"$50,000."

218

"What?" Samantha asked incredulously. She had to sit down.

"Yes. The full amount of that loan you took out for the new mill. I'm sorry, Miss Christiansen. Nothing personal. Business is business. It's just bank policy."

Samantha exhaled slowly. "Could you do one thing for me? Could you please freeze our accounts, immediately, all of them, so no more money can be withdrawn?"

"Not a problem. That I can do for you. Consider it done." She paused. "I don't enjoy doing this, I hope you know."

Samantha didn't respond.

"If you had any other means of restoring the loan, we might be able to work something out—"

"Thank you, Miss Lawton, but we're tapped out." Samantha hung up the phone, tried to take a few deep breaths, and called Nonna. No answer.

Samantha went over to the farmhouse and found Kathleen in bed, sound asleep. "Kat, wake up. Get up! Something's happened. I need your help."

But Kathleen could barely rouse herself. Slowly, she raised an elbow to pull herself up, then slipped back down on the bed. Shocked at how lethargic Kathleen had become, Samantha forgot about the problems of Running Deer, forgot about being kidnapped, and worried only about Kathleen's condition. She tried to call Pete at the office, but no one answered. *Oh God, please help*, she prayed. She didn't know what to do next.

Just then, the house phone rang. It was Kathleen's doctor. "Kathleen?"

"No, this is Samantha."

"Oh. You sound just like your sister. I hadn't heard from her this week, and I just wanted to make sure she had turned the corner."

"No! She's *worse*. She isn't even able to sit up in bed for more than a few minutes."

Dr. Utley exhaled loudly. "Sam, I think we should consider hospitalizing her. I mean, you can only do so much, being…"

"Blind."

"Well, yes. You've got a lot to deal with. I know her husband has been busy, too. Maybe Kathleen would be better off in a hospital setting."

She knew he meant a psychiatric ward. "No. Please. Give us a few more days. I can take care of her. I'll just work harder. I'll get her up."

"Well, listen, I'm going to drop by in a short while. I'm leaving the office now and driving past Running Deer to get home."

Twenty minutes later, Dr. Utley stopped by. After checking on Kathleen, he prescribed medication for her and gave Samantha stern orders. "She has a clinical depression. It's a reaction to the miscarriage, but it's gotten worse than I had anticipated. No more letting her sleep all day. She has to get up. She has to eat. She has to get some exercise, even if it's just a short walk to the end of the driveway. And I don't want her left alone. My nurse tried calling a couple of times this afternoon, and there was no answer. Listen, your sister *has* to be a priority." As he walked to the door, he said, "And just *where* is her husband?"

Where were Pete and Lily? Where was Nonna? Where were Jack and Lucy? And what has happened to my business? All Samantha really wanted to do was sit down and have a good cry. Instead, she only shrugged her shoulders and meekly said, "Pete is probably out in the orchards. This is the busiest time of year for us."

How could this doctor walk in and make her feel so bad? So guilty?

Because I've always felt so responsible for Kathleen. With a flash of insight, she realized Jack was right. *Again.* Her family *was* dependent on her.

"And Sam, I have to warn you, this is going to take time. It might be as long as six weeks before you see significant improvement." He gave her sample pills for Kathleen and wrote out a prescription for Samantha to get filled. "It's important she takes these like clock-work."

The doctor drove away as Pete pulled up the driveway in the truck with Lily. He hopped out and ran over to greet Samantha, gripping her by the shoulders. "Was that the doctor?

Are you okay? Did those guys hurt you at all?" He calmed down as he realized she was unharmed. "What a crazy afternoon! I just came from Lucy's house after picking up Lily. Met Lucy's mom. Man, she's a piece of work." He whistled. "When Lena brought me your phone message and I got it to…wait a minute…was the doctor here for Kat?" he asked, interrupting himself, worried.

"Pete—he said Kat is clinically depressed." Samantha gently picked up a sleeping Lily out of the car and hugged her close. "The doctor is threatening to hospitalize her if we leave her alone at all. He started her on medication. She needs someone here constantly."

Just then, Nonna pulled up in her Buick Riviera.

"*Who* are those people with her?" Pete murmured to himself.

"What people? Do you recognize them?"

"There's a man and a woman…oh…my…gosh…" Pete stopped abruptly.

The woman jumped out of the car and called out, "Samantha! Pete! It's us! Mother and Daddy! Home for good!"

* * * *

As they sat down at the kitchen table in the farmhouse, Samantha's parents explained that they had retired from the mission field. "We have a big surprise!" said Samantha's mother. "We bought the Mitchell's house, right next door to Running Deer!"

"*What?*" Samantha asked in disbelief. "How?" She knew they didn't have two spare nickels to rub together.

"Did you know that you can wire money, from one bank to another, and buy a house?! It's a miracle," her mother clapped her hands together in delight.

"But *where* did you get that kind of money?"

"Nonna!" explained her father. "Months ago, she wrote to say she had come across a bit of extra money and wanted to do this."

Some puzzle pieces floating in Samantha's mind started to find their proper place.

"Sam, you look upset," noted her mother.

221

"Lily's favorite blanket is over at my cottage. She'll need it to get to sleep. I'll be right back."

The truth was that Samantha desperately needed fresh air. As she walked over to the cottage, she stopped. Running Deer's newest financial disaster suddenly made sense, if anyone could call it 'sense.' She felt as if she was draining the sea with a pail. "So, God, talk," she said, out loud, lifting her head to face the black sky. "If you're there, I'm listening. Tell me what you want from me."

It wasn't that Samantha didn't believe in God. She had always believed in God; she just didn't think God believed in her.

But the heavens were silent. No thundering voice responded to her question. The only sound came from an owl overhead in a tree; it hooted once, then twice. Samantha listened patiently for any kind of sign, but nothing came.

She wasn't sure what she expected God to say or do, but she expected *something*. A sudden river of cool wind washed over her face, giving her a chill. "Yeah. That's what I thought." Disappointed, she took a deep breath and went into the cottage.

After finding Lily's blanket, Samantha washed her face and went back over to the farmhouse to help Pete put fresh sheets on the bed in the guest room. Finally, she had a chance to tell him privately about the conversation with the bank today.

"*What*?" Pete fairly thundered the word, outraged. "We're bottling the best olive oil we've ever had. Can't the bank give us some time? Just until Christmas!"

"Apparently not. We've lost our good standing. And please lower your voice. I don't want my parents to hear this. We owe the bank $50,000. Within ten business days," she added miserably.

"Let's tell your folks about this. Maybe they'll give up the Mitchell property."

No, they wouldn't. They're receivers not givers. "There's got to be another solution."

"Look, Sam. I know you and Kat have problems with your folks. But at least they're here. Maybe it'll be different this time."

222

Samantha *wanted* to believe that. But she had needed her parents before, and they never failed to disappoint. As she slipped a pillow into a pillowcase, her mind drifted back to their college graduation day. Her parents happened to be in California on furlough but had missed the ceremony because they had an opportunity to raise funds. "You can understand this, girls," her mother explained over the phone. "It's a unique chance for us to build a relationship with an organization that wants to support our work."

Kathleen had pleaded with her, trying to change her mother's mind. "But, Mom, Sam is receiving the highest honors!"

"Nonna will take lots of pictures," her mother added, as if that would suffice.

Ironic, Samantha remembered thinking at the time. And still thought. *My parents were building relationships with others while dismantling the one they had with their daughters.*

"Why can't you just *talk* to your parents about the house?" Pete asked, breaking her muse.

"I just...can't!"

"Why *not?*"

"My folks left us to figure things out on our own; I'm not going to ask them for help now."

"So you will let this company go *under* because you have to prove something to your parents?" He turned and stomped away, closing the guest bedroom door with a decided bang as he muttered about stubborn Swedes.

Later, when Samantha was back in her cottage getting ready for bed, her telephone rang.

Jack's voice was husky with emotion. "Samantha! Are you all right? Where have you been? Why haven't you answered your phone?"

Just hearing the concern in his voice made her smile. It felt so good to have someone worry about her. "I was over in the farmhouse." Five minutes ago, if anyone had told her that she'd find anything to smile about tonight, she'd have said they were crazy. "Where are *you?*" she asked.

"I'm sorry. I couldn't...there was something I had to do..." he sputtered.

"Are you at home?" She heard a lot of voices in the background and the click-clack of a typewriter. "You sound like you're in an office." Kind of like the sounds in the police station.

"Uh, sort of. You're all right, aren't you? And Azure?"

She noticed that he neatly avoided her question. "I'm fine. But, Jack, there's something you need to know."

Jack inhaled and exhaled. "If it's about Chance, I already know."

"How could you possibly know?"

"Look, it's late, and I can tell you're tired. I need to go, too. Get some sleep. We can talk tomorrow."

She hung up, wondering where he was that could be so important, but she was too tired to dwell on it. She flopped on her bed and tried to push the troubling day out of her mind.

The next morning, Samantha was awakened early by the shrilling ring of the phone, rousing her out of a deep sleep. "Um, hello?" she mumbled in her pre-coffee voice.

"Officer Brent here. We need you to come down to the station and identify these guys so we can book 'em. An officer will be up to get you in an hour."

She was suddenly wide awake. Samantha quickly got ready, fed Azure, turned Spitfire into the corral, and guiltily threw hay into the corral for his breakfast.

The phone rang again. "Sam? It's Jack. Would you mind if I run up to your cottage now?"

"I'll get the coffee pot started," Samantha said, smiling.

* * * *

As soon as Jack turned up the gravel lane to Running Deer, he saw Samantha outside, waiting for him. He broke into a run and grabbed her for a crushing hug as he reached her. He stepped back and looked her over, just to make sure she was unharmed. He'd been worried sick about her. Then he hugged her again.

"Smells good in here!" he exclaimed, breathing in the coffee-scented warm air as they walked into the cottage, arm in arm. He pulled off his jacket. "Lucy offered to skip school today on your behalf, but I told her 'no.'"

Samantha smiled then her smile quickly faded. "Have you told her about Chance?"

Jack groaned. "Not yet. I will. I just…don't want to…ruin the moment."

"What moment?"

He still couldn't believe it. "When Lucy called me in a panic from the supermarket, guess what she called me?"

Samantha tilted her head curiously. "What?"

"Dad. She called me 'Dad'," he beamed proudly. "Twice." He still couldn't believe he had heard *that* word come out of Lucy's mouth.

Grinning, Samantha poured him a cup of coffee. "But you will tell her about Chance soon, right?"

"Yes. Today. Not looking forward to it, though." He took a sip of the coffee and reached for Samantha's hand. "You're sure you're okay? You look tired."

"I am tired. I didn't sleep well." She gave him a quick rundown of what occurred last night with Kathleen and with the bank loan. "What about you? Where *were* you last night?"

Just then, a police car arrived to take Samantha downtown. "Can you come with me?" she asked.

He glanced at his watch. Relieved, he said, "Can't. I'm late for work."

* * * *

At the station, Officer Brent explained that they had confiscated some incriminating evidence from the Volkswagen bus. "There were drugs. And there's a newspaper article with your by-line about some blind athletes. They had circled a sentence that says the worth of a service dog is over $5,000."

Samantha's hands flew to her face; she thought she might get sick. To think she had provided information to inspire them to kidnap Azure! Then another thought bounced into her head. "You said there were drugs in the car. What kind? Marijuana?"

"That. And hashish."

"What's hashish?"

"A very potent type of marijuana."

Samantha's fists clenched. She *knew* Chance was doing drugs. Just how involved had Lucy gotten with him?

The officer interrupted the frantic cycle of worry in her mind. "Ma'am, a group of men are lined up behind a one-way mirror. You need to point out which two tried to kidnap your dog."

Samantha tried not to look exasperated. "Uh, officer, I really can't point them out to you. I'm blind."

Officer Brent smacked the palm of his hand against his forehead like he was trying to hit a mosquito. "I'm sorry. I should have thought of that. It's just that you don't—"

"I know, I know. I don't look blind." *I wish I had a dollar for each time someone made that remark. I could pay off Running Deer's loan.* "How about if each one makes a statement and I'll try to identify their voices?"

"Good thinking. Can you remember something specific that they said?"

Samantha thought for a moment. "The driver said, 'Lady, you are a sensible hostage'. And the one who tried to take Azure told me to 'hand over the dog!'"

The officer had the men in the line-up repeat those phrases. Samantha picked out Chance right away. When Nate repeated the phrase, he loudly objected, "That ain't what I told her!"

There was a stunned silence as he realized he had just incriminated himself. Then the other men in the line up howled with laughter. "I thought I'd seen everything," murmured the officer. "Well, anyway, you picked the same two guys as the ones the CCAB driver cornered last night. Helps build the case."

After an officer dropped Samantha back at home, she stopped in at the farmhouse. She found Nonna feeding Lily applesauce in the kitchen. Her parents were still asleep, exhausted from jet lag.

Good. I'm not in the mood to deal them right now.

She woke Kathleen up and made her take a shower, eat something, swallow her medication, and walk down the driveway to the mailbox and back again to the farmhouse. Then she helped Kathleen head back upstairs, called Nonna's doctor, and set up an appointment. Finally, she made a cup of peppermint tea for Nonna.

"I made a doctor's appointment for you. Just for a check-up," Samantha told her as she handed her the tea. She reached down and picked up Lily, who had crawled up to her and was clinging to her leg like a sock just out of the dryer.

Nonna sipped on her tea, not responding.

Gently, Samantha added, "You seem a little confused lately."

Nonna put down her tea. "I was just thinking the same thing about you!"

Samantha's jaw dropped. "Me? Me?! Do you have any idea of how many problems we're facing?"

Nonna stood up and reached her arms around Samantha and Lily for a hug. "Well, no wonder you're confused. I know it will all work out, Sammy. You'll do the right thing. You always do."

Samantha nearly cried. *Not this time, Nonna. I don't even know what to do.*

* * * *

As Samantha's key turned in her lock to her cottage, she heard the phone ring and hurried inside to get it.

"Samantha? Ted Collins with California Canine Academy for the Blind. Heard about your big day yesterday. You okay? Good? Good! So…Channel Two wants to do a follow-up story on this, and they're sending a crew over to your house right now for an interview."

"Right *now?*" Samantha asked, her hand automatically going to her hair, wondering what it looked like. She had planned to get to the office this morning to try to rescue her company.

"On their way. I was sure you wouldn't mind. I'll come, too."

Samantha barely got a comb through her hair and fresh lipstick applied when she heard the TV van pull up with Mr. Collin's car right hustling up right behind it.

She could hardly believe it! *This man has serious pull in this town.*

"Hello, Samantha," called out Mr. Collins. "You remember Anita Perez. She did your interview at CCAB a few months ago."

227

Samantha shook hands with Anita Perez and the cameraman as Mr. Collins walked around, sizing up the best place for the interview.

"Shall we do the interview inside? It's starting to rain."

Samantha nodded, admiring how Mr. Collins worked a group of people so skillfully.

Mr. Collins stopped abruptly when he walked into the cottage. "Hmmm....this is a very little house," he said. "Very, very little. Whoa. A lot of pink."

"Well, not *that* much pink," Samantha said, frowning, as the cameraman started rolling the film.

As Anita Perez expertly began the interview, she asked Samantha questions to explain the sequence of events of the kidnapping experience. Samantha answered questions as if she knew what to anticipate. But then Anita brought up a piece of information about the kidnapping unknown to Samantha, something that stunned her, caused her to stammer and stutter, to lose her train of thought. So much so that they had to do a re-take. And another. And another.

* * * *

Later that afternoon, Samantha took Nonna for a doctor's appointment. After the nurse took Nonna down the hall to get some blood drawn, the doctor swiveled in his chair, facing Samantha. "We'll need to run more tests," he paused, "but I want to prepare you for the possibility of senility."

"Senility?" asked Samantha.

"Some form of dementia. Seems like the family would have noticed symptoms for a while now. Any chance that you've been missing signs of it?"

"An excellent chance," said Samantha dolefully. "My family seems particularly fond of denial."

When she returned home, Samantha knew she should be heading down to the office, but she just couldn't make herself go there. Instead, she did something she hadn't done in months. She changed into her riding clothes, groomed and tacked up Spitfire, opened up the corral gate, and led Spitfire out. Just as she lifted one leg into the stirrup to climb up on him, her mother ran out of the farmhouse.

228

"Samantha! You *can't* be serious! I saw you put the saddle on that horse, but I thought you were going to ride in the corral. You *can't* be thinking that you're going out on the property!"

"Sure I can." Samantha lifted herself up on to Spitfire, adjusted the stirrups, and gathered the reins. "I've done it for years."

"But Samantha! You might get hurt! You *can't* go! Think of the risk! You'll hit your head on a branch!"

"I've got a riding helmet on. Spitfire is pretty good with overhanging branches, too." She pulled Spitfire's reins around to go.

"But you'll get lost!"

"No, I won't," Samantha said, irritation rising. "Like I said, I've done this for years." She didn't add that she hadn't actually ridden Spitfire out of the ring *in* years. As she gently kicked her heels, Spitfire picked up his pace and trotted away to their well-loved trail. His ears were forward, his tail was up, as if he, too, shared Samantha's happiness with their brief escape.

As Spitfire stretched his neck out to climb up a hill, Samantha leaned forward in the saddle and pondered her mother's reaction to her riding.

Almost as though she had just met her mother for the first time, Samantha suddenly had an evanescent insight into a peculiar contradiction. Even though her mother had lived in a remote part of a Third World country, faced all kinds of personal challenges, hardships and sacrifices, she was *afraid* of Samantha's blindness.

Samantha wondered what she might have been like had her grandmother not carried her through those teen years—as her vision deteriorated. Had she remained in Papua New Guinea with her mother's anxious overprotection, she might have grown up afraid of everything.

She knew herself well enough to know she had that tendency. Especially the last few years. The last few months! She was afraid of going to New York. Afraid of dogs. Even afraid of falling in love.

Maybe Dr. Sommers is right. Maybe, just maybe, God *had* been alongside her all of the time, even providentially sending her to her grandmother right when she needed her the most.

A little piece of resentment that she held toward her mother dissolved, like a chunk dropping off of a thick block of ice.

* * * *

Later that afternoon, Lucy frantically bicycled to Samantha's cottage. She exhaled a sigh of relief when she saw Samantha through the kitchen window. She didn't know where else to go or who else to turn to. She knocked on the door, shivering. When Samantha opened it, Lucy said quietly, "Sam? I need help. I'm...I'm in trouble." Then she rushed into Samantha's arms, sobbing.

Stroking her hair and patting her back, Samantha said softly, "So Jack told you?"

Lucy pulled back. "No. The cops called my mom. They found my book sack in his car. With drugs in it! Chance stashed his drugs in it before the police arrived. He told them the drugs were mine." She started to weep all over again. "But that's not true, Sam! I had no idea!"

"Did you tell the police that?"

Lucy nodded. "They said that I might have to testify at the trial."

"I'll back you up. I know the book sack didn't have drugs in it."

Lucy got up and went to the bathroom to find a box of tissues. She blew her nose and wiped her eyes then plopped down on the sofa. "Chance never cared about me! He never meant any of it. He was just trying to find out about your dog and your grandmother!" She choked out the words in big, gulpy breaths. "He was always asking me questions about places you like to go in town. I thought he was just interested in blind people. Even yesterday, Chance had asked me where we would be in the afternoon," she took a deep breath, "and I told him we would be at the grocery store. He knew you would be there! He set me up."

She pulled more tissues out of the box and wiped her eyes. She looked at Samantha to see if she believed her. "Sam, I never would do anything to hurt you or Azure or your family."

"Of course I know that. Don't even worry, Lucy." Samantha bit the corner of her lip. "Lucy, did he introduce you to drugs?"

How did she know? Oh, I feel like I'm going to puke. "No! Well, I mean…he tried. Once, I smoked some dope." She glanced at Samantha but was amazed that she didn't seem horrified. Then she realized why: Samantha had already guessed. "But I didn't like it! Chance said it's better than drinking because you don't get a hangover, but I felt sick after, and my throat felt so raw…oh, my mom is going to kill me." She blew her nose into a tissue. "Chance is just…he's…just a jerk. I don't know how I could have been so stupid. It's just that…he made me…feel…" her voice drizzled off.

"Special?"

How did you know? Lucy's eyes filled up with tears.

"Lucy, you *are* special. You don't need a guy to make you feel that way."

Samantha's kindness made her feel worse, as if she believed Lucy to be a better person than who she really was. That started her tears flowing all over again.

Afterwards, Samantha and Azure and Lucy waited patiently on Jack's front steps for him to return from work. Next to Samantha was a big basket filled with the very best bottles of Tuscan extra virgin olive oil from Running Deer Ranch. She explained to Lucy that she had promised a gift for the man who had driven the CCAB van on a wild chase, trapped the kidnappers' car in a dead end street, and didn't budge until the police arrived to arrest them. During the interview with Anita Perez, Samantha learned who that man was.

"And that was *Jack*?" Lucy asked in disbelief. *Jack never drove anywhere!* "Jack *drove*? He actually drove a car to rescue you?" She started sobbing all over again.

Samantha said she was glad she had thought to grab a fresh box of tissues before leaving the house. "Lucy, you cry like a fountain," she told her, amazed, handing her a tissue.

* * * *

A few hours later, Samantha left Lucy at Jack's house. Jack sounded a little panicky when she said she had to go. "But what do I do if she starts bawling again?" he whispered to her as he helped her on with her coat. "I hate it when women cry. I never know what to do."

"I really don't think she has a drop of water left in her body; she's cried it all out. But if she does start up again, just pat her on the back and hand her tissues," Samantha answered as she gave him a quick kiss goodbye.

She was eager to go, relieved to hand Lucy over to her father. She wasn't sure she was cut out for this parenting gig, especially with a teenager. Especially with a teenager who has a delinquent boyfriend. *This was hard work!* She felt exhausted and was getting ready for bed when the phone rang. She almost didn't answer, it but she thought it might be Jack.

"Miss Christiansen? My name is Vinny. I'm an acquaintance of your grandmother's." Vinny's voice was raspy, smoky, like he had puffed on one too many cigars.

Samantha's mouth went dry. "How did you get my home phone number?" she asked accusingly, trying to keep her voice from quivering.

"Your very helpful secretary gave it to me."

Tomorrow morning, fire Lena!

"I heard that my collection agents have been…temporarily detained…but you need to know that your grandmother's loan is not going away. I'll call you soon to arrange a meeting. Let's keep this conversation just between you and me. We don't want anything to happen to that sweet little old lady, now do we?" Click.

Samantha shrank from the phone. Her nerve endings sizzled and zinged all over her body. Running Deer's problems just took a back shelf to this one.

Samantha breathed deeply and tried to clear her mind. She didn't know *what* she was going to do. And the one person, whom she had so often turned to for help, whom she counted on more than anyone in the world for more than twenty years, couldn't help her anymore.

Chapter Fifteen: **The Pool Hall**

The next morning, Samantha went over to the farmhouse to check on Kathleen before heading down to the office. Her mother was in the kitchen opening a can of Pringles potato chips. "Oh, hi," Samantha said flatly. "How's the jet lag?"

Her mother came over to give her a hug. "Oh, I haven't really slept well yet. I'm concerned about Kat. And now Nonna with the news you gave us yesterday." She poured the chips out on a plate. "Have you ever seen anything like these potato chips?"

"They've been out a couple of years," Samantha answered, trying hard not to roll her eyes. "Well, Kat is getting help now. And Nonna will get some answers later this week after the doctor runs more tests."

"Somehow, I just knew that Dad and I needed to be here. A mother's intuition. And not a minute too soon. How could you possibly manage all of this alone? You really needed us to be here."

Right. Again, Samantha tried not to roll her eyes. "I'll go down to the office then."

"Oh Sam, before you go, help me with this telephone."

"What do you mean?"

"Where's the dial?"

Samantha picked up the receiver and turned it over. "It's called a Princess phone. No dial anymore. We use push buttons." Now she did roll her eyes. "I *really* need to go." Pointedly, she added, "You should ask Nonna to explain all of these things. She's very adept with modern gadgets." *At least she used to be.* Samantha turned to head out the door.

"Sam, wait, taste this!" She handed Samantha a glass.

Samantha sniffed it. "It's Tang, Mom."

"Right on the label, it says it's what the astronauts drink!"

She handed her mother back the glass. "I really, really need to go." She buttoned up her coat before her mother could find another new or improved consumer product. "Well, then, as long as you've got Kat and Lily covered, I'm going to go down to the office. I have a lot to get caught up on." She threw her purse over her shoulder. "You'll make sure Kat takes her medication?"

Her mother hesitated.

Something in that hesitation tripped a hammer in Samantha's mind. "The anti-depressants. Kat started them a few days ago. "You're making sure she takes them, right? Like clockwork, the doctor said." When her mother still didn't answer, realization dawned on Samantha. She tried to catch her breath. "*What* have you done?" she accused her mother in a cold, staccato beat.

Her mother put her hands on Samantha's shoulders. "Dad and I had a long talk the other day. We feel that this is a spiritual battle for Kathleen. She needs to confront this head-on. With faith. And prayer. And—"

Samantha remembered a summer when she was only ten years old when the family was on furlough to the United States. Her parents had taken her to hear faith healer Kathryn Kuhlman. "If you just have enough faith," she remembered her parents telling her afterwards, imploring her, "you will be healed." She tried to have enough faith. She prayed every day. She didn't want to disappoint God. Or her parents. Both, really. But still, her vision kept deteriorating. So did her belief that God heard her prayers.

"Sam?" her mother asked, snapping her back to the present. "What's wrong?"

She shook off her mother's grip. She was so angry she wanted to scream at her mother and tell her to go catch the next plane, or boat, or canoe, back to Papua New Guinea. She knew that she would never be able to change her parents' mind once it was made up. She spun around and left the house, furious, deciding she would call that bossy Dr. Utley directly and let him deal with her parents.

* * * *

After a battery of diagnostic tests for Nonna, the doctor sat at his desk, facing Samantha and her father with the findings. "We can't really tell until an autopsy, but it's looking like Alzheimer's disease," he announced with finality.

234

"But we don't have that in our family," objected her father.

"Actually, it's pretty common in the elderly."

"I thought dementia caused people to lose their memory," Samantha said. "She has some short-term memory loss, but a bigger concern is her poor judgment which is not typical for her. And she is vulnerable to…" she suddenly remembered that her father had yet to be informed about the sweepstakes scams, "…to people who can confuse her."

"Well, dementia is a progressive brain disorder that gradually destroys a person's memory and ability to learn, reason, make judgments, communicate, and carry out daily activities. As the disease progresses, she may also experience changes in personality and behavior," explained the doctor.

"Is there any cure?" asked Samantha hopefully.

"Not yet, but new treatments are on the horizon. They're making breakthroughs all the time. It won't be long until we have this licked. And effective care and support can improve the quality of life."

"How long can we expect her to…?" her father's voice trailed off.

"To live?"

I'm glad Dad asked that. I couldn't. Besides Nonna is his mother.

The doctor sighed. "Well, a patient usually lives an average of eight years or more from the onset of symptoms. Your mother is in very good physical condition, so that has probably helped to slowdown the progression of the disease." He paused, letting Samantha and her father take in this information.

"But there are days when she seems perfectly fine," Samantha said, clinging to a last, tiny thread of hope.

"It's a funny thing. It's almost like electricity that dims a little and then gets brighter, then dims again. The important thing is to savor those days when she seems like her old self. Cherish them. They're not going to last," the doctor said grimly.

On the car ride back to the farmhouse, Samantha's father said, "Guess it's a good thing you and Kat already moved Nonna into Shady Acres."

"She moved herself." It occurred to Samantha that Nonna might have realized something was wrong. Maybe *that* was why there was such an abrupt decision to move. *That would be just like Nonna.*

* * * *

Later that day in the office, after Lena had gone home, Samantha told Pete she needed to pay back Nonna's loan to the loan shark.

"What?! They tried to kidnap Azure!"

"I know. But sooner or later, it's going to be a problem for Nonna. It's not going to go away." She took a deep breath, as if a decision had been made. "So I'm going to tap into my savings." That was only partially true. Samantha had been saving money for as long as she could remember, but that was only a part of the full amount. Her grandfather had given her savings bonds every year on her birthday until the year he died. She had never cashed them in like Kat had. Samantha had planned to use those bonds as retirement income when she grew old. Maybe then, she would write her novel.

"What a minute, Sam. Didn't that Alice Lawton say that if you could find some cash, she would try and stop calling in the loan?"

Samantha nodded.

"Then let's use your savings to hold off on bankruptcy. That would buy us time so we can figure out a way to help Nonna."

Samantha didn't want to tell Pete about the threatening call from Vinny; she was concerned he would tell everyone and that would only make it worse for Nonna. "I thought of that, but we need to take care of Nonna first. I'm sorry."

Pete was silent for a moment. "Then I should help. I'm the one who got her in this mess to begin with."

"No, you didn't. Not intentionally. You have a family to consider. I have time to earn the money back. My finances aren't expansive, but I can swing it." *Besides, you don't have any savings.* Pete and Kathleen lived paycheck to paycheck, trusting that the future would take care of itself. That and they never thought they would grow old.

"Seems like there's got to be a way to take care of both. The business and Nonna."

"Maybe," she said. "There are still a few days to go." But she didn't hold out any hope.

The next morning, Samantha dressed up in her most business-like suit, wore stern looking boots, put her hair in a no-nonsense bun, and put on a heavy dark wool dress coat. She wanted to be taken seriously for this errand. She had decided not to *wait* for Vinny's next phone call.

And so she forged ahead, a woman on a mission.

Outside of Vinny's Pool Hall, Samantha leaned against the wall and tried to ignore the carbonation brewing in the bottom of her stomach. She took a deep breath and said to Azure, "Okay, work with me on this, girl." Azure wagged her tail sympathetically. The smell of stale beer inside the pool hall nearly made Samantha gag. She asked the bartender if he knew where to find a man named "Vinny."

The bartender lowered his voice and asked her, "Ma'am, you sure it's Vinny you want?"

Samantha gave a terse nod. As the bartender went to get Vinny, Samantha sat on a plastic red leather stool. Unsure of where to put her hands because the top of the bar was sticky, she finally decided to keep them on her lap. Her foot tapped nervously.

"You lookin' for me?" asked a gravelly voice that Samantha recognized from the phone call.

"Vinny?"

"Yeah. Would you like to go somewhere to talk in private?" he asked, sounding smarmy.

"No, I'd prefer to stay right here," she answered. She tried to sound bold, breezy, confident, but her lungs froze, and her heart skipped a beat.

Vinny leaned against the barstool next to her. "Somethin' I can do for you?"

She opened up her briefcase and pulled out a file.

"Ah, geez, a lawyer?"

Samantha said, not answering, trying to look as officious as possible. "Now, Mr. Vinny, I'll get right to the point. I understand that an elderly woman, known as Anna Christiansen, borrowed money from those two...ahem...boys...and that they, in turned, borrowed money from you."

"Got that straight, lady. And when those two kids get out of the slammer, it's gonna be cement shoes for them."

"How much?"

"Huh?"

"How much did this elderly woman borrow from you?"

"And just who's doing the askin'?" he asked.

"I'm acting on behalf of this woman. Just answer my question, Mr. Vinny."

"In the neighborhood of $50,000."

"My records state she currently owes you $15,000."

"But that's just the original amount. It doesn't take into consideration my interest rates. And my fees. And my personal aggravation. That old lady has been a bad loan risk."

"I see," Samantha said, tapping her chin with her finger. "Would you mind showing me your license?"

"What license? My driver's license?" he asked as he reached for his wallet.

"No, no. Goodness, no. Your *lending* license," she said, sounding out the words very carefully, using her professorial voice. "Any financial lender in the state of California is required to have a license so that they are a *licensed lender*. Surely you're aware of that. It's part of the regulations that govern the financial industry. It would be most unfortunate if you were operating a lending service illegally."

"What's so unfortunate about that?"

"Well, when a lender operates illegally, it falls under the criminal category of being a 'loanshark.' By providing unofficial sources of money, loans sharks have a nasty habit of charging their clients exorbitant interest rates and using threats of violence...well...come to think of it...much like that remark you made about your two colleagues finding themselves in *'cement shoes'* when they get out of the *'slammer'*."

Vinny stood up and leaned close to Samantha, so close she could smell his sour breath. "Now look, lady—"

As if on cue, Azure stood up, hackled, and growled a throaty growl. Even Samantha was surprised by Azure's bravado, though she tried not to show it.

"Please sit down, Mr. Vinny. We're not quite done with our interview."

Vinny sat down obediently. "I never agreed to no interview."

"Now, Mr. Vinny," Samantha ignored his protest. "Anna Christiansen is prepared to repay you the $15,000 that she owes you, in full, and you, in turn, will leave this woman alone. You are not to have *any* contact with Mrs. Christiansen, at any time. Ever. Or—"

"Or what?" interrupted Vinny.

"Or…I will be forced to share the non-licensing information that I have uncovered about you with the local law enforcement. They, in turn, will notify the FBI," Samantha said, trying to sound like Detective Joe Friday from *Dragnet*.

Vinny was silent.

"Now, on the other hand, if you had lent Mrs. Christiansen money as a favor, kind of an 'all in the family' type of favor…in which you didn't charge her the interest on the loan…" Samantha slowed down, letting Vinny catch her meaning.

"You got the $15,000?" he asked, peering into her briefcase.

"If I give you the money, this loan would be considered paid in full."

She heard him inhale and exhale, heavily through his nostrils, as he debated his options. Finally, he said, "Yeah, sure."

"Do I have your word on that, Mr. Vinny? Because I heard you're not a nice person." As soon as the words left Samantha's mouth, she regretted them.

Vinny stiffened on the stool. "Yeah, yeah. You got my word."

Samantha could tell that something just went wrong. *I'd better get out of here.* She reached into her briefcase, took out an envelope with a cashier's check for $15,000, and handed it to Vinny.

"Thank you, Mr. Vinny. And good-bye." Samantha snapped her briefcase shut, stood up, told Azure "Let's go," and left, holding her head high, walking briskly out of the pool hall.

As soon as Samantha was outside, she took a deep breath, colossally relieved. She walked quickly up the street, stopping only to listen for traffic before crossing the street. Then she heard Vinny call her name from the fence gate of the back of his pool hall. She turned around as an ominous foreboding squeezed her breath.

"Hey, lady!" Vinny opened the gate. "You can tell your grandmother that *now* her interest is paid up." He unhooked the leash of a snarling and hackling Doberman Pinscher and let it go.

* * * *

Jack had been at home when he received a call from the vet clinic at CCAB about the attack. He found Samantha sitting in stony silence in the waiting room of the clinic while Azure was being examined. Samantha seemed dazed, still in shock. She wasn't even crying. She just sat there, head hung low, hands folded together, as if she was praying.

He crouched down in front of her. "Sam? Let me see your hands." He turned them over, tenderly wiping the blood off and examined them. "Oh, Sam, you've got some bite marks. Don't they hurt?"

Sullenly, she shook her head.

"I've got to get you to a doctor. You might need a few stitches, and you're definitely going to need a rabies series."

Again, she shook her head. "I'm not leaving here."

Gently, he said, "Sam, why didn't you let go of the harness? You know you were supposed to, if you were *ever* involved in a dog attack. We lecture and lecture that to our students. You can't risk your own life, too."

"Azure is an extension of me, Jack. I just couldn't let her go. I couldn't let her down," she tried to explain, voice wobbling.

Jack put his arms around her. "How did you get that other dog away from you?"

"The bartender turned the hose on Vinny's dog and kept it on him until the dog finally ran off." Her chin quivered; she was trying not to cry. "It only lasted less than a minute, but it felt like slow motion. The bartender drove us directly here. He was a godsend. It could have been much, much worse. Jack, that dog was *insane.*"

Jack sighed. "Why would you go there in the first place?"

"I went to repay my grandmother's loan," she answered in a flat monotone voice. "Vinny called and threatened her."

Jack stood up, alarmed. "*What? When?* Why didn't you tell me? Or Pete?"

"I thought I could take care of this myself. I was afraid he would come after Nonna. I just wanted to protect her."

Jack hung his head, shaking it in disbelief. "Why would you put your head in the lion's mouth?"

"Because I underestimated Vinny. I thought I could handle him. I thought I could outsmart him. I thought he would be like those two guys who tried to steal Azure. I made a *huge* mistake. And Azure is paying the price for it."

She looked so miserable. Jack felt helpless. He knew what this could mean for her. For Azure. He'd seen it before.

* * * *

Minutes later, Mr. Collins and a policeman came in to the vet clinic, looking for Samantha. Jack helped her stand up. She dreaded this encounter almost as much as she had dreaded facing Jack, but Mr. Collins' tone was kind, avuncular almost. "It's not your fault, Sam," Mr. Collins said kindly. "Don't blame yourself."

Tears were falling now, streaming in ribbons down her cheeks. *Don't be nice to me! Anything but that. Arrest me for being negligent. Aren't there laws against stupidity? There should be.* She had to swallow back the boulder of a lump in her throat. "But it *was!*" she said forlornly, her voice cracked painfully. "It was entirely my fault."

He patted her arm. "Almost a third of our guides have had some kind of problem from dog attacks—either harassment or interference or an actual unprovoked attack like you had today.

It's all too common an occurrence. But we're going to throw the book at this guy, Sam. We're going to nail him."

The officer interrupted. "Hold your promises, Mr. Collins. It isn't that easy to get a conviction when a blind person is involved. She didn't really *see* anything."

In the chaos and aftermath of the attack, Samantha had completely forgotten that she had turned on the tape recorder in her coat pocket before heading into Vinny's Pool Hall. Samantha reached in and pulled it out. It was still running. Grateful that she had just put new batteries in it because Lena forgot to turn it off yesterday and the batteries had gone dead, she looked at them hopefully, asking, "Would this help?"

Mr. Collins took the tape recorder from her, clicked it off and, delighted, gave her a loud peck on her cheek.

As the police officer took Samantha's statement, Jack went to the back of the clinic to speak to the vet. Much later, the vet came back out with him and explained to Samantha that Azure was sedated, had her ears stitched up, and her bite marks irrigated. Fortunately, Azure's rabies shots were up to date. The vet reassured Samantha that Azure was going to be fine, but that she needed to stay at the clinic and be watched for a while.

With that news, Samantha felt enormously relieved. After the vet left, Samantha said to Jack, "I haven't talked to Lucy for a few days. How is she? Is she getting over Chance?"

"She's…pretty unhappy. It's going to take some time."

"So sad. What a hard lesson to learn about love." Samantha tilted her head. Jack's voice sounded funny. Distant. "What else did the vet tell you? You were gone a long time."

Jack sat down beside her. "We can talk about it tomorrow."

Something in his voice sounded portentous. "Jack, what exactly did she say to you?"

He sighed a deep sigh, filled with awareness of the enormity of the unpleasant task that lay ahead of him. "Sam, CCAB is going to have to evaluate Azure before she's returned to you."

"The vet already told me. She said Azure needed to be watched for a while."

He hesitated before clarifying, "She will need to be re-evaluated as a guide."

"*What*? The vet said she was going to be all right," she asked.

"It may not even be an issue. I'm just telling you this to prepare you in case they make the decision to career change her." Jack's voice was calm and controlled. "Often, after an attack, the guide loses self-confidence. She may be fearful of other dogs, or loud noises, or going down certain streets."

"But I don't mind. That doesn't have to be a reason to drop her."

"It *is* a reason. Those inhibitions can create distractions for the dog, and we need to have you be able to rely on her at all times." He spoke in his instructor's voice, carefully and clearly.

Samantha looked up at him, wide-eyed, not quite hearing. "But I count on her, Jack. That's what you wanted me to do all along, wasn't it?"

"That's exactly why. You need a guide to count on. This is one of the reasons we do follow-up visits with graduates each year. People get so attached to their dogs that they overlook some problems. Even normal aging. We don't want that to happen. I realize this is hard to cope with after all that's happened, but Sam..." he paused, "it's not your decision to make."

"How could I have no input in the matter? She's my guide! She's *my* dog."

"No, Sam. She belongs to CCAB, and they make the decisions for her." He reached out to touch her shoulder.

She flinched at his touch. "Who will make this decision?" she asked coldly.

"A couple of people who work there. Including the vet."

"Including you?" she pressed.

"Yes. I'll have a recommendation, too."

Samantha's voice rose, despite trying to keep her rising fury controlled. "Jack, I am struggling on many fronts right now. Do *not* take Azure away from me. Not *now*."

"Look, Sam, please don't personalize this. It's a system at CCAB. It's a playbook. We work with the system. That's how we make decisions."

A switch tripped. "Don't you dare try to make a football analogy out of this! This is my *life*!" She spoke faster and faster, the words rising inside her like steam. "Jack, you're not even listening to me! How *could* you? How *could* you take her from me? You know how attached I've become to her!"

"I'm going to make the best decision for you. You can trust me." He sounded pained.

"Make a decision *for* me? Jack! You're *always* trying to make decisions for me! You're always so sure...about...everything! You aren't *listening* to me!" She felt herself getting sucked into the maelstrom of pent up anger. "And you probably don't listen to Lucy, either! Her mother certainly doesn't!"

"Settle down, Samantha," he said, his voice hammered thin.

She shook her head stormily. "Don't *tell* me to settle down! My entire life is falling apart, and now you want to take my dog away from me!" Her frustration erupted like a storm cloud.

"Running Deer is facing bankruptcy, my sister can barely get out of bed because she's so depressed, my grandmother is losing her grip on reality, my parents have just arrived back in the United States for...*forever*...and took Kat off of her medicine, and bought the last remaining property that I hoped we could purchase for Running Deer. And Lucy got mixed up with...that *Chance*. And it's all *my* fault!"

"How is it *your* fault?"

"Because I became distracted!" she answered.

"Wait *just* a minute, Sam. You're not being logical."

By now, she was too mad to link her thoughts. "I should have been paying attention to the ranch the month that I was at CCAB. It was a critical month with the loan going through to buy the press, and I was...*distracted*. Everything had been going so well up until then. I was so—"

"Safe?" he offered, irritation starting to rise in his voice.

"Yes! I was safe. My life was safe. It was fine! Everything was—"

"Mise-en-place," he said loudly, sarcastically, throwing his hands up in the air.

"Yes! That's it exactly. Everything was in its place. Then *you* had to come along."

Now *he* was angry. "How are Running Deer's financial problems *my* fault?"

Emotions she hadn't even realized she felt were flying past her now. "They're not your fault; they're *my* fault. It's *all* my fault! And I can't fix anything! I can't fix my grandmother! I can't fix Kathleen! I can't fix Running Deer! Or Azure! Or Lucy! And I'm not even cut out for this parenting stuff. It's too hard! None of this would have happened if…if…I hadn't gotten so distracted."

She broke off to catch her breath. "And I do blame you for Azure's dognapping! If I hadn't written that stupid article and been in that stupid television interview, then she wouldn't have been seen by those two idiots, and Chance wouldn't have tried to meet Lucy, and Azure wouldn't have been dognapped!"

"Wait just a minute! Let's back up and see this clearly. They tried to take Azure because your brother-in-law borrowed money from those two idiots! *Not* because of Lucy!" Jack pointed out, sounding upset. "And he borrowed money from those goons because your grandmother was losing it, and no one in your family was willing to admit it!"

Samantha dismissed his argument. "And now, you're telling me that I might not get Azure back! And *you* might be the deciding vote who keeps her from me! From the first day that I met you, you have tried to tell me what is best for me. In every single area of my life. My blindness, my business, my family. And now my *dog*!"

She wasn't really sure why she was being so hard on Jack. Her mouth was acting like it had a mind of its own.

"Just answer me this, Samantha. Why is it that you have to feel so responsible for everybody? For Kathleen, for Pete, for your grandmother, even for Lucy! Why can't you ever ask anyone for help? What is it that you think you have to prove by being so independent? Or *to* whom? Because *that's* why you went into Vinny's Pool Hall today. Whatever the answers are to those questions, *that's* the reason that you're in this mess now."

Coldly, Samantha said, "I'm in this mess now because I got on the wrong bus one day last summer."

Jack was silent for a long time. In an icy tone he said, "I'll call a taxi for you. Have the driver take you to the emergency room for stitches and a rabies shot." Without another word, he got up and left, gently closing the door behind him.

* * * *

During the night, Samantha woke up, feeling the ache of every muscle in her body from the tension of yesterday's attack. It was so dark that she felt for the hands on her watch and was alarmed to discover it was already morning. She waited in bed for a while. She was accustomed to her eyes taking a long time to adjust to light and dark, but this morning, they didn't adjust. She got up to flick on the light switch. Nothing. She went over to open the blinds. Nothing. She went quickly to the door and opened it, straining to see the morning light. *Nothing!*

Panicking, she called Dr. Freeman's office and begged the answering service to connect her to him at home despite the early hour. When she finally got through to him, she explained what had happened to her vision.

"Oh, Sam," he said, sounding disappointed.

"Can't something be done?" she asked hopefully, desperately. "There's *got* to be something. Medicine? Rest? Anything?! There's got to be *something*!"

He was silent. Finally, in a gloomy voice he answered, "I think you know the answer, Sam. You knew this was inevitable."

The stress of the last few weeks had taken their toll on the last little bit of crummy vision she had left. She had always known this day would come. She told herself she wouldn't cry, but before she knew it, she was doubled over, sobbing so hard that her chest hurt. Unrestrained, from-the-gut, inside-out, eyes-swollen-shut weeping.

Chapter Sixteen: **A Cup of Tea**

When Samantha finally got up for the day, she knew she had to get out of the cottage and go somewhere, but she didn't want to go over to the farmhouse; she wasn't ready to tell anyone about the dog attack. Besides Azure's unexplained absence, the bulky bandages that the doctor had wrapped around her hands would broadcast the event. So would her puffy eyes after her crying jag; her eyelids still felt like sandpaper. She just knew she had to get out of the cottage and go *somewhere.*

She found her white cane buried in the back of the closet, put on her parka, and started walking down the street, heading to the bus stop at the end of the road. She *hated* the sound of the white cane. Each tap, tap, tap caused a lump of sadness to tighten up her throat, reminding her of Azure lying in the vet clinic, bandaged up.

Half an hour later, she found herself knocking on Nonna's apartment door. "Samantha!" said Nonna, opening the door wide open. "Come in! What a nice surprise. Let me fix tea."

Tea! Samantha felt comforted, at least momentarily. *What a good idea. Drinking tea would help to clear my mind. Tea was like that. It just worked.*

"Let me make it, Nonna," she volunteered. Samantha couldn't forget that the last time Nonna made tea, she had ripped open the tea bags and handed her a cup of floating tea leaves. Samantha went into the kitchen and turned on the hot water kettle. After the kettle whistled, she poured hot water into two tea cups and steeped the tea for a few minutes before dumping the tea bags in the sink.

"Samantha, before you sit down, will you turn off the television?"

"Oh, Nonna, you aren't watching *Lawrence Welk* again, are you?" Samantha crinkled her nose.

"Don't make fun. That show will be a classic."

Don't bet on it, Nonna. Samantha flipped off the television and sat down at the kitchen table, sipping her tea, feeling sad. *Nonna hasn't even noticed that Azure isn't with me.*

Nonna added a teaspoon of sugar into her tea cup and stirred. Then she started to rummage through on an old box of photographs, an assignment by the doctor to help aid her long-term memory. "Oh, here's one of you and Kat as babies. Such beauties." She sighed happily. She sifted through the box. "I don't have very many of you girls once your folks went off to..." she had an attack of tip-of-the-tongue-it-is, losing the word Papua New Guinea until she substituted, "... the mission field. Oh, my, look at this!"

"Describe it, Nonna," Samantha said.

"Grandpa took it of your family in front of our house right before your parents returned after furlough. The year they left you here. Oh, look, your mother is crying. Must have been so hard on her."

"Think so?" Samantha said sarcastically.

"Well, Gramps was so determined."

"What do you mean?"

Nonna added a second teaspoon of sugar into her tea cup. "He just couldn't rest easy, knowing you were losing your sight, and your folks weren't doing anything to help you learn how to live with blindness. He was adamant that you should remain here. Even wrote a letter to the Mission Board to tell them about the situation."

Samantha was stunned. "But they weren't bad parents..."

Nonna put her hand over Samantha's. "Of course they weren't." She added some sugar into her tea and stirred it.

"Did you support Gramps? Did you think Kat and I should stay in the States?" Samantha asked.

Nonna sighed. "Yes, I did. We had tried to convince your folks to return to the United States for good, but they refused. So we begged them to at least let you come live with us, but they weren't open to that, either. Finally, Gramps went to the Mission Board, and they convinced your parents to let you live where you could get help." She put a third teaspoon of sugar into her tea.

Nonna went to the refrigerator to get the carton of milk and poured it into her tea. "Your parents and Gramps never healed that rift. That's one of the reasons I wanted to buy your parents a home nearby. It's high time we all became a family again."

Samantha tucked her bandaged hands in her lap. "Mom and Dad won't give Kathleen the anti-depressants that her doctor prescribed. Mom said this was a spiritual battle for Kat. Not a medical one."

Nonna took a long sip of tea. She put a fourth teaspoon of sugar into her cup and stirred it in. "Sometimes people can be very sincere in their beliefs, in what they think is so important, and be sincerely wrong."

With that thought came the dawning of objectivity for Samantha. She felt the old pull of gratitude toward her grandmother, if someone had just washed a window in her mind and she could see clearly through it for the first time.

Nonna sipped on her tea and shuddered. "I'm sorry, dear, but you make the worst tea. Much too sweet and much too milky." She poured her tea down the sink.

An hour later, as she left Nonna's apartment, Samantha knew exactly what she had to do.

That afternoon, Samantha made a phone call to the food corporation that had approached her with an offer to buy Running Deer Ranch, months ago, when she was in New York City.

Later that day she went over to the farmhouse and found Pete in the kitchen alone. Grateful for the privacy which was becoming increasingly rare in the full house, she told Pete what she had done.

He sat down at the kitchen table, shocked. He put his head in his hands. Hoarsely, he said, "Well, I knew you would figure something out."

"I only had two choices, Pete. To sell or to face bankruptcy. The sale price will be based on what happens when we close the books on December 31st. But thanks to this year's harvest and all of the publicity we've been getting this fall, it might be more than we could have ever hoped. They're going to wire earnest money next week. I've already spoken to Miss Lawton at the bank; she's agreed to take the earnest money as an installment on the loan so we can avoid bankruptcy. She said she'll help in any way that she can." She smiled bleakly, still stunned by Miss Lawton's magnanimous offer. "So maybe using a small bank is turning out to be a good thing."

"Isn't there anything else we can do?"

"Well, have you heard anything about the value of those stock certificates?" she asked.

"No," he said glumly, chin to his chest, hands folded on the table. "I haven't had time."

Just what I thought. "So," she continued, "this company wants the orchards, but the five acres surrounding the farmhouse will remain ours. And I negotiated a job for you."

"Why not for you, too?"

"Marketing is a duplicate function. They don't need me. I'm not worried. I'll find another job or maybe take some time off." She smiled reassuringly. "Maybe I'll finally have time to finish that novel."

* * * *

Kathleen actually had a little bit of energy today, at least enough to make her want to come downstairs when she heard her sister's voice. She stood by the kitchen door listening to Sam and Pete's conversation before letting them know she was there. "Good. It's about time you finished that novel," she said when she heard Samantha mention that novel. "I know I'm the main character anyway."

"Kat? You're up!" Samantha went and hugged her. "And you've showered! Twice in one week. This is turning into quite a day!"

"Mom made me."

"You've been taking the medication, right?" Samantha asked, forehead wrinkled in concern.

"Faithfully," Pete answered. "I give it to her myself. That doctor read me the riot act."

Shocked at the sight of Samantha's bandaged hands, Kathleen asked. "*What* happened to you?"

"Uh, long story."

Kathleen looked at Pete. He mouthed silently that he would tell her later. She shrugged and sat down at the kitchen table as a wave of fatigue rolled over her. "Just think, Sam, after all of these years, we finally have parents. Just in time for Christmas."

Pete added quietly, "They look so much older since our wedding."

Kathleen agreed. "I know. Their hair has gotten so gray."

"And your dad's shoulders are slightly stooped," Pete said.

"What?" Samantha asked, visibly stunned. "I've always thought of them as young." She swirled cold coffee in her cup. "Silly, I guess, but I must have locked images of them in my mind. It honestly never occurred to me that they were aging."

Kathleen saw the sadness that covered Samantha. She understood. They both had such conflicted feelings about their parents. She covered Samantha's bandaged hand with her hand. "They're here now, Sam. Try to focus on that."

"That fact would be hard to miss," Samantha said sarcastically, dumping her coffee down the sink.

* * * *

Samantha unlocked the door to her cottage as the phone began to ring. "Sam!" Lucy cried out, "Jack told me what happened to you and Azure. I've been so worried about you! Azure, too. I've been calling and calling. Where have you been?"

Just as Samantha opened her mouth to say something, Lucy interrupted her, her voice cold and flat. "Oh, my mom wants to know who I'm talking to. She says she doesn't trust me any more because of…Chance. Look, I'd better go. She's just standing at the door staring at me, listening in. Call me later!" Click.

Samantha frowned, holding the receiver in her hand. Lucy didn't give Samantha her phone number. And Samantha was *not* about to call Jack to find out what it was. Not yet. She wasn't ready. *Besides he hasn't called me.*

The vet clinic at CCAB called her the next day to come and get Azure. Pete drove her over and waited in the parking lot for her.

"She's such a great dog," said the vet, patting Azure's head. "How are you mending, Samantha?"

"Better each day, thanks," answered Samantha.

The vet hesitated for a moment. "I'm sorry to be the one to tell you that we've decided to career change Azure. She's showing signs of being afraid of other dogs. I sort of expected that after such a vicious attack." She paused. "Or did Jack already tell you all of this?"

Samantha kept her face expressionless. "No, I haven't spoken with him."

"He was just in here. Shall I send someone to find him?"

"No, thank you," Samantha said firmly, still smarting from their argument.

"You could keep her as a pet. Or if you don't want her, the next in line is her puppy raiser."

Didn't want her? She had missed Azure terribly these last few days. And how could she ever tell Azure's puppy raiser that she had been career changed? After providing foster care for her for eighteen months, training her and socializing her, only to have her dropped as a guide within three months. *And I'm the one to blame!*

"We hope you'll consider coming back for another dog. I even have the paperwork here for you."

Reading the guilt on her face, the vet said, firmly and clearly, "No one blames you for this attack. It happens all too often. Now," she said decidedly, "let's talk about your options."

As the vet described the retraining program, fat tears floated in front of Samantha eyes. How could she ever learn to count on another dog the way she counted on Azure? How could she ever love a dog the way she loved Azure? *I'm not sure I can.*

The vet handed Azure's leash to Sam. "Such a sweet girl," she said, stroking Azure gently around the large Elizabethan collar surrounding her neck to keep her from licking injuries. Bravely, Azure wagged her tail, as if she knew she was the object of conversation.

* * * *

Samantha and Pete were painfully aware of the importance of Running Deer's balance sheet as of December 31st. Each new day brought a stack of fresh orders, and the temporary work crew scrambled to stay on top of the workload.

Samantha woke early one morning and hurried down to the office as quickly as she could. Lena met her at the door, fizzing with frustration. "Miss Sam! You can't believe all of the orders that are backed up! How are we ever going to get these orders fulfilled?"

"Don't worry, Lena. We're going to manage. We're not going to let one single order slip through the cracks."

Suddenly, a silence filled the air. Then there were loud voices, shouting in alarm.

"Oh, no, please no! Not *today!* Not *now!*" Samantha clapped her head in her hands.

Lena ran to her office. "What is it? What's wrong?"

"The generator to the mill shut down," Samantha muffled from behind her hands. "This is terrible!"

Pete opened the door and called to Samantha, "Get an electrician out here!"

"Lena, start calling every single electrician, and don't stop until you find one who can come out today. No matter what it costs."

Thirty minutes later, Lena knocked on Samantha's door. "Miss Sam, no one can come until after Christmas."

"No one?! Not a single electrician? Not even a Jewish one?"

"Not a one. There are only four in the county anyway." Lena closed the door then opened it up again, poking her head into Samantha's office. "What about that boyfriend of yours? The old boyfriend. The one who wears the pocket protector."

"You mean...Bob?" Samantha bit her lip, hope rising. "Lena, that might just be the best idea you've ever had. Remind me to give you a raise." *It might be the only idea Lena ever had.*

"I will!" Lena said, sounding delighted.

Right at his desk, Bob answered Samantha's SOS call. "So," he said, sounding pleased, "you need my help." Rushing over, he found the problem with the overtaxed generator and fixed it by the end of the business day.

As the sound of the mill eased back to life, Samantha said, "I can't tell you how much I appreciate your help, Bob. Please, let me at least fix you dinner before you go."

253

As Samantha fumbled with the lock at her cottage door, Bob inhaled the star jasmine. "I've missed this cottage. I've always loved it. Everything is calm and orderly."

"Thank you. I completely agree," Samantha smiled. "I need to go feed Spitfire. I can hear him kicking his stall. That's his version of ringing a dinner bell."

When she got back inside, Bob had made himself at home and started supper. "Hope you don't mind but I threw together a stir fry from leftovers. I found some brown rice and vegetables."

"No, I don't mind at all. I'm amazed there were enough ingredients in that fridge to pull anything together. I've been so busy lately that I've hardly had time for the basics. You're a miracle worker." She pulled out a cutting board to slice a red pepper. "I thought I heard the phone ring while I was outside."

"It did. Twice," Bob answered. "First time was the receptionist for Kat's doctor, reminding you to make her an appointment. Second call was a wrong number; somebody asked who I was. When I said 'Bob,' he said 'oh.' And then he hung up." He took the cutting board from her. "And there's a stray cat that keeps clawing at the door to get in. I thought I'd take it away tonight and dump it off at some farm."

"No!" Samantha said, a little too loudly. "I mean, he's not a stray. I, uh, got him for the barn mice. He's a mouser. A good one."

As they prepared dinner together, silently working side by side in her tiny kitchen without bumping into each other, not even once, Samantha started to wonder why she had ever broken things off with Bob. *Things were so easy with him.* Even Azure seemed to have a new appreciation for him. Once she even gave his hand a lick.

Bob lit the candles and held the seat out at the table for Samantha to sit down. "I was glad you called today. I've wanted to call you. I've missed you, Sam." He clinked his glass with hers. "Here's to a fresh start."

* * * *

The next morning, Samantha's parents arrived, uninvited, to her office. "Sam, you've hardly made time to see us," said her mother as she pulled up a chair to sit down. "So we came to find you. It's been so hectic with Nonna, Kathleen, and your problems with the dog. And we've never even gotten an update about your eyesight."

"An update on my eyesight?" Samantha gave an awkward laugh. "That will be quick. I have no vision. Completely, irrevocably blind." As silence filled the room, Samantha wondered why their conversations were always so stilted and awkward. Finally, she said, "Look, it's a very busy time right now. Busiest time of the year for the company. We have a lot of orders to fulfill before Christmas. I really need to get back to work now." She straightened, putting even more distance between them.

Meekly, her father offered, "Maybe we could help out?"

"I thought you felt the world didn't need another bottle of olive oil," Samantha said accusingly.

"When did we ever say that?" asked her mother, confused.

"Dad said it. When Gramps wanted him to take over the olive ranch, but he wanted to be a missionary." She looked straight at her father. "You told him you needed to do something really important and significant with your life. That 'Gramps had sold his soul to earthly mammon,' I believe, were the exact words."

"He told you that?" her father asked, obviously shaken.

"Yes. I think it hurt him pretty deeply. Not because you wanted to do something different with your life than continue in the family business, but because you felt he wasn't doing something significant and important with his life."

Her father didn't respond.

"Funny, though, how he ended up raising your daughters for you, so that you could continue being so important and significant," she said curtly.

Another awkward silence hung suspended in the air until her mother asked, "Samantha, you seem…upset that we've returned."

She sank back in her chair and shrugged, a silent admission.

"Well, if you're going to act sulky…" her mother said, sounding like Samantha was ten years old and in a bad mood over what was served for dinner.

255

Samantha's anger bubbled up and over. "You just don't get it, do you? Frankly, aren't you a little late on the scene? After all, you shipped us off years ago. You *made* your choice. You chose your work over your children." She gripped the arms of her chair. "Don't blame me if I'm not pulling out the welcome mat just because you suddenly decide to be interested in your family."

"We did what we thought was *best* for you. For everybody! You needed to be in the States. And Kathleen needed to be with you," defended her mother.

Her father leaned forward in his chair. "That's what missionaries in Third World countries do, Samantha. When children reach school age, they are sent to boarding school."

"That doesn't change the fact that you chose work over us."

"Do you think it was an *easy* choice to leave my two daughters and get on a plane without them?" objected her mother, her voice shaky. "To say goodbye to you and Kathleen? To entrust your upbringing to your grandparents? Especially knowing that you were...going blind?"

"An easier choice than helping me to cope with it," Samantha said coldly. *There. I said it.* Her anger subsided like a popped balloon.

Lena interrupted and brought everyone coffee, chattering about the weather, oblivious to the tense atmosphere in the room.

After she left, her father cleared his throat and said, "Look, Sam, the real reason we came to your office this morning was because Pete told us about Nonna's money problems. About those sweepstakes scams, too. He told us everything. Even about his part in setting Nonna up with that awful loan shark."

"We had *no* idea that Nonna had squandered her money," added her mother. "Samantha, why didn't *you* tell us?"

She shrugged her shoulders. "I wanted to handle this myself. I wanted to find a solution that made everything work out. But I just couldn't."

"Why would you think you had to handle all of this yourself? How could one person try to unravel all of this herself? *Especially* one who is..." her mother abruptly stopped herself.

"Blind." Samantha finished the sentence for her. She shook her head. "Don't you see why? Can't you even hear what you just said? 'How could one person unravel this? Especially one who is blind?' As if I am half a person! You never believed I was capable of having a full life. You've always seen me as handicapped." She threw her hands up in the air. "But *Nonna* knew better. She's the reason I've had the self-confidence to build this company. I always wanted to live up to her expectations. To *surpass* them."

She wiped her face in a weary gesture. "But I let her down. I got so busy with work, and I didn't even see how much Nonna had declined. I checked her bank accounts and found she had been getting scammed for months. She had given away thousands of dollars to those horrible, slimy con-artists who have preyed on her. *And I let that happen!* I allowed myself to get distracted by the business, and by having a guide dog, and by..." she stopped herself, not wanting to tell them about Jack. "And all of this happened while you and Mom were doing whatever you do in PNG."

"Doing *whatever* we do?" asked her mother. "You know how important our work has been! It's God's work, after all."

Hearing that last phrase jump out of her mother's mouth nearly made Samantha want to scream. She had heard that excuse more times than she could count. Most recently was when Lily was born and her parents weren't able to find the time to come home to meet their granddaughter.

"It wasn't an easy life, for any of us, but we answered God's call, and that required sacrifice. For all of us," added her father.

"Did it?" Samantha said bitterly. "I really don't think so. I think you chose that life because it made you feel important."

That remark hung in the air, waiting for someone to act. Her father quietly got up and left, her mother trailed behind. The conversation remained unresolved. *Like always*, Samantha rued as the door closed behind them. *If only they could have at least offered to do the one thing that could help everyone: cancel escrow with the Mitchell house and return the funds to*

Running Deer. If they did, selling Running Deer could be avoided.

Why can't I ask them? she wondered.

But why wouldn't they offer? she wondered even more.

Swirling the cold coffee in her mug, she suddenly realized they simply didn't "get it." It was as simple as that. She had been looking most of her life for *something* from her parents—affirmation, acceptance, validation, maybe all three—that they couldn't give. It was as simple as that.

In a strange paradox, they were wonderful missionaries but terrible parents. They really *had* done the best they could as parents. It just wasn't enough. *But God is enough.* The profound knowledge that God was enough permeated her entire being, smoothing out the rough places, filling the interstices.

All of the tension she had carried for months left her. She exhaled, releasing something deep inside. She could let it go. She could stop expecting more from her parents. She could stop feeling disappointed. That big block of ice she harbored within her cracked down the middle and shattered into a thousand splinters.

* * * *

In the afternoon, Pete burst into her office. "You won't believe it, Sam. You just won't believe it!"

Curious, she spun around in her chair to face him.

"The stock certificates." He sounded stunned. "My stockbroker friend just called. A couple of the stocks add up to nearly $20,000. He's still tracking down the other stocks."

Samantha sat back in her chair, equally stunned. "Do you know what this could mean?"

"We might not have to sell?"

A tidal wave of emotions washed over her—joy, relief, disbelief. "Oh, I hope! Say a prayer, Pete!" She picked up the phone to call the bank.

Pete stood up to leave. "Samantha, do you realize those stocks are worth the very same amount that Nonna lost in the sweepstakes scam? Nearly to the penny?" He sounded overjoyed.

Slowly, Samantha nodded.

"Kind of makes you think, doesn't it?"

She put down the receiver. "What do you mean?"

"Well, what are the odds? The same amount? Isn't that a little, well, spooky? Like Jack said."

"Jack said that?"

"Well, I don't remember the exact words, but once he said that God can turn rotten stuff into good stuff."

She inhaled sharply, sorely missing Jack. She knew just what Pete meant. Jack had always given her the feeling that everything would come out the way it was intended, all for good.

After calling the bank, she decided to make another call.

"No, I'm sorry. Jack Shaw isn't here," said the receptionist at California Canine Academy for the Blind.

Where is he? Why hasn't he tried to get in touch with me? She raked her hair with her hands. *Who could blame him?* After all, she had told him she regretted ever meeting him. She couldn't forget that frosty tone in his voice when he told her he was calling a taxi for her. It sounded so final, like he was saying good-bye. She recognized that tone. It was the one she had used for Bob, months ago.

Late on Christmas Eve, Samantha and Pete locked up the office doors, ready to keel over in happy exhaustion. Every member of the family, even Nonna, though heavily supervised, helped to pack up the orders. And every order was fulfilled. Running Deer spent a fortune on shipping to keep the promise of delivery by Christmas morning.

"It's okay," Samantha gulped, after signing off on the last delivery charges for the local trucking company. "We're creating good will with our customers by keeping our promises." But it did irk her to admit that the expensive boxes the bottles were placed in, thanks to Kathleen's bottle order blunder, actually made the packaging go swiftly.

When Samantha and Pete reached the farmhouse, they were surprised to find Kathleen in the kitchen helping to prepare an elaborate feast, though still in her pajamas.

At dinner, her parents explained that they planned to move into the Mitchell house after the first of the year, insisting that they would take on the bulk of Nonna's care.

Samantha was dubious, wondering how long it would be before her parents felt called to something else, but she couldn't deny some relief that they were staying nearby. She knew they would be needed. Nonna had just been given thirty days notice to move out of the retirement facility because it didn't have a dementia unit. Since she had been diagnosed, she was now considered a liability. That, and she had recently caused a small fire by putting her gloves in the toaster oven to dry.

Her parents had yet to volunteer having Nonna move in with them, but Samantha held out hope. *And I'm so grateful that my own cottage only has one tiny bedroom.*

The entire family, except for Kathleen and Lily, went to the midnight service for Christmas Eve.

"Immanuel, God is with us," were the first words the minister proclaimed.

God is with us. Right here, right now.

For the first time in her life, Samantha felt, with a quiet certainty, that God was there. She thought back over the last few weeks, savoring the peace of releasing the buried rancor she had held against her parents for nearly twenty years. With stinging awareness, she realized she had even gathered strength from that bitterness. Her drive to be successful and independent was rooted in a determination to prove that her parents had been wrong. To prove that while she may be blind she *wasn't* handicapped.

All those years, she had been looking in the wrong place. Her parents were human. Fallible. It had finally gotten through to Samantha that what she needed was to forgive her parents.

It took that conversation with Nonna, over tea, that sweet, sweet tea, to help her realize she didn't have to prove anything. *Not to God anyway.* Her mind wandered to Jack. *Where is he?*

She kept hoping he might call. Despite her doubts, she realized she wanted to trust Jack, wanted to be with him. She hoped she could have another chance. She hoped he could forgive her for the things she said. But even if he didn't, she knew she would survive. She would miss him, but she would survive. Jack might have left, but God was here.

☐

Christmas dawned cold and foggy and dismal, but one of the most satisfying mornings Kathleen could ever remember. After opening a mountain of hastily purchased presents, the family lingered around the dining room table for a leisurely brunch. Afterwards, they sat in the living room by the crackling fire in a state of pure contentment. She looked around the room, her heart full, as she saw Lily asleep on Pete's chest, who was sprawled out on the floor, napping. Her parents were sharing the newspaper on the sofa. Samantha was curled up next to the fireplace. *She looks...so...peaceful.* Kathleen hadn't seen her sister look so relaxed in years. The sight brought her a wisp of happiness, like a glimmer of sun breaking through the clouds.

"Is Boring Bob invited for dinner?" Kathleen asked Samantha. Instantly, the pleasant look on Samantha's face froze.

"Kathleen, please stop calling him that. Sometimes you are positively puerile. And yes, he is coming."

"Who is Boring Bob?" asked her father from behind the newspaper he was reading. "I thought his name was Jack."

"No, Dad. Jack is out of the picture," answered Samantha, "so please don't make a mistake and call Bob by the wrong name. Not Boring, not Jack. Just Bob."

"What happened to Jack?" asked her father.

"They had an argument," volunteered Kathleen. "But his cat is still here." Somehow, she found that to be comforting. A sign, a good omen.

Samantha rolled her eyes.

"What's so bad about arguing?" asked Nonna as she walked into the living room carrying a tray of mulled cider in large mugs. "A good relationship is like good food. Contrasts and surprises keep life interesting."

Kathleen grinned at her. "Ah, Nonna, our kitchen philosopher," she sighed, feeling warmly satisfied. Today was a good day for Nonna. Just last night, Samantha had reminded her to savor them.

Later that afternoon, Bob arrived as they were putting the final touches on the evening meal. Kathleen searched in the kitchen cupboard for a package of walnuts for a Waldorf salad but couldn't find it. "I have to have those walnuts," she insisted. "Pete, I put it on the shopping list." She scowled at him.

"Kat, that list was three pages long, and the store was closing," Pete objected.

"I have a bag, Kat. I'll go get it," volunteered Samantha.

Bob jumped up. "Let me go, Sam."

"I left the door unlocked," Samantha said. "It's in the kitchen cupboard to the left of the fridge, second shelf—"

"Alphabetized," Bob supplied. "I know just where it will be."

"Oh, gross…" said Kathleen, after Bob left the kitchen. "He actually likes that you alphabetize your food." She tossed the chopped celery into the large salad bowl. Pete put his hand in the bowl to grab a few bites, and she slapped it away.

Samantha opened a package of bread rolls and placed them in a basket. "We both happen to prefer the predictable."

Kathleen reached for an apple on the counter and started dicing it. "Watching the two of you together is like watching grass grow. Like watching Jell-O set. It's painful. Mindnumbing."

Samantha threw a bread roll at her and hit her right on the forehead. "Gotcha! Might be blind, but I have great aim."

"Stop it, you Bicker Twins," scolded Nonna as she came into the kitchen from setting the dining room table.

Kathleen looked at Samantha, and they both burst out laughing, as if on cue, having heard that very phrase repeated from Nonna for twenty years. *Wow, it felt good to laugh again.* Even her laugh sounded rusty.

Bob walked back in the kitchen with the bag of walnuts. "Just where you said it would be," he said. "And your phone rang while I was there. I picked it up, but it was that same wrong number guy."

Kathleen took the bag from him and opened it up, pouring it into the salad bowl.

"What same wrong number guy?" Samantha asked.

"That guy who called last week when I fixed your generator. It was the same fuzzy connection. A guy asked who I was, and I said 'Bob' and he asked, 'What the heck are you doing there?' So I hung up. Twice he's done that. Probably a pervert. You might want to get your number changed."

"I bet it was Jack, Sam!" Kathleen declared triumphantly. "I'm sure it was him. Calling to apologize. That weird cat *was* a sign! I *knew* he would come back! He was trying to call you on Christmas day!"

A deafening silence filled the room. Bob cast a sideways glance at Samantha, who kept her head down as she concentrated on arranging the rolls.

"Aw, sweetheart, it's good to have you back," said Pete, reaching out to hug his wife. "Big mouth," he whispered in her ear.

After Christmas dinner, Bob and Samantha put on their coats to go on a walk with Azure. Bob had been quiet through dinner. Kathleen knew he was peeved about her offhanded remark about Jack. *But Jack was so right for Sam, and Bob was so...Bob.*

Too weak and drained to work through any more thoughts about Boring Bob, she tiptoed upstairs to lie down. She hated this depression and wanted it to be over. She was starting to have moments when she felt like herself again but then a wave of fatigue would hit her, knocking her over like a wave. As she was pulling back the covers on the bed, she noticed that Samantha and Bob were right below her window. She saw Bob wave his arms in the air. Quietly, she opened the window to listen.

"So...want to tell me about Jack?" Bob said, hands on his hips.

Samantha shrugged. "There's really nothing to tell. He was an instructor at CCAB."

"And he's your neighbor."

"Yes. He bought the house down the street."

"And that cat belongs to him."

Samantha nodded. "Well, sort of. Kind of a long story."

"Kat's hoping there's more to it then?"

You bet I am, buddy! Kathleen wanted to shout as she kneeled down to hear more.

Slowly, Samantha nodded her head.

"What about you?" He crossed his arms against his chest. "Are you hoping there's more to it?"

Samantha didn't answer.

Bob took her hands in his, but Samantha gently pulled them away and put them in her pockets.

"So," he said quietly. "It's like that?"

Samantha kept her head down, hesitating. Then she looked up at him. "Yeah. It's like that."

Kathleen could barely contain a cheer. *Yes! Samantha is finally admitting what I've known all along!*

Bob lifted her chin with his fingers. "Do you love him?"

Samantha didn't respond right away. She looked down the driveway toward Jack's house.

"I asked," Bob said. "You answered." He gently kissed her cheek and walked off toward his car. When he unlocked his car door, he turned and said, "Good luck, Sam. But next time your generator dies, you'd better pay an electrician." He glanced back at the house, taking it in for the last time, and did a double take when he saw Kathleen in the second story window. He gave her an icy stare before getting into the car. He unrolled the window and said loudly, for Kathleen's benefit as well as Samantha's, "I just hope this guy is everything you want, Sam. You deserve that."

As Bob's car drove down the gravel driveway, Kathleen heard Samantha say out loud, "He is. I'm just not sure I'm what he wants."

Kathleen's jaw dropped open. *Oh dear. I hadn't thought of that.* Frowning, she quietly closed the window.

Chapter Seventeen: New Year's Day

New Year's Day broke on a beautiful, cold morning. The sun shone gloriously. Samantha couldn't wait to get to the office to start closing Running Deer's books and check the final numbers. Eagerly, she bundled up in her parka, wrapped a scarf around her neck, put on gloves, and headed down the path to her office. Her breath formed gray puffs in the stinging air as she exhaled. As she reached the ridge above her cottage, she heard a faint whistle. Azure turned back, started barking, straining at her leash, tail thumping furiously.

"Azure! What is it?" Samantha called out in alarm.

"Not what. It's 'who'," huffed a familiar voice, soft and deep, as he ran toward them.

A bubble of happiness rose up inside of her. "Jack!" Samantha dropped the harness and gave Azure the okay to take off to greet Jack. Jack stopped to grab Azure's leash and pat her affectionately before walking to meet Samantha.

For a long moment, they both stood there, neither breathing, neither saying anything. Then she took a step forward and slid her arms around his waist, burying her face in his chest. He wrapped his arms around her, and they hugged silently, until she finally whispered, "I thought you quit on me."

"Never. I like a challenge," he whispered back confidently.

She pulled away and pushed at his chest. "Then where in the *world* have you *been*?" She wiped tears away with her gloved fingers.

"Texas. I just got back late last night. Came right over as soon as I thought you might be up. I saw you already heading up the hill."

"No one knew where you went! Your mail in your mailbox is overflowing. And Pete said your newspapers are all piled up on your porch."

Jack groaned. "Oh, I noticed that. I forgot to put a hold on my mail and cancel the paper. But I must have told you that I'd be gone for Christmas."

"You never said you were *leaving* the *state*! Jack, you have the *worst* memory for details."

"Are you sure? I *must* have told you. I meant to."

"Jack, I'm *so* sorry," she said, miserably.

"Sam," he interrupted.

"I should never have said those things—"

"But there's something you should know—"

"I was angry and upset, and I took it out on you—"

"Sam, I understood. I really did."

Jack's response gave Samantha a catch-in-her-heart feeling. It was undeservedly kind. "Then why didn't you call? Or even send a lousy postcard?"

"I did try. Twice! That little Bob guy kept answering."

"As soon as I stopped being angry, I tried to call you, but there was never any answer, and CCAB wouldn't tell me where you were. And I haven't even spoken to Lucy in weeks."

Jack laughed. "Lucy came with me! We had a family reunion at my brother's house. The one who owns the restaurant with the crazy chef. Lucy met my parents and my brothers and their wives and their kids. It was good timing for her, kind of jolted her out of her funk. We had a really good time together. She even said she doesn't hate me anymore."

Samantha grinned. She could just hear Lucy make that announcement. Jack led her over to a large rock, basted by the early morning sunlight. They sat down on it, facing each other. He tucked a loose strand of hair behind her ear and said, "So I understand that Azure has to turn in her harness."

Samantha nodded.

"Look, Sam," he started, hesitantly. "There's something you need to know. There was a reason I left on my trip without saying goodbye."

Samantha tilted her head at him curiously, waiting for him to elaborate.

"I was the swing vote that decided Azure was to be released."

She didn't say a word.

"Sam, I know how independent you are, and how hard it was for you to finally learn to rely on Azure. I was concerned you would start asking less and less of her, even subconsciously, and not get the kind of help you need from a guide."

Samantha remained silent.

"I'm sorry. I really am." Now *he* sounded miserable. "But I *had* to make the right decision, even knowing what it might do to you. To us."

She bent down to stroke Azure's head, taking time to gather her thoughts. Then she said, "You were in a hard position. I trust your judgment." Then she stood up to face him. "No, let me re-phrase that. I trust *you*."

Framing her face in his hands, he said, "Wow...*that* was a long time coming."

"But... you were wise to give me a few weeks to cool off," she said, putting her hands on top of his.

"Oh, yeah. No doubt about that. I knew you needed time." He gave a short laugh. "But I didn't expect that little Bob guy to pop up. What's up with that?"

She waved a hand, dismissing the topic. "Long story." She liked that Jack was jealous of Bob. She could imagine Kathleen asking, "Who could *ever* be jealous of Bob?"

"But he's gone, right?"

"Yes, gone," she answered, grinning. "Jack, after Azure was hurt, after you and I had that horrible argument, I woke up the next morning, and my vision was completely gone. I knew it was inevitable, but I just hit rock bottom. I went to see Nonna one morning and, well, that's a long and confusing story, but it wasn't long before I realized that God was enough, and He was with there with me in the midst of this big mess. And from that moment on, things fell into place, but in ways I could never have expected."

She explained how she had nearly sold Running Deer. "I was at peace about the decision to sell. I could let it go. I couldn't believe I would ever part with Running Deer, but it was okay. It's important, but it's not everything. Not anymore." She leaned over and stroked Azure's head. "And now I think I can hang on a little less tightly to Azure."

"Have you thought about applying for another guide?"

"Already sent in the paperwork. This time, I filled it out and signed it myself." She smiled. "I leave in two weeks."

"I won't be able to be your instructor. I'm back in the kennels with a new string this month."

"That's okay."

"But I'll be able to check in and see how you're doing."

She bent over to stroke Azure's head. "Do you really think I'll be able to bond with another dog the way I've bonded with Azure?"

"Absolutely!" Jack answered, with great confidence, in his instructor's voice.

"Jack, I called the supervisor of the bus line the other day. They've agreed to let me ride the bus—any bus—with my guide dog. They even apologized."

"See? Not so hard," Jack said. "I'm proud of you."

"Me, too! I should've called months ago when Jimmy first bounced me off. I might even try going into the Mexican restaurant one of these days." She laughed. "Yesterday, I realized that I am going to have not one, but two dogs in my tiny little cottage. I've become one of those dog ladies that everyone makes fun of." She grinned, thinking of how Bob would have hated that. "Do you think Azure will be okay with the new dog? She doesn't like to be around other dogs. She starts to tremble when she hears another dog bark."

"Might take time, but I think it would be good for her."

"I'm not sure if it'll ever get published, but I want to spend some time this year to finish that novel."

"I've been thinking about that novel. I thought of a new ending." He wrapped his arms around her. "Instead of *offing* the instructor in a gruesome death, I was thinking that the blind woman realizes she's crazy in love with him and insists he marry her. He finally relents, knowing that this woman is desperate for him, and they all live happily ever after."

She wrinkled her brow. "I don't know. I sort of like *offing* the instructor."

"Then how about this ending: The instructor realizes he's the one who needs the blind woman. He's the one who's crazy in love and insists she marry him."

It dawned on Samantha that Jack, in his missing-the-important-details-style, had just asked her to marry him. "Yes!" she nearly shouted. Then his mouth was on hers, and it was all she could do not to collapse at the effect of the kiss. Her head felt dizzy, and her knees actually went soft. She thought that kind of thing only happened in the movies.

"Hey—I have a great idea for a honeymoon," he whispered in between kisses.

A horrifying thought fluttered through Samantha's mind. She put a hand up on his lips. "Wait just a minute. I am *not* going to Canton, Ohio for a honeymoon." She was *not* about to spend her honeymoon at the Football Hall of Fame.

"Oh," Jack said, sounding crestfallen. "Well," he said, brightening, "maybe we'll save that for our first anniversary."

Samantha shook her head, trying to clear it of that thought. "Jack," she said, "if I can put this in terms that everyone can understand…football is a metaphor for life. The groom is the *visiting* team. Thus, he makes *no* decisions. The bride is the *home* team. The bride gets to make *all* of the decisions," she explained knowledgably.

Jack laughed. "Samantha! I'm impressed! You've been doing some homework!"

"Pete and Kathleen gave me a book-on-tape for Christmas. *Understanding Football in 10 Easy Steps.*"

Jack burst out laughing. "Hey, I have another idea for your novel," he added, "how about if after they get married, the blind woman lets her grandmother live in that little pink dollhouse, and she moves into the instructor's house down the street?"

Samantha gasped. "But I love Mise-En-Place. I love everything in its place. From the moment I've met you, everything has been out of place."

"Sam, that's the whole point! There's no such thing as everything staying in its place." He gazed down the hill toward her little cottage. "And, seriously, I can't live in that little house. Every time I'm in it, my head gets scrambled. One time I went home and watched a soap opera." He shuddered.

"But your house is so big and has so many stairs, and I'll end up setting a sleeve on fire on the gas range in the kitchen."

"We'll make it work for you. I'll build an extra railing on the stairs and get an electric stove, and we'll throw out all of the old furniture, and you can buy round furniture so you won't bang your shins." He paused, looking at her skeptically. "Just no *pink* furniture. Any other colors. Like black and silver would be fine."

She smiled. "Don't think I don't realize those are the colors from your football team."

He kissed her before she could find anything else to object to.

"I've missed you," Samantha said sincerely. "Lucy, too. How is she?"

"Lucy? She's heavily campaigning to have me finally buy myself a car. So tomorrow, I promised her we would go and look. I'm ready. It's overdue. I'm leaning toward a Pontiac Trans Am, but she's adamant I should get a pink Volkswagen Bug. I would feel like I'm driving an Easter egg." He shuddered. "Can you *imagine*?"

Pink? "Actually, I can."

Jack groaned.

A chill breeze blew around them. "I'm freezing!" Samantha said, rubbing her hands together. "Let's go down to the farmhouse and get a cup of coffee. You can meet my folks." She stamped her feet to warm them up. "Gotta warn you, though. My folks might seem a little…odd."

Jack stood up. "That bad?"

Samantha grinned. "They're not as bad as I made them out to be. They're not so bad at all. Let's go."

Arm in arm, happily reunited, they walked down the hill to the farmhouse, Azure trotting alongside them. Suddenly, Jack stopped. "Wait a minute. Samantha, were you on your way to the office? *At eight o'clock in the morning of New Year's Day?* You were, weren't you? Checking the books on New Year's Day." He sounded like she was a hopeless alcoholic and he had just found her with a newly opened bottle of *Dewar's* Scotch Whiskey.

Samantha glanced in the direction of the office. *Closing the books could wait.* She looked back at him and took his hand. "Jack, Jack. How you misjudge me," she gently chided.

In her sweetest voice, she added, "Now Jack, about Mr. Malcolm's property. What if we just converted some of the acreage to olive orchards? Leave the house but surround it with this type of new olive tree that I want to import from Spain?"

"Our property, not Mr. Malcolm's," Jack corrected patiently. "And not a chance, Sam."

Available Now from Vintage Spirit
www.vrpublishing.com

Grit for the Oyster: 250 Pearls of Wisdom for Aspiring Writers
Written by *Suzanne Woods Fisher, Debora M. Coty, Faith Tibbetts McDonald, Joanna Bloss*
Writing/Non-fiction/Inspirational

A powerful motivator for aspiring writers, *Grit for the Oyster* offers wit, wisdom, and inspiration to take that first step and persevere through the writing journey. More than a how-to, this confidence-building book is designed to draw readers to a closer relationship with God, to affirm their calling to write, and to offer pithy practical guidance from successful writers like Terri Blackstock, Martha Bolton, James Scott Bell, Liz Curtis Higgs, Dr. Gary Chapman, and David Kopp.

Including such quotes as:

"In these pages, you'll find a helpful and soul strengthening community." ~David Kopp, best-selling co-author of *The Prayer of Jabez*

"This is definitely a book you want to keep within close reach as you work. It's like having your own personal writer's group and cheering squad right in your own home!" ~Linda Danis, best-selling author of *365 Things Every New Mom Should Know*

"To those who feel called to write for the glory of God, *Grit for the Oyster* is like the 'Writer's Bible.'" ~Ruth Carmichael Ellinger, award-winning author of *The Wild Rose of Lancaster*

Suzanne Woods Fisher

Reading Group Questions and Topics for Discussion

With which characters in *For the Love of Dogs* do you most closely identify? Why?

What kind of a person is Samantha Christensen? What motivates her? As you were reading, what were your reactions to her?

Unpack Samantha's emotional baggage. Describe the change she undergoes in the course of the book.

Way back when, what happened between Samantha, Kathleen, and their parents? How did that experience color and complicate the twins' life choices, whether personal or professional, ever since?

What effect does the intimate relationship Samantha forges with Lucy and Jack have on her sense of self?

What role does Dr. Sommers play? Why is he such a significant person to Samantha?

Consider Lucy. What does Samantha come to mean to her? Why? How does that relationship parallel the one between Samantha and Nonna?

Of all the book's characters, who would you say finally comes to "see" things most clearly? Samantha? Jack? Lucy? Explain.

How does Samantha's perception of faith and prayer evolve during the novel?

What aspects of *For the Love of Dogs* particularly resonate with you?

Samantha said that she always believed in God, she just wasn't sure He believed in her. Have you ever felt that way?

Samantha finally resolved that fundamental issue when she realized God had always been in her life—she just hadn't seen Him. Did her new perspective illuminate anything for you in your life? About knowing that you are significant to God? Scripture tells us that no one is beyond the reach of God's love (1 John 4:10). Like Samantha, maybe it's time to give God another chance.

The author gratefully acknowledges the use of the following trademarks:

Milk-Bone
Del Monte Foods
1 Market St.,
San Francisco, CA 94105.

Fresca and Tab
The Coca-Cola Company
P.O. Box 1734
Atlanta, GA 30301

Ruffles Potato Chips
Frito-Lay,
PO Box 660634,
Dallas, TX 75266-0634

Breck Shampoo
In 2006, Breck was acquired by <u>Dollar Tree</u> of <u>Chesapeake, Virginia</u>.
Dollar Tree
500 Volvo Parkway, Chesapeake, Virginia 23320
Chesapeake, Virginia

Cheerios
Betty Crocker ® **Bac-Os** ®
General Mills, Inc.
P.O. Box 9452
Minneapolis, MN 55440

Pringles
Procter & Gamble
One Procter & Gamble Plaza
<u>Cincinnati, Ohio,</u> <u>USA</u> 45202

Tang
Kraft Foods Global, Inc.
3 Lakes Drive
Northfield, IL 60026
www.kraft.com

Dewar's Scotch Whiskey
Aberfeldy, Perthshire
PH15 2EB Scotland

Bayer Aspirin
Bayer Direct Services GmbH
51368 Leverkusen
Germany

FAO Schwarz –
875 Avenue of the Americas 20th Floor
New York, NY 10001

Birkenstocks
Birkenstock USA, LP Novato, CA 94949

Rapanelli Mill
e-mail: info@rapanelli.com. WEB: rapanelli.com -
sinolea.com. MILL AUTOMATION PROCESSING AND
TEMPERATURE .
www.rapanelli.com/inglese/Quadro_temperature.htm

Volkswagen
Volkswagen
P.O. Box 3
Hillsboro, OR 97123-003

Camel Unfiltered
RJ Reynolds
Winston-Salem, North Carolina

Good Housekeeping Magazine
300 West 57th Street
New York, New York 10019

Velcro USA Inc.
406 Brown Avenue
Manchester, NH 03103
United States

Sesame Street
www.sesamestreet.org

Pop-Eye
King Features Syndicate
300 West 57th Street
15th Floor
New York, NY 10019-5238

Twilight Zone
CBS
51 West 52nd Street,
New York City,New York 10019

Twilight Zone music (composer Bernard Hermann, who is
deceased)
Mail
The Bernard Herrmann Estate
32, Beacon Lane
Grantham
Lincolnshire
NG31 9DL
 Lincolnshire
NG3I Dream of 1 9DL

I Dream of Jeannie
Bewitched
Screen Gem Network
Sony Pictures Entertainment
10202 West Washington Blvd.

Suite 3900
Culver City, CA 90232-3195

Dragnet --Original Series (1951)
Most episodes of this series are in <u>public domain</u>, and have
been released by many DVD labels.

Lawrence Welk television shows (part of PBS now)
OETA Foundation
P.O. Box 14190
Oklahoma City, OK 73113

Buick Riviera
Buick Customer Assistance Center
P.O. Box 33136
Detroit, MI 48232-5136

Princess Phones
AT&T
Corporate Communications
175 E. Houston St.
San Antonio, TX 78205.

Western Union Corporate Headquarters
PO Box 6992
Greenwood Village, CO 80155-6992